GERMANY IN THE HIGH MIDDLE AGES

Germany in the High Middle Ages opens with a wide-ranging and yet detailed description of the conditions under which men lived and their attitudes of mind during the period 1050–1200; against this background it proceeds to analyse the fundamental political, social, economic and cultural changes of the period in central Europe. Professor Fuhrmann considers the social transformation brought about by the emergence of new classes such as ministeriales and burghers, and examines the intellectual renewal reflected in the rise of scholasticism and the foundation of the universities. He also describes the gradual erosion of the power of the German rulers, which led to the Empire losing its position as the leading power in Europe, and yet was accompanied by a last flowering under the Staufen emperors and the chivalric culture with which they were closely associated. Throughout the book these changes are contracted with contemporary developments elsewhere in Europe, especially in France, England and Italy.

HORST FUHRMANN is President of the *Monumenta Germaniae Historica* and Professor of History at the University of Regensburg.

———— · ————

GERMANY IN THE
HIGH MIDDLE AGES
c. 1050 – 1200

———— · ————

HORST FUHRMANN

Translated by Timothy Reuter

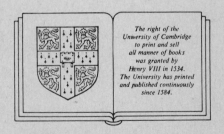

The right of the
University of Cambridge
to print and sell
all manner of books
was granted by
Henry VIII in 1534.
The University has printed
and published continuously
since 1584.

CAMBRIDGE UNIVERSITY PRESS

Cambridge

New York   New Rochelle   Melbourne   Sydney

Published by the Press Syndicate of the University of Cambridge
The Pitt Building, Trumpington Street, Cambridge CB2 1RP
32 East 57th Street, New York, NY 10022, USA
10 Stamford Road, Oakleigh, Melbourne 3166, Australia

Originally published in German as *Deutsche Geshichte im hohen
Mittelalter von der Mitte das 11. bis zum Ende des 12.
Jahrhunderts* © Vandenhoeck & Ruprecht in Göttingen 1978.
Übersetzung aus dem Deutschen mit Genehmigung des Verlages
Vandenhoeck & Ruprecht in Göttingen.

English translation © Cambridge University Press 1986

First published 1986
Reprinted 1987

Printed in Great Britain at the University Press, Cambridge

British Library cataloguing in publication data
Fuhrmann, Horst
Germany in the high Middle Ages c. 1050–1200. –
(Cambridge medieval textbooks)
1. Germany – History – 843–1273
I. Title   II. Deutsche Geschichte im hohen Mittelalter. *English*
943'.02   DD141

Library of Congress cataloguing in publication data
Fuhrmann, Horst.
Germany in the high Middle Ages c. 1050–1200.
Translation of: Deutsche Geschichte im hohen Mittelalter.
Bibliography
Includes index.
1. Germany – History – 843–1273.   I. Title.
DD141.F8313   1986   943'.023   85-29988
ISBN 0 521 26638 6 (hard covers)
ISBN 0 521 31980 3 (paperback)

CONTENTS

I

GERMAN HISTORY IN THE HIGH MIDDLE AGES – CONCEPTS, EXPLANATIONS, FACTS

·

Master Hugo of Saint-Victor (†1141), probably a Saxon by birth, and a man held by his contemporaries in high esteem for his learning, wrote a treatise on history in about 1130. He saw history as 'the basis of all knowledge', and identified its three 'essentials' – the things which determined its nature – as space, time, and man. Space, time, and man are indeed in a formal sense the determining categories used by history as a branch of knowledge, and they were referred to as such both in the methodological considerations of J. G. Droysen (†1884) and in the *Historian's toolbox* by A. von Brandt (†1977). Hugo of Saint-Victor admittedly regarded *historia* as allowing only a preliminary form of understanding, because it was based on the appearances of this world. It did not in itself allow men to perceive the real significance of an event in God's plan for the salvation of the world; this could only be perceived by the mind from a higher plane.

To take an example, in 1080 Archbishop Wibert of Ravenna was elected as Pope Clement III in opposition to Gregory VII by the partisans of the German king Henry IV, an act which marked the beginning of a long schism. Provost Gerhoch of Reichersberg (†1169) wrote that 'for many faithful and wise men' this division of the church seemed like the fulfilment of the prophecy of the Book of Revelation that after a thousand years of peace the devil 'must be loosed a little season' (Revelation 20.3). 'May the Lord remember his promise', wrote Gerhoch, almost as if to remind God to stick to his timetable, for the church had found itself in darkness for seventy years, and that was long enough for a 'little time'. The attitude of mind evident here was widespread at the time. Space and time had another dimension, foreknown and foreordained by God; it was in this context that man as God's creation had to see himself.

1 *The medieval view of space, time, and man*

(a) Space How was the world visualized at that time? The earth was thought of as lying in the middle of the universe, generally as a flat disk swimming on the universal sea. Antipodeans, cut off by this sea from the known inhabited world, could not exist, for if they had done they could not have been reached by God's message of salvation. At the centre of the earth lay Jerusalem, the earthly counterpart to the city of God in heaven with its twelve gates; here the three continents met, Europe, Asia and Africa. World-maps of the high Middle Ages show the three continents surrounded by a circle. The top of the map does not show north, as on modern maps, but usually east; within the circle the continents are set out in the shape of a letter T, with Asia filling the whole of the top half of the map, and Europe and Africa filling the bottom left and right quarters respectively. This was derived from a statement by Augustine (†430) in his *City of God* that Africa and Europe together were as large as Asia, a view confirmed by the encyclopaedist Isidore of Seville (†636). Until the thirteenth century such maps were produced without any practical purpose – the intention of the cartographers was to enable the user to understand the progress of God's plan for salvation, rather than to orientate himself on the basis of precise measurements. Questions like: where was Eden? or where did Christ take up his cross? were of far more importance than the mere location of a place or a region on the map.

The microcosm reflected the macrocosm. It was not just the inheritance of Pythagorean and neo–Platonic thought that led medieval intellectuals to see space as organized even in its smallest particles according to a harmonious and divinely ordained plan. The 'significant' measurement and the 'significant' number played a crucial role. Church architecture became a carrier of symbolic meaning: the cloisters of monasteries reflected the proportions of the Holy Sepulchre, whose size and shape were the object of much speculative interpretation. The measurements used in daily life were derived from man, God's image: the ell, the foot; the pace and the day's journey as measurements of distance; the ploughman's 'daywork' or 'morning' as measurements of area, and so on. Germanic law determined distance by reference to man's senses: the distance on which one could still perceive the shining of a red shield or of a door-bolt, or hear a man's shout. The dead, inhuman, normalized measure still lay in the future.

(b) Time   Here too men sought to trace God's plan. When was the world created? When will it come to an end? What stage is it at now? Ever since the cyclical view of world history current in antiquity had given way to the Christian linear view there had been repeated attempts to calculate the time of the beginning and end of the world, in spite of Augustine's forcible reminder that Acts 1.7 had said 'It is not for you to know the times or the seasons, which the Father hath put in his own power.' The statement in the ninetieth Psalm that a thousand years are but a day in the sight of the Lord was often interpreted as meaning that the world would last for six millennia, corresponding to the week in which it had been created; the sixth and last *aetas mundi* was reckoned to have begun with the birth of Christ, a point used to reckon dates from the time of Bede (†735) onwards. At the end would come the Last Sabbath. But such chiliastic calculations seemed to many to be too crude and inaccurate, especially from the eleventh century on, when a whole series of world chronicles were compiled. A more sophisticated reckoning can be seen from the example of Marianus Scotus († c. 1082). Marianus, an Irishman by birth with the name Maelbrigte, had gone into exile 'for the love of Christ' and settled as an *inclusus* first in Fulda and then from 1069 in the cathedral at Mainz in a cell which he did not intend to leave before his death: a hermit as world chronicler. After studying many chronicles Marius produced his own calculations. According to the tradition of the fathers, Christ was crucified on 25 March and rose again on 27 March; these dates did not match with the dates of Easter given for AD 34 in any of the tables he had consulted. Consequently the usual date was erroneous. The date of the Creation had also been calculated wrongly. Sun and moon had both been created on the fourth day; this was by consequence the spring equinox, 21 March, and Easter in year 1 of the world fell on 25 March. The customary date for the Creation, 3952 BC, should be put back by 241 years and the dates reckoned AD were to be increased by twenty-five years.

Marius' calculations were only one example among many; world chronicles were all intended as a precise description of the course of

world history on its way between the Creation and the Last
Judgement. There were terrifying predictions of the end of the
world: the French conciliar theologian Pierre d'Ailly, who died in
1420, reckoned that it would come in 1789, the date of the French
Revolution, which was indeed to change the world. The year itself
was often determined by reference to events of significance in the
history of salvation. The chancery of the German kings and those of
most bishoprics began the new year with Christmas Day, as was
general in Europe in the early and high Middle Ages; the Annun-
ciation (25 March) or Easter (as a movable feast a particularly
awkward starting-point) were also used as the beginning of the year.
The particular nature of the days throughout the year, the degree of
their holiness, was carefully noted. Important acts of state, such as
the election and coronation of kings, court cases, diplomatic negotiations, peace treaties, and general assemblies, were arranged to
take place on especially holy days. H. M. Schaller has estimated that
'at least ninety per cent of such acts took place on particularly holy
days', for example the feast of the Circumcision (1 January), Epiph-
any (6 January), Candlemas (2 February), Palm Sunday, Maundy
Thursday, Good Friday, and Easter. There were special mnemonic
verses to assist in memorizing the list of holy days: the first half of
January was compressed into the line *Cisio Janus Epi sibi vendicat*,
which may be translated as 'January claims for itself the Circum-
*cisio*n of the Lord, *Epi*phany.' On Maundy Thursday the king, as a
second Christ, washed the feet of twelve poor men – a custom
followed by the Austrian Emperor Franz Josef I until 1916. On
Good Friday one laid oneself in the grave in imitation of Christ.
There was to be no fighting between Wednesday evening and early
Monday, the period of Christ's passion and resurrection. Many feast
days were used to fix obligations and transactions: Michaelmas (29
September) and Martinmas (11 November) were favoured for the
payment of rent, the ending of leases, the close of the accounting
year or the dates of contracts. For things like blood-letting, bathing
or travelling some days were particularly favourable, while 'Egypt-
ian' (unfavourable) days were to be avoided. The day itself began
liturgically on the previous evening with vigils (a fact still faintly
commemorated in the term 'Christmas Eve'); divine service was
celebrated at sunrise, and the day ended at sunset. Day and night
were each divided into twelve hours, whose length naturally varied
with the time of year. There were normally only two mealtimes;
during Lent there was often only one, and we not infrequently find a
person taking a pious vow to eat only once a day for the rest of his

life. Besides such divisions the day was also organized according to the seven or eight canonical hours – these too were intended to commemorate and bring to mind significant events, the morning representing the resurrection, midday the crucifixion and evening the incarnation of Christ.

(c) Man Medieval anthropology was inexhaustible and full of contradictions. On the one hand man was God's image, on the other hand he was all too much a sinner, a perfected natural creation and yet subject to desires which prevented him from leading a holy life. The cardinal deacon Lothar of Segni – later to become pope as Innocent III – wrote in 1194–5 a treatise 'On the misery of the human condition' (*De miseria humanae conditionis*), a work which in spite of its frequent lapses into banality dealt with a subject of burning importance for contemporaries and found a wide reception: nearly five hundred manuscripts have survived. Lothar dealt with three aspects of the misery of human fate: birth, life and death. 'Why did I crawl forth from my mother's womb, that I might see such poverty and misery, and live my days in shame?' is the opening question, taken from the prophet Jeremiah, and Lothar added a whole series of depressing illustrations – the stars were created from fire, wind from air, fishes from water, but God made beasts and man from earth, 'dirt'. Man is born as a living proof of a previous act of lust and sin, nourished in his mother's womb by poisonous juices which produce rabies in dogs. Naked we come into the world, naked we leave it, and life becomes shorter and shorter: at the beginning of time men lived to ninety and more, nowadays only a few reach sixty and only a very few seventy. This tone is continued for nearly a hundred chapters, and at the end Lothar lists the punishments in the world beyond: 'Brimstone and glowing fire for all eternity'. It was indeed a terrible predicament: no sooner had a child been born than care had to be taken to have it baptized, for if it should die unbaptized it would be damned. Care had to be taken with the baptism as well: an exorcist (the third grade of the four minor orders, one of the preparatory stages for anyone who became a priest) had to exert himself to ensure that evil spirits did not disturb the baptism or even succeed in rendering it invalid. The salvation of man's soul was in constant danger. What happened if simoniacal priests, men who had received their orders in return for payment, bestowed the sacraments? What happened if one unknowingly had contact with excommunicates, which could bring automatic excommunication as a consequence? If a layman made a gift to

monks, could he be certain that they would really take care of his salvation? True, it was said of the monastery of Cluny that its prayers could free sinners from purgatory, but was that true of one's own foundation? Perpetual anxiety about one's own salvation could give life a gloomy seriousness; but had Christ himself ever laughed? 'We read that Christ wept on three occasions, but never that He laughed, He who said "Woe to you that laugh now, for ye shall mourn and weep"': so wrote Petrus Cantor around 1170. One could quote hundreds of similar statements; both monastic rules and moral treatises regard laughter as a defect in human nature, and if not forbidden, then certainly not encouraged.

Many people of the high Middle Ages must have felt severe pressures and impossible expectations as a consequence of their view of space, time and their own nature. There were any number of regulations governing the righteous way of life in existence before the mid eleventh century, but they were not necessarily taken very seriously; the reform movement produced a new seriousness, a disturbing discussion about the appropriateness of received ideas of order and righteousness to the Christian way of life. First, however, we must leave medieval anthropology and examine the realities of space, time and man in the period.

2 *Space, time, man: facts and findings*

(a) Space   The landscape of central Europe looked very different in the period between the eleventh and the thirteenth centuries from the way it does now. We should remind ourselves at the beginning of any description that the people of those times did not share our enthusiasm for nature or the protection of the environment. True, men lived from nature, which had to be protected as a source of the necessities of life; but the wood which overgrew clearings again, the water which flowed where it wished, and the weather which determined harvests and famines all gave nature the aspect of something mysterious and uncontrollable.

What did Germany look like at that time? The inhabitants on the North Sea and Baltic coasts adopted a largely passive attitude to the power of the sea. Storms led to floods and changes in the coastline: the islands at the mouths of the Scheldt and Rhine became smaller, and many disappeared; the estuary of the lower Meuse and the Bay of Biesboch only came into existence in 1421, an event which caused the destruction of seventy villages. Around 1200 Texel, Vlieland

and Wieringen became separated from the mainland, and the large island of Borkum was divided up into a number of islets. Dyke-building, checked and endangered by floods, had been in progress since Carolingian times, but it was not until the fifteenth and sixteenth centuries that the bulk of the marshes were protected by dykes, in contrast to the great rivers, whose banks had been built up much earlier, partly in order to provide roads and towpaths. The dyking of the Weser marshes is well recorded: it was begun in the early twelfth century, and by 1181 the whole of the north-eastern half was enclosed and under cultivation, followed in 1201 by the south-western half. The Baltic coast suffered very little alteration in this period, in contrast to the regions bordering on the North Sea. South of the marshy regions around the North Sea lay a broad stretch of sandy heathland and moorland; here lay the great oak forests of what was later to become the Lüneburg Heath, and here also lay the centre for the colonizing activities of numerous monasteries. South again there was a band of sandy and loamy soil with centres of settlement around Brunswick, Hildesheim and Hanover. Here as elsewhere in Germany a more intensive cultivation set in around the turn of the eleventh to the twelfth century, organized and spurred on by a more intensive exploitation of rights of lordship. Clearance was practised so extensively that it had to be forbidden in some areas as early as the thirteenth century.

The woods which were turned into arable land consisted almost entirely of deciduous trees. If a statistical survey of the oldest place-names is to be trusted, then it is clear that deciduous woods were far more common than coniferous ones: 6,115 of the oldest German place-names have elements referring to deciduous trees, but only 790 indicate conifers. The most widespread deciduous tree was the beech. Apart from the Harz Mountains and the Thuringian and Bohemian Forests, the Alps and the Black Forest there were scarcely any coniferous woods: such trees were regarded as 'unfruit-ful' (*arbores non fructiferae*) and consequently as less valuable. Wood was only a by-product of forest cultivation: isolated trees were cut down as necessary here and there, and reafforestation was almost never practised. The woodland was much more important as grazing for livestock, especially for pigs, but also, where meadows were scarce, for oxen, horses, and goats. Trees which produced fodder, like oak, beech, and wild fruit trees, were specially protected. The value and the size of a wood was measured not according to how much wood lay in it but according to the number of animals – usually pigs – it could provide with nourishment during the fattening season and during winter.

(b) Time   It was not only in the context of the history of salvation that men calculated time; in the study of astronomy, a part of the quadrivium, men learnt and improved the scientific calculation of time. Sundials were in use from the early Middle Ages on, and from the tenth century the astrolabe – an instrument invented in antiquity which allowed the accurate measurement of the positions of the stars – was used for precise calculations of time. Throughout the Middle Ages water-clocks were used to reckon the divisions of the day, and there was a guild of clockmakers in Cologne as early as 1183. Clocks with clockwork are first found in the thirteenth century. The monastic life demanded a careful observance and observation of the division of the day; the earliest sundials (like the earliest real clocks) were installed in monasteries and priories, though the simpler method of judging the time of day according to the length of one's shadow was never forgotten, and there were elaborate tables to assist in this. In each monastery a monk was deputed to keep watch over the time. When he rang the prayer-bell at two in the morning he had reckoned the time from the beginning of night (the time when stars had first become visible) by singing a çertain number of psalms: the number varied according to the seasons. In the high Middle Ages this primitive method of calculating time was often replaced by machinery.

The great experts in time-reckoning of the Middle Ages used divisions of time ranging from the century (*saeculum*) to the unit of time which could not be divided further (*atomus*). Between these lay the *lustrum* (five years), *annus* (year), *mensis* (month), *hebdomada* (week), *dies* (day), *hora* (hour), *quadrans* (quarter of an hour), *minutum* (minute), *momentum* (the period of time in which one can discern that time has moved on) and *ostentum* (the time needed to take something in with the eyes). The smallest unit of time was the *ictus oculi* ('a twinkling of an eye'), which was equated with the *atomus*. Ratios were established: the *ostentum* consisted of 370 atoms, the hour of 22,560. The 'human time' of the Middle Ages, according to J. Leclercq, was 'measured by the rhythms of nature and the liturgy, and favoured an attitude of expectation and longing'.

The connection between time and the seasonal rhythms of nature was felt much more strongly in these centuries without much technical protection than it is today. *Tempestas* was both a storm or tempest and time:

> Lo, the awaited
> and beloved
> spring brings forth its joys once more.

So the *Carmina Burana* show the longing for spring. The change of the seasons was felt keenly, so that one could say that fifteen seasons had passed in order to indicate that nearly four years had passed.

The climate associated with the seasons is subject to long-term fluctuations: periods of damp and cool weather are followed by warmer and drier phases. The famous winter of 1076–7, when the German king Henry IV crossed the Mont Cenis pass to Italy at the beginning of January together with his wife and his two-year-old son, lay in a period of cool and damp weather lasting from 1014 to 1089. In that year the great rivers of Europe were frozen over from Martinmas (11 November) until well into April: the Rhône, Rhine, Elbe, Danube, Weichsel, Po and even Tiber were said to have been 'impassable to ships, but passable for men, horses, donkeys and carts as if it had been solid ground'. Time and seasons meant heat and cold, dearth and plenty: an accurate timepiece would not have given much useful information.

(c) Man Those who visit museums and armouries frequently remark to one another that the men of the middle Middle Ages must have been smaller than they are today, judging by their armour. Although physical anthropologists have tended to neglect questions of body size in their study of medieval skeletal remains – the distinctions between racial and ethnic groups depend rather on skull measurements, on the relationship between the length and width of the skull – we can make a few generalizations. It is generally agreed that the people of the period of the barbarian invasions were quite large, and that the average body size had dropped considerably by the end of the Middle Ages. This process had not gone very far by the twelfth and thirteenth centuries, to judge by the results of excavations. A number of reasons have been put forward to explain the decline: plague and other epidemic diseases; increased urbanization, which meant living in cramped quarters and surrounded by dark unhygienic alleys. It is also noteworthy that the shape of skulls tended to alter along with body size: 'During the period from the early Middle Ages to the modern era we observe that skull-length declines, but skull-width and the height of the cranium increase', according to E. C. Büchi. It should be borne in mind, however, that the size of excavated skeletons is not necessarily typical of the

population as a whole, since there is an unusually high number of members of the upper class among them, and these were generally taller than the masses. The Salian kings Henry IV and Henry V, for example, were very tall men, both around 5 ft 11 in. The grave of a high aristocratic family in Komburg (near Schwäbisch Hall) held human skeletons of around 5 ft 8 in.; in another grave in the family church at Öhringen there was a male skeleton of 5 ft 10 in., and so on. The non-aristocratic population was probably noticeably smaller than this.

An average expectation of life of just over thirty years has been calculated for the population of central Europe in the period from the tenth to the twelfth century. Here too there were substantial differences between different groups. If we take the German kings from Henry I (†936) to Henry VI (†1197), none of whom fell in battle or died an accidental death (apart from Barbarossa, who drowned at the age of sixty-eight), we can calculate an average age at death of not quite fifty. What lowered the average was the very high infant mortality in all classes, and the generally low expectation of life of the lower classes, who were exhausted by heavy physical labour and particularly exposed to sickness and natural disasters. As in life, so in their death they remained anonymous, without gravestones or records of their names in the *libri memoriales*. The best chance of finding out their expectation of life is the investigation of skeletal remains, and if we use the data from some one hundred cemeteries which have been excavated north of the Alps, ignoring differences of time, climate and geography, we arrive at the following statistics. The majority of those who died were aged between fourteen and twenty (30.1% of males; 24.8% of females) or between twenty and forty (28.4% of males; 23.2% of females). Only one in four lived to be over forty. In spite of this low expectation of life, the maximum life-span was much the same as it is now: if nothing intervened, men could reach very high ages, as in the case of the popes Lucius III (1181–5) and Celestine III (1191–8), both of whom died around the age of ninety. Women were worse off than men throughout the Middle Ages; apart from frequent births, which were often fatal for mothers, women were weakened by heavy work in the fields and very susceptible to illnesses, especially to tuberculosis of the lungs, which seems to have been endemic.

The numerous infant deaths seem to have kept the average family size down, though here again there will have been class differences. Documents from Fulda reveal the existence of 196 married couples with 518 children – an average of 2.6 per marriage. The ratio of

males to females among the total population, including the un-
married, was 318 to 237: the high proportion of males is very
noticeable. It has been observed for the peasant population in west
Francia that the number of female births declined in proportion to
the number of females already on the holding. From this fact it has
been deduced that there was a kind of birth control through female
infanticide, though this cannot be directly demonstrated, and it has
been argued that one of the reasons for the population explosion in
Europe in the high Middle Ages was the abandoning of such
practices. It is certainly significant how frequently the penitentials
and synods of the early Middle Ages dealt with the problem of
mothers who crushed or suffocated their children in sleep.

The population of Europe seems to have grown steadily up to
about 1000, when it totalled about 42 million. From there to 1150 it
grew slowly to 50 million, but in the following half-century alone it
increased again by about a quarter to some 61 million, the largest
increase until the fifteenth century. For the German kingdom, with
a surface area of some 700,000 square kilometres, the population has
been estimated at 5–6 million for the time of Henry III (†1056) and at
7–8 million for the time of Barbarossa (†1190). This compares with
estimates of 12 million for France and 2.2 million for England for the
period around 1200, that is after the great increase. Some regions of
Germany with very intensive internal colonization saw a much
greater rise in population: the population of Saxony is estimated to
have increased by a factor of ten between 1100 and 1300. The
numbers of emigrant settlers which need to be added to these figures
do not seem to have been large, not at any rate in the twelfth century
when the eastern colonization had only just begun; perhaps 100,000,
or 4% of the total. There were scarcely any serious epidemics in the
eleventh and twelfth centuries; the great outbreaks of plague in the
fourteenth and fifteenth presupposed a more mobile population and
the existence of numerous densely populated towns as centres in
which the infection could develop and from which it could be
transmitted. In the twelfth century, according to H. Mottek, at
most 10 or 15% of the German population lived in towns. The main
causes of death for those between fifteen and thirty-five were
malaria, smallpox and dysentery, and in particular lung tuberculosis, which was hard to diagnose. Leprosy also claimed not a few
victims, as did ergotism, the result of fungal contamination of grain,
known as 'Holy Fire' and against which the help of the hermit
Anthony was invoked; this reached epidemic proportions in some
years, for instance 1076, 1089 and 1094. Man was surrounded by the

danger of illness of the body as well as of the soul. The record of miracles worked by the saint Anno II of Cologne (†1075) includes references to some fifty human ailments, and mentions the following cases: thirty of lameness or paralysis, thirty of blindness, fifteen of dropsy and ulcers, ten of water on the stomach and haemorrhaging, nine of heart disease, nine of drowning, nine of deafness, seven of epilepsy, five of demoniac possession. All these were healed by Anno's miraculous powers, which also restored twenty-four persons to life.

Besides illness there was also famine, which affected the lower classes in particular. Monasteries were by their nature concerned with the care of the poor, and frequently received a third of their tithes with the provision that it was 'for the use of the poor'. Besides this there was the monastic custom of feeding a poor man on the anniversary day of a monk's death; the anniversary of an abbot's death might mean the feeding of several poor men. Many monasteries gave out several thousand such meals in a year. The need of the poor was naturally also exploited by the wealthy, the *potentes*, who appear in the sources as the counterpart to the *pauperes*, and the wealthy also included ecclesiastics 'who oppressed the poor people so that many died of hunger'; royal ordinances had little effect here. The chronicler of the monastery of Saint-André (near Bruges) praises his abbot for having so managed his affairs that 'the poverty of his neighbours brought him abundance'.

Famines drove crowds of people through the land begging; sometimes they came together to form gangs which sought food by plundering. The rich monastery of Fulda was attacked by such a gang in 1145 and stripped bare. It is scarcely a coincidence that the First and Second Crusades had been preceded by famines in 1095 and 1145–7, and the Bamberg monk Frutolf of Michelsberg noted drily in his chronicle under the year 1095 that the 'western Franks' had easily been persuaded to leave their fields, for 'the lands of Gaul had for some years experienced civil war, famine, and high mortality'. Necessity knows no law. The Archbishop of Trier, Poppo (1016–47) was on his way to church in great pomp when he was met by a group of starving men; they refused the money offered them, forced the Archbishop and some of his companions to dismount, and before the eyes of their pastor the hungry mob tore the animals to pieces and ate them. Such attacks were not the revolutionary expression of social tensions but were dictated simply by need, even though it was at this time that the first complaints about fat priests and well-fed monks appeared. Famines were often local affairs, but there were years in which the whole of central Europe was afflicted by dearth, usually as the result of harvest failures: 1043–5, 1099–1101, 1124–6, 1145–7, 1150–1 and 1195–8 appear to have been such periods. In a period when agricultural production was largely intended for consumption by the producers and there was little interest in surpluses (and in any case little spare cash available to buy them) an inadequate harvest hit the population like a natural disaster.

Up to the eleventh century over 90% of the population lived on the land, mostly in small hamlets or in nucleated villages located near some favourable natural feature such as a spring, a stream or a terrace. Two-course rotation had been replaced by three-course rotation before 800 in parts of Germany, but it was to take centuries before it was generally adopted. Three-course rotation meant sowing winter wheat or rye in the autumn, and in the spring oats, barley, peas, lentils or beans. By the end of the eleventh century pulses were as important as corn; a chronicler noted for the year 1094 that because of the drought 'grain and pulses' had been ruined, a sign of the latter's importance. Ploughs and harnesses were improved. In the course of the eleventh century the horse began to replace or at least supplement the ox as a draught-animal for ploughing, especially after the advantages of the horse-collar, introduced from the East, had been generally recognized. The horse is faster moving than the plough-ox and has greater strength and stamina, so that it was possible to work one to two hours per day longer. It was not only ploughing which benefited; the speed of land transport was increased and its cost reduced, by the use of properly shod and properly harnessed horses. The *caretta longa*, the wagon with four wheels, took the place of the two-wheeled cart. From the eleventh century onwards we can observe that settlements were increasing in size, and the question why this was so has been answered as follows by Lynn White Jr:

The answer seems to lie in the shift from ox to horse as the primary farm animal. The ox moved so slowly that peasants using oxen had to live close to their fields. With the employment of the horse both for ploughing and for hauling, the same amount of time spent going to and from the fields would enable the peasant to travel a much greater distance . . . Even a slight increase in the distance which it was convenient to travel from the village to the farthest field would greatly enlarge the total arable which could be exploited from that village. Thus extensive regions once scattered with tiny hamlets came to be . . . dominated by huge villages . . .

The extension of the arable land and its more intensive exploitation, the increase in food supplies and the widening of the range of what was available were probably all causes of the rapid increase of the population in the eleventh and twelfth centuries.

Rye was the grain most frequently used for bread. Selective breeding of dwarf wheats had produced one of the most important kinds of grain used in the Middle Ages, spelt, which was particularly widespread in the South-West; wheat, which is more sensitive to soil and climate, was grown mainly in the West. Grain was eaten raw or roasted or in the form of porridge as well as in bread and flatcakes. The rise in the numbers of horses kept led to an increase in oat-growing, though oats had always been used as a foodstuff, generally in the form of a primitive porridge. Barley was the preferred grain for beermaking; beer was drunk especially in the North, while wine – in contrast to present-day drinking habits – was preferred in the South and was drunk even by the poorer groups in society. Hops were used for medicinal purposes as early as the Carolingian period; they contain lupulin, which was thought to lower the libido, and it has been observed by K. and F. Bertsch that hops are mentioned surprisingly often in connection with monasteries, churches and bishops. Hops were used in brewing from the eleventh century onwards.

The question of what was eaten and how much was eaten in this period is naturally hard to answer. There are some indications in contracts for annuities such as are recorded in the biography of Bishop Meinwerk of Paderborn (†1036), perhaps written by Abbot Conrad of Abdinghof (1142–73). A nun of the 'upper middle class' (F. Irsigler) secured for herself an annuity of thirty-six bushels of rye, twenty-four bushels of barley, sixty cheeses, four sheep and a ham. On a smaller scale, and evidently intended for the recipient's personal use, was the annuity granted to the mother of a donor: seven malters of corn, thirty bushels of barley, one malter of cheese and a ham. It is apparent that the diet consisted primarily of bread and cheese, only occasionally varied or supplemented by meat. A free man with his wife made a contract of annuity with the abbot of Abdinghof in 1118 which tells us something about the weekly diet of two persons. Every day except Friday there were two loaves of rye bread, two loaves of barley bread and two pots of beer. On Sunday, Tuesday and Thursday this was supplemented by two pieces of meat and green vegetables or pulses; on Monday, Wednesday and Saturday there was a cheese instead. On Friday there were to be two dishes 'which it is lawful to eat on that day', presumably fish. The food provided for the poor was less plentiful and varied: we hear of a ration of one loaf of white bread, three jugs of 'strong beer' and three herrings per person per day.

Human life was extraordinarily hard at that time. Most people, even those who lived in urban or quasi-urban settlements (the number of markets has been estimated at two to three hundred for Germany at the beginning of the eleventh century), lived in draughty wooden huts. Only those buildings which we would nowadays call public buildings – palaces, monasteries, urban fortifications, and so on – were constructed in stone. It was only in the twelfth century, with the rise of the knight's castle and the rich burgher house, that building in stone became more widespread. The house-dwellers pressed up close to the smoky and sooty open fire, especially in winter; light came in only through the door or through the smoke-hole in the roof. If there were openings for windows, these were closed with wooden frames and bars or wickerwork, occasionally by oiled parchment or linen; window-glass scarcely existed, and was used even in the twelfth century almost exclusively in churches. Windows were often simply blocked up with straw, which also served as a mattress on the hard-packed earth floors. Clothing, which was almost without exception produced domestically up to the twelfth century, varied little with the centuries, and was more like wrapping than tailored garments. Over a shirt men wore a short tunic reaching down to the knees, and broad linen trousers with leggings drawn over them and wrapped round with garters; women wore a long undergarment with a cloak with wide arm-openings over it. From the eleventh century on clothing became more elegant, partly under the influence of Byzantium; with increasing skill in clothes-making tailoring emerged as a separate occupation. In northern France and the lower Rhine we find as early as the beginning of the twelfth century a division into the specialized occupations of 'cutters' and 'sewers'. The man's tunic became longer and was trimmed with rich borders; the leggings, now often coloured, became more like stockings, so that garters were no longer necessary. Women began to wear clothes which were close-fitting above the waist, so that outraged clerics claimed that they 'bared' their bodies to show their charms to their lovers. A warm coat, preferably lined with fur, was a luxury, a princely gift, which would be worn for decades.

Such depressing living conditions might well have led men to wonder whether such a life in dirt, drudgery, constant fear of death and without much hope for improvement was worth living. Why not escape nerve-wracking need and perhaps persecution and cruel punishments by committing suicide? However, such a thought was virtually unknown up to the high Middle Ages, especially after the church fathers (especially Augustine) had formulated a prohibition

of suicide which prevailed over the more favourable attitude to it
among the Germanic tribes and the citizens of antiquity. Suffering
had to be borne; the suicide was more reprehensible than the
murderer, for he deprived himself of his own free will of the means
of salvation. Judas Iscariot was the prototype of the suicide: his
corpse burst open as he hanged himself and the fig-tree he used
withered. Up to the thirteenth and fourteenth centuries we scarcely
hear reports of suicides. If a convicted heretic flung himself into a
well, that was a proof of the depravity of his doctrine. If we regard
suicide as a 'social symptom' (Marc Bloch), then we must see
medieval society in its archaic phase, up to the twelfth and thirteenth
centuries, as having been largely free of the kind of tensions which
lead to such acts of despair. An analysis of cases of suicide in France
in the late Middle Ages shows that it was craftsmen who were most
liable to kill themselves, whereas peasants were largely immune; the
society of the early and high Middle Ages consisted almost entirely
of people who lived and worked on the land.

GERMANY IN THE EUROPE OF THE HIGH MIDDLE AGES

1 Middle Ages and 'high Middle Ages' – Europe and the 'West'

The term 'Middle Ages' was first popularized by the Professor of
'Rhetoric and History' at Halle, Christopher Keller, or, Latinized,
Cellarius, who died in 1707. In his academically worthless but
widely read book *Historia medii aevi*, which first appeared in 1688, he
used the term to describe the period between the Emperor Constantine the Great (†337) and the conquest of Constantinople by the
Turks in 1453. Since then there have been countless reflections on
the appropriateness of the label. The name has survived in conventional usage, especially as certain characteristics of a society have
come to be regarded as 'medieval': feudal structure, an aristocratic
society, a unified world-view and the early stages of urbanism, for
example. The characteristics of a 'Middle Age' have seemed so
clearly defined to scholars working on comparative history that the
term has been applied to other cultures, and even the order can be
reversed: according to the Viennese historian of art and culture
J. Stzygowski (†1941) the period of antiquity *follows* the Middle
Ages in Chinese history.

The thousand years of European medieval history (to speak
approximately; the limits are generally set at *c.* 300/500 at one end
and *c.* 1500 at the other) are generally further subdivided. The

so-called bourgeois historiography of the West uses the term 'high Middle Ages' freely, though different things are meant by this in different countries. For an Italian historian the *alto medioevo* is the early Middle Ages up to the time of the Carolingians; the Spaniards see their *alta edad media* as reaching up to the time of the *reconquista* in the mid eleventh century, while French medievalists – apart from Marc Bloch and the *Annales* school, who use a different periodization – see the *haut moyen âge* as lasting at most up to the beginning of the Capetian dynasty in 987, more usually up to the end of the ninth century. What follows is for the French often termed the 'classical Middle Ages', *le moyen âge classique*. England is a special case. The Norman Conquest meant a radical break with the Anglo-Saxon period, which does not easily allow a schematic division of English history; the term 'high Middle Ages' applied to European history generally refers to the period from the mid twelfth to the early fourteenth centuries. In German historical writing it has long been usual to refer to the era from the beginning of the tenth century to the middle of the thirteenth century as the 'high Middle Ages': this period stretches from the foundation of the Empire up to the Interregnum, from the powerless Franconian king, Conrad I (†919), to the equally powerless last Staufer king, Conradin (†1268).

This period used to be described by a German nationalist school of historiography as the 'imperial period' (*Kaiserzeit*) or 'the old German Empire' (*Das altdeutsche Kaisertum*), which is the title of a book by Johannes Haller (†1947) first published in 1926 and reprinted on numerous occasions since then. The 'old German Empire' was 'old' by contrast with the German Empire of 1871, though the implied comparison was in many ways misleading. The medieval Empire of the German kings was 'Roman', not 'German', and eschatologically it stood last in the series of world empires (Babylonians, Medes and Persians, Greeks, Romans). It claimed authority over the whole of the West. The 'German Empire' of the Prussian king William I proclaimed in Versailles was consciously *kleindeutsch*; it was not intended to infringe 'the rights of territorial rulers in the non-Prussian territories'. To think of a 'new German Empire' as succeeding to the 'old' one founded by Otto I in 962 and abolished by Francis I in 1806 is just as much an offence against the spirit of the Middle Ages, against its concept of empire and of the Last Judgement, as it was to talk of the First and the Second Reich, a practice in any case brought to an end by the fate of the 'Third Reich'.

The catastrophe of 1945 eliminated many political and ethnic structures which had survived from the Middle Ages. The preamble to the Weimar constitution of 1919 could still confidently talk of 'the German people, united in its tribes' – a formulation which might almost have come from the pen of an author of the high Middle Ages. In the opening of the constitution of 1949 for the Federal Republic of Germany it is stated instead that 'the German people in the states of Baden-Württemberg, Bavaria, Bremen' etc. is 'filled with the will to preserve its unity as a nation and as a state and to serve world peace as an equal member of a united Europe'. The federal structure of West Germany is certainly not lacking in 'gentile' elements, but the idea of a German people 'united in its tribes' has been abandoned in favour of the idea that the German people wishes to preserve its unity and serve peace 'in a united Europe'.

If the history of Europe is to be taken back as far as the high Middle Ages, then – at least from a German perspective – the appropriateness of the term must be questioned. In 1932 a book by the Englishman Christopher Dawson appeared with the title *The making of Europe*; it dealt with the period up to the end of the first millennium AD. The German translation, which appeared in 1935, was entitled *The making of the West: an introduction to the history of western unity* – in other words, the English expression 'Europe' was replaced by the German 'West' (*Abendland*). It is customary to speak of the 'western', not the 'European' Empire, even though Charlemagne for example was apostrophized by contemporaries as *rex, pater Europae* and as *Europae veneranda pharus* ('the venerable lighthouse of Europe'). Europe meant humanism and the idea inherent in the humanistic view of history of a unity which stretched from the history of the Greek city-states to the age of the world empires of the civilized 'white man'. Christianity was in the history of 'Europe' only a subordinate element, though one with an important integrating role, 'which was at its most important in the medieval West' (O. Köhler). Although 'Europe' and 'the West' are sometimes used as synonymous terms, there seems to be a difference between 'western unity' and 'European pluralism and freedom', and one may ask when the 'European' element came to predominate over the 'western' in the history of the Middle Ages. Friedrich Heer entitled his book which appeared in 1949 *The rise of Europe*: it deals with the emergence of nation-states and of a rationalistic world-view in the twelfth century. Historians who study comparative constitutional history also talk of the beginnings of the 'old European' era in this period.

2 Germany, the Germans and their neighbours

The land and people whose history in the high Middle Ages is to be the subject of this book were known by a number of names which were not entirely congruent with one another. In the tenth century the term 'kingdom of the eastern Franks' (*regnum Francorum orientalium*) still indicated the origins of the kingdom as a part of the Frankish Empire; but the term *Germania* came to be used with increasing frequency, and not just in its Roman sense of the lands to the right of the Rhine (though the phrase *Gallia et Germania*, which preserves this Roman distinction, was still often used to describe the German kingdom). It was only from the eleventh century onwards that the term *regnum Teutonicum/Teutonicorum* came to be generally used; it was paralleled by Gregory VII's use of the term 'king of the Germans', which was intended to deny the German king the unique title of a king of the Romans (*rex Romanorum*) and put him in the same category as the kings of the Danes, Hungarians, and so on. If we look through the writings of Bishop Otto of Freising (†1158), the most important historian of the German Middle Ages, we find a whole range of names used alongside one another: *Franci orientales*, *Franci Teutonici*, *Teutonici*, *Germani*, *Alemanni*, and correspondingly *Francia orientalis*, *Francorum regnum orientale*, *Teutonicum/Teutonicorum regnum*, *Germania*, *Alemannia*. What is apparently the oldest use of the term *regnum Teutonicorum*, found in a twelfth-century copy of tenth-century annals made in the monastery of Admont in Austria, may in fact not be so; it is an open question whether the phrase was already in the original from which the copy was made or whether the copyist, influenced by Otto's work, introduced it himself. There is no Old High German word for 'Germany': *diutschen lant* and similar phrases first appeared in the twelfth and thirteenth centuries and even then remained rare. It was only from the sixteenth century onwards that the word *Deutschland*, 'Germany', became widely used. *Deutsch* and *Deutschland* were the concepts familiar to the nationalistic way of thought prevalent in the nineteenth century, and took in the Germans of antiquity as well: examples of this range from the student drinking-song by Victor von Scheffels (†1886) about the 'insolent Romans' who marched into 'the north of Germany' to serious studies like that of Adolf von Harnack (†1932), who sought to show that Pope Boniface II (530–2), because he had a Gothic father, had been 'the first German' to become bishop of Rome.

The history of the German kingdom is even today generally

subdivided into dynastic periods. The Carolingian dynasty, named after its most distinguished member Charles the Great, remained in power in the various parts of the Frankish Empire after this had ceased to be a unity. It was succeeded in east Francia or Germany by kings from the Saxon house (919–1024); these in turn were succeeded by the Salians (Salians here meaning Salian Franks, a reference to the ancestry of Conrad II) from 1024 to 1125, and these in turn – after an interlude under Lothar of Supplinburg (1125–37) – gave way to the Staufer (1138–1254). These terms appear at first sight superficial and uninformative, but they do in fact indicate a structural change of some significance. The earlier kings were identified with one of the old tribes of the German kingdom (Saxons, Frisians, Franks, Thuringians, Suabians or Alemanni, Bavarians), in which they had previously been dukes and from which they continued to find their principal support after they became kings. The Staufer, by contrast, took their name from that of a castle, Stauf near Göppingen. From the king whose rule is based on a tribe we move to the ruler who takes his name from a castle or from allodial property. The ability of a king to make his will prevail came to depend more and more on the extent of his allodial lands – and not on the possession of ducal office or of the crown domains: one more reason why the electoral princes who controlled the elective kingship tended from the thirteenth century onwards to look for 'a small count' who could be elected as king.

The German kingdom, whose ruler was also king of Burgundy and imperial Italy, and so of three kingdoms in all, had the following border regions – we cannot speak of borders yet – around the mid eleventh century. In the north Danish settlement began beyond the River Schlei – the role of Haithabu as a harbour and trading-centre had already begun to decline, while the region between the Schlei and the Eider, the northern border of the county of Holstein, remained largely uninhabited. In the West, beyond Frisia, which was never wholly integrated into the kingdom of Germany, lay Flanders, rich in markets, which formed a kind of buffer state between the kingdoms of France and Germany. The count of Flanders was a double vassal – he held imperial Flanders as a fief from the German king, and royal Flanders from the French ruler. In the eleventh and twelfth centuries there were constant conflicts between the German king and the rebellious counts of Flanders, who provided a haven for rebels. To the south of the two duchies of Lotharingia lay the kingdom of Burgundy, divided into Upper Burgundy (later Franche-Comté) and Lower Burgundy, with important towns like Besançon (an imperial town until 1674), Lyons, Vienne, Geneva and Lausanne. The kingdom had come to the Empire in 1034 on the death of King Rudolf III, but the bond was a loose one, and it was only Barbarossa's marriage to Beatrice of Upper Burgundy in 1156 which brought the two kingdoms closer together. Beyond the Alpine barrier lay Lombardy and imperial Italy up to the borders of the papal state; the hold of the German rulers on Italy constantly needed renewing.

The eastern border of the kingdom of Germany had a quite different character; right through into the high Middle Ages relations between the Empire and its eastern neighbours were characterized by more or less permanent warfare. From Charlemagne's first campaign against the Slavs in 789 to Barbarossa's Polish campaign in 1157 no fewer than 175 armed clashes have been counted, and this does not include minor skirmishes or border conflicts. Much more effort was put into these wars than into the Italian expeditions, without much to show for it – about half the campaigns must be regarded as unsuccessful. Until the twelfth century there were invasions and expeditions almost annually, using the same tactics each time and almost always the same invasion-routes. One of the main problems for the Germans was securing their supplies: a large army had a baggage-train which could stretch out over sixty miles on poor and narrow roads. In order to remain mobile, it was customary to plan to live off the land. 'Only when the harvest was ripe, around the first of August, could the army be assembled. After eight to ten weeks a withdrawal was necessary, in order not to be overtaken by winter' (K. Schünemann). Rivers offered little help to eastern invasions, for the majority of central European rivers flow from south to north rather than from west to east, with the important exceptions of the Danube and the Havel; these rivers were in practice the favoured invasion-routes, along with the two routes into Bohemia over the Erz Mountains through the Kühner Pass and along the Regen past Cham in the direction of Pilsen. The growth of state organization in these regions brought with it the erection of a wide network of frontier fortifications, such as the so-called Preseka in Poland. These were designed to block the paths of invaders, and consisted of great blockades of felled trees and trenches, which could not easily be taken with the usual siege-machinery. The marches which lay around the heartlands of Germany were intended to ward off attacks as well as prepare for invasions; even in the twelfth century their inhabitants had 'to be tough and not fear to risk their lives', to quote a marcher count cited by the Holstein priest Helmold of Bosau. Only gradually could the borders be made secure, and they remained uncertain and dangerous, especially as brutal razzias were still being carried out in the twelfth century on the Slav borders to capture wares for the European slave-market, which had its centre in northern Italy. It was only after a more orderly colonization had led to the Germanizing of the lands of the Elbe Slavs that the situation was stabilized.

East of a line running roughly from the mouth of the Schwentine in the Firth of Kiel down to the bend in the Elbe at Lauenburg lay the border region of the *Limes Saxoniae*, a waste zone with a few scattered settlers; beyond this lay Slavs, the Abodrites and Wagrii. Here and in the mid-Elbe region there were numerous Slavonic tribes; though these might join together in a religious confederation they never formed substantial political units. The situation was quite different in the lands to the east and south-east: Poland, Bohemia and Hungary. Here there were states with established dynasties and a degree of political organization, a substantial military potential and something like an incipient feudalism. The name *Polonia* first appears for *Sclavinia* under Boleslav the Bold (†1025) from the legendary Piast dynasty. It expresses an attitude of mind which regarded Poland as a state alongside the German Empire, just as the Polish church had freed itself from its missionary and suffragan relationship to the German church and acquired its own organization under the metropolitan see of Gnesen. The so-called castellany organization was established – castles with dependent districts and associated settlements of craftsmen run by royal *ministeriales* – which gave the Polish state a considerable degree of centralization; this was enhanced by the fact that the Polish ruler, in contrast to the German king, had a fixed residence, first at Posen, then at Gnesen and finally at Cracow. In Bohemia the Premyslids consolidated their rule, though it was constantly under threat. The Premyslid Duke Wenceslas, whose murder in 935 (?) soon came to be regarded as a martyrdom, rose to the status of a patron saint of the new country; the whole Bohemian people became his *familia*, a closed group bound to their lord as his vassals and servants. Here too there was an attempt to establish a separate archbishopric; Duke Bretislaw kidnapped the relics of St Adalbert from Gnesen and carried them off to Prague in 1039. In Hungary the Arpads were the ruling dynasty. St Stephen I (†1038) had carried through the Christianization of the country with unusual energy; he had set up a church organization under an archbishopric at Gran, had his kingship confirmed by the pope with the agreement of the German king, and was crowned and anointed on Christmas Day 1000. In the civil wars which followed Stephen's death the Arpad Andreas established himself against the will of the German king; in 1055 a compromise was reached by which Andreas agreed to pay tribute. At this time all three eastern states – Poland, Bohemia and Hungary – were tributaries of the Empire, but their rulers had shown again and again how much independence and equality with Germany meant to them. The south-eastern border was protected by marches whose number and extent fluctuated: from 976 Austria was a march under the Babenberger; the march of Carinthia was later split off from it; there were further marches in Styria, Krain and Istria. The border county of Verona had the function of linking Germany with the kingdom of Italy; beyond the borders of the kingdom lay the papal state.

3 The economy of the Empire

The manorially organized rural society which had developed in the Carolingian period was largely self-sufficient economically. There were admittedly centres which produced for the needs of churches and monasteries as well as for the court, particularly in the artistic sphere, but in the villages everything from house-building to cloth-making was produced domestically. Within a particular manor there might well be craftsmen – smiths, millers, waggoners – but their output, even though it might be substantial, was destined for consumption within the manor itself. The transformations which came about in the high Middle Ages had numerous causes. The crown stepped up the working of silver-mines and used the money to purchase additional supplies at the palaces and royal manors. Already in Otto the Great's time, when the silver-lodes were first discovered near Goslar, it was reported that the court spent thirty pounds of silver per day. The Staufer had an annual income of 65,000 pounds of silver from towns, crown lands and the Italian *regalia*, and most of this they put back into circulation. This circulation was generally in the form of coinage, though ingots were also used. Many ecclesiastical and secular lords had secured minting privileges and ran their own mints, making their profits out of the coinage fees.

The coinage was silver; not until the fourteenth century were gold coins in circulation in Germany. The pennies and halfpennies of the Ottonian and Salian period were stamped on both sides; in the twelfth century one-sided coins, bracteates, also circulated. The mark was the main unit of account; within Germany the most favoured (because of its stability) of the various marks was that of Cologne, which was probably also the oldest. It amounted to 233 grams of silver in coined form, and was divided into twelve shillings (*solidi*) or 144 pennies (*denarii*). The increase in the number of mints and the variety of different pennies – whose weight was often reduced by the owners of mints, sometimes with royal permission – led to the 'regional penny coinage, no longer valid throughout Germany but in general only in the place it was minted and its immediate vicinity. A traveller was forced to exchange his coinage at each stopping-point' (A. Suhle). The weights on which the coinage was based were subject to such variation that there was a tendency to value coins by their weight: the 'pound', meaning a pound by weight of pennies, became a new unit of account.

Finds of coins from the Ottonian and early Salian periods show the rapid rise in the production of mints and the growth of long-distance trade: 38,000 German coins from the period have been found on the island of Gotland alone, 9,000 in Russia, 4,000 in Denmark and 2,500 in Norway. The increase in trade was accompanied by an increase in the number of toll-stations. It has been estimated for a slightly later period that there were toll-stations on average every ten kilometres along the Rhine between Basle and Rotterdam; the tolls on the fifty-kilometre stretch between Bingen and Koblenz put the cost of the goods transported up by about two-thirds.

The routes in use in the Carolingian period remained largely unchanged until the twelfth century; only in the Staufer period was there some improvement in the number and quality of the roads. The extension of the West through the crusades and trade with the Near East, the spread of German settlers and German influence eastwards, and the increase in the size and mobility of the population led to a greater density of traffic. By the thirteenth century most of the routes taken by the roads of the present day (motorways excepted) had probably already been established, with north–south routes better represented than those running east–west. The main north–south artery came from the Great St Bernard (Mons Jovis) to Basle, where it was joined by the road from the Septimer, 'king of the Bündner passes'. From Basle the road ran along the left bank of the Rhine to Strasburg, where it divided. One fork went via Speyer and Worms to Mainz; the other led via Koblenz to Cologne and the Rhine delta. A road along the right bank of the Rhine via Frankfurt and Neuß led to Frisia, with branches off to Münster, Osnabrück, Stade, and via the lower Elbe to Itzehoe and Schleswig. Bremen and

Hamburg were linked to Würzburg and Augsburg by a road which went via Verden and Frankfurt; from Augsburg a further road through Memmingen and Reutte led across the Reschen pass to Meran. The more the frontier of the Empire shifted eastwards after 1000, the more the Brenner pass rose in importance. The Great St Bernard was preferred by pilgrims and merchants, but the Brenner was the main military route: 66 of the 144 Alpine crossings made by the German kings used the Brenner, whose importance also increased with the growing prominence of Venice as a trading centre. The opening up of the Baltic and the growth of the power of the Welfs gave a new importance to a road which went from Lübeck via Lüneburg to Brunswick and from there via Halberstadt to the valley of the Saale and via Goslar to Eisenach. Thuringia was linked to Nürnberg by a road through Coburg and Bamberg.

Up to the Staufer period Germany had played only a peripheral role in European long-distance trade, but from now on the roads along the Rhine which linked Italy with the lands around the Rhine delta and even with England and Scandinavia, together with the routes taken by the Russian and Scandinavian trade from Lübeck through Brunswick to Westfalia and Cologne, were major trade arteries. Nevertheless, the German North and the German South were two largely independent trading regions: the differences have been summed up in the slightly exaggerated statement that the towns in the South were primarily those of craftsmen, those in the North those of merchants. The incorporation of Germany into the European long-distance trade network led to an increase in the number of markets; a more widespread circulation of coinage and the increasing use of trading partnerships led to a growth in credit and money-lending. In the communities laying along the Rhine between Cologne and Worms we find Jews acting as money-lenders – taking interest on loans was forbidden to Christians – but also as dealers in dyes and medicines. They were under episcopal, and sometimes also royal, protection, and lived mostly in their own quarters, though sometimes side by side with Christian merchants. It was only towards the end of the eleventh century with the first pogroms instituted by the crusaders that walls were erected around the Jewish quarters: the first recorded instance was in Speyer in 1084. The settlements of wandering merchants were also surrounded by palisades, walls or even fortifications to protect the market. Such market settlements under the protection of the lord of the market had a church which was also the centre for the merchants organized together in a guild. Each guild would have its own church in the larger trading centres: there were fifty-five in Durestad (now Wijk-bei-Duurstede near Utrecht) and sixteen in Wisby on Gotland. The customs of the market which grew up with trade and guaranteed protection to merchants were gradually transformed into a merchant's law (*ius mercatorum*); in the case of a new settlement such a law was conceded to the merchants from the beginning. Once the number of merchants had passed a certain point it became attractive to craftsmen to settle in such centres; craftwork might also be commissioned by merchants intending to sell the products elsewhere. Rhineland pottery, for example, has been found in remote villages in the Harz from the eleventh century. The craftsmen also met the demand from the immediate hinterland of the town; markets grew up which had as their customers not just the merchants and burghers of the town (some of whom also owned farmland) but also the rural population of the surrounding region. Some of the basic crafts are for this reason found in towns from a very early period: baking, smithery, cobblery, milling, weaving, pottery, and so on. As early as the eleventh century we meet a *ius fori*, a law covering the local market, which had its origins not in the royal monopoly of market rights but in the powers of the town's landlords. The abbot of Reichenau, for example, granted Allenbach such a local market law in 1075.

In many towns in the twelfth century we can find closed settlements of craftsmen – weavers, dyers, cloth-cutters, wood-turners – and the town lords began to grant the first confirmations of liberties to such corporate bodies. Specialization began, and we find the first craft branches specializing in work for luxury consumption or distant markets: furriery, glovemaking, and swordmaking. Around the middle of the twelfth century there were coopers and cupmakers working in wood in Strasburg and in Regensburg in 1156 there was a street called *inter tonsores panorum*, 'alley of the cloth-cutters who refined raw cloth'.

From the twelfth century onwards German merchants appear all over Europe. Trade with Scandinavia was almost a German monopoly, especially after the foundation of Lübeck: Russian furs were transported inland, as was the herring which was caught off Rügen and the coast of Scania, salted down with the salt from Lüneburg, and packed into barrels produced locally; German craft products went in the opposite direction. Germans appeared in England and Italy trading in glass, swords, and linen; Aachen and Cologne were part of a region of specialized cloth production with its centre in Flanders. But raw materials and basic foodstuffs were also exported, such as wine to England and grain to Scandinavia. The aggressive merchants from Regensburg, Cologne, Aachen and Ulm were soon the object of defensive measures; treaties between the cities of Italy, which had become an object of interest to German merchants as the Staufer re-established their power there, formally excluded Germans from the Mediterranean trade, a sign of the strength of their competition.

The craftsmen also became more self-confident. They joined together in corporations, which represented their collective interests externally and internally acted as a kind of supervisory inspection for the trade in question. The oldest such corporations were probably those of the weavers of Mainz (mentioned in 1099), the fishmongers of Worms (1106/7) and the glovemakers of Würzburg (1128). There were as yet no tensions within the corporations, which were firmly organized under a 'father' at the head, and at this stage they did not demand a say in the government of their towns.

4 The period from 1050 to 1200 as a turning-point in European and German history

The idea that there was a dramatic transformation of western society around the middle of the eleventh century is a view which has become ever more prevalent in recent years, and is common ground to both 'bourgeois' and Marxist historiography. The beginning of the 'second age of feudalism' or of 'high feudalism'; the end of the 'archaic epoch' and the 'rise of medieval society'; an 'intensification of cultivation, craft production and trade' which altered both the landscape and the structure of the economy; 'population growth', a rise in both 'vertical' and 'horizontal mobility'; 'communal movements'; the final breach between and mutual cursing of the eastern and western churches in 1054; a 'church reform' brought about by a 'papal revolution'; a 'new mentality' which showed itself both in a more rigorous orthodox theological discussion and in heterodox expressions of opinion; 'dialectic' and 'antidialectic': these and other phrases have been used to emphasize particular aspects of the radical changes which took place in the eleventh century.

The political map of Europe also began to change around the middle of the eleventh century. In southern Italy the Norman Hauteville family established itself around 1050; within a few decades it was to build up the most modern state in Europe. In 1066 the victory of Duke William of Normandy over the Anglo-Saxon king Harold and his *huscarls* took England out of the Scandinavian sphere of influence and into that of the Continent. In Spain the *reconquista* began, the Christian reconquest of the lands occupied by the Moors. Beyond the Latin world, but not without consequences for it, there were large-scale shifts of power. The Turkish Seljuks from Central Asia conquered the eastern half of Islam with breathtaking speed, and blocked the path of Christian pilgrims to the Holy Sepulchre. As late as 1064 Bishop Gunther of Bamberg organized a pilgrimage to Jerusalem with, we are told, 12,000 pilgrims, on which the German 'Hymn of Christ's wonders' by the schoolmaster Ezzo was sung and to which the Byzantine purple cloak in the treasury of Bamberg Cathedral still bears witness. In 1071 the Seljuks of Rum defeated the Byzantine emperor; the petty empire of eastern Rome, from now on perpetually threatened in its very existence, sought backing from the West, though in its eyes the West was barbarous and deviated from the orthodox faith.

The social and political structures of the German Empire had shown a remarkable stability until immediately before this period of transformation, and no one questioned that the German emperor had a special responsibility for the well-being of Christendom. It was a halcyon period, and there seemed no reason for it to come to an end: stability was seemingly assured by a kingship whose hereditary basis was scarcely questioned, a designated successor to the throne, and an apparent absence of social and political tensions.

The period around 1200, where this book ends, was already perceived by contemporaries as a turning-point. 'The Year 1200' was in 1970 the object of an exhibition and of a scholarly conference, and a number of books have dealt with the twelfth century as an epoch of its own, whether characterized as a 'renaissance' (C. H. Haskins, C. N. L. Brooke), a 'pluralism' (P. Lehmann) or simply as 'Twelfth Century Europe' (S. Packard). The Frankish crusader states had collapsed in 1187 under the onslaught of the new Sultan Saladin. Jerusalem was lost, and after the Third Crusade had ended in catastrophe, with the German king Frederick Barbarossa dying in 1190, the French king returning almost immediately and the English king Richard Lionheart unable to achieve much, the diversion of the Fourth Crusade against Constantinople marked the final perversion of the knightly ideal of an armed pilgrimage to the Holy Sepulchre. After this the kings of Germany, France and England never again joined together to go on crusade, and the former crusading states became mere bridgeheads, which had to be abandoned one by one. Around 1200 there were drastic changes within the kingdoms of

France and Germany and in the relations between the two kingdoms. Philip Augustus (1180–1223) was able to consolidate the
power of the French crown and establish the principle of *ligesse*,
which set fealty to the king above all other feudal claims. Secure in
the power conferred by his extensive possessions in the Île-de-
France, Philip II had the English king's continental fiefs adjudged
forfeit in a feudal trial in 1202; John's ancestor had conquered
England as Duke of Normandy and he was thus a vassal of the
French crown. France became a unified state with a modern
centralized administration; Philip was able to quadruple the crown
domain and win a brilliant victory over the Anglo-Welf alliance at
Bouvines in 1214. It was not the whole German army which was
defeated, but only that of the supporters of the Welf king Otto IV;
nevertheless it was seen as a decisive defeat for the Germans: 'it is an
established fact that from this time on the reputation of the Germans
declined among the Welsch [i.e. foreigners who spoke a Romance
language]', wrote a contemporary chronicler. Philip had the broken
wings of the imperial eagle repaired and sent it to his Staufer ally, the
twenty-year-old German king Frederick II. The defeat at Bouvines
also meant that the English king John had to give up his plans for
reconquering his continental possessions. Internally his struggles
against the barons led in 1215 to the issuing of the most important
document of English constitutional history, Magna Carta. France
and England were in their different ways on the way to becoming
unified states in 1200. Such constitutional changes were accompanied by social and economic changes of equal magnitude, so that
it has been suggested that we should consider the period from 1200
to the French Revolution as an era in itself, 'Old Europe' or 'the
early modern era'. Similarly, ecclesiastical historians have seen in
the pontificate of Innocent III (1198–1216) the 'turning-point for the
medieval church', and the 'orientation of all Christendom towards
the Roman curia', i.e. the beginnings of the modern papal church
(B. Moeller).

What was the position of the Empire? The death of the young
King Henry VI in 1197 at the age of thirty-two while he was
preparing for a crusade to be waged by German knights has been
called 'the greatest catastrophe of the German Middle Ages'; it had
seemed that he would have succeeded in achieving a unification of
the Sicilian, Italian and German kingdoms. The civil war which
followed between the three claimants to the throne, Philip of
Suabia, Otto IV and Frederick II, with Pope Innocent III acting both
as referee and as the man who conferred the imperial title and hence

could judge the suitability of the German king, showed how a new
situation had arisen, dominated by a hierocratic papacy. The princes
and the towns went their own ways, ignoring the crown; town
leagues and merchant guilds organized their own protection, since
the king was no longer able to keep the peace. The feudal structures
ossified into the *Heerschild* (see below, p. 171). The old tribal duchies
were replaced by territorial lordships. The fall of Henry the Lion in
1180 and the constitutional changes which accompanied it showed
what was in process: the establishing of large stable territories which
were to survive the following centuries, for example in Bohemia, on
the lower Rhine, or in Bavaria, of which P. Moraw has said that 'the
later Middle Ages last from 1180 to 1506'. The prestige of the
Empire, so high under Frederick Barbarossa and Henry VI, sank
almost to insignificance, and Frederick II's reign has been described
as 'an epilogue to the great days of the imperial period'.

New forms of piety emerged. Communities were set up outside
the official church, consisting of people who sought salvation in
poverty and penitence, free of the ballast of earthly possessions. The
Waldensians (named after the Lyonese merchant Waldes, † before
1218), sought to recapture the way of life of the early Christians
even in their clothing, and converted many by their moral and
evangelistic fervour. Orders of friars like those founded by the
brilliant figure Francis of Assisi (†1226) or the penetrating theologian Dominic (†1221) opened up new opportunities for the church
and won back groups whose orthodoxy was insecure; prophets and
mystics like the Calabrian abbot Joachim of Fiore (†1202) provided
new perspectives on man's place in the history of salvation.

The period between 1050 and 1200 has been characterized as that
of the 'discovery of the individual' (C. Morris), and indeed there
was a change in intellectual consciousness, a new belief that the
world could be understood through reason. The question thrown
up by scholasticism, 'what holds the world together in its innermost
being?', took on a life of its own. The great dispute over universals
began; Averroes (†1198) revealed to the West his view of the
world based on Aristotle, in which a world to come was no longer a
necessary assumption. Education, which had been frozen in the
tradition of the 'seven liberal arts', was transformed into the
specialized study practised at universities, with new academic
professions and a ceaseless intellectual unrest. There has perhaps
been no period in which Europe turned with such enthusiasm to the
new and the modern as in these decades between 1050 and 1200.

2

'PROGRESS AND PROMISE': THE GERMAN EMPIRE IN THE MID ELEVENTH CENTURY

In 1944 the British historian Geoffrey Barraclough published a learned and in many ways original book, *The Origins of Modern Germany*. Its chapter on the period 1024–75 is entitled 'The era of progress and promise'. Compared with its state at the beginning of the tenth century and measured against contemporary France and England, eleventh-century Germany

was a homogeneous land, held together by great and enduring traditions, ruled over by energetic and intelligent sovereigns, who had proved competent to resist and counteract the disintegration of society which accompanied the ravages of invasion from north and east. The leadership of Europe was firmly established in German hands . . . by the middle of the eleventh century the realm was firmly united under its ruling dynasty, and all traces of particularism seemed on the point of disappearance . . . The only question was whether the crown, which had worked hard to release the new forces in German life, would continue to control and profit from the economic and social movements of the century . . . Germany had already far outstripped France and England . . . and was already on the path leading to a more modern form of government.

SOCIAL STRATIFICATION AND THE STRUCTURE OF GOVERNMENT IN THE OTTONIAN AND SALIAN PERIOD

The medieval form of rule was monarchy. Both in the iconography of the Old Testament, and in mirrors for princes, where reference was made to the natural order of things as seen in swarms of bees and in other examples, it went without saying that the person who ruled was a monarch. Nevertheless, many things about the king were not self-evident. Did he come to his office by hereditary right or by election? If by election, who elected him? was he elected for life, or could he be deposed? The king was surrounded by his court; but the German rulers of the high Middle Ages had no fixed residence and the Empire no capital. The king 'exercised his rights in travelling around the country', as one commentator has put it, and an impressive entourage, including the queen as *consors regni* ('co-ruler of the kingdom'), moved about the land with the king. The itinerant ruler had constantly to renew his rights by his presence, and as one of his first official actions he would go on a progress through the kingdom to receive his subjects' allegiance. The route the king travelled was dictated mainly by political considerations, but also took into account the need to eat up the produce of the royal estates. Not much is known about the royal lands and how they were organized; the most important source is a list of 'estates serving the table of the king of the Romans', which according to the most recent research probably belongs to the period around 1152, though it has been dated as early as 1064 and as late as 1189. Theoretically the king had the right to claim food and lodging from anyone, but this remained theory, and he would often break his journey at a palace that was directly served by a royal estate. The fact that kings over the centuries travelled more or less the same roads may largely be attributed to the problem of feeding themselves and their followers. Some regions were rarely or never visited by the king. When Henry IV came to meet the Danish king Sven Estridsen at Bardowick/Lüneburg in 1071, a Saxon writer observed that there was no previous record of a king's having come 'into those parts'. From very early times the noble and great secured exemption for themselves from such 'royal service' (*servitium regis*), from providing hospitality for the travelling king. One nobleman is reported on his death-bed to have warned his son against two things: waging war, and receiving the king as his guest. By contrast, the imperial church – bishoprics and royal monasteries – was having increased demands for hospitality made on it by Henry III's time, and the burden was a heavy one. It has been calculated that the king was normally accompanied by anything from three hundred to four thousand persons. Warning of the king's arrival had to be given four to six weeks beforehand, so that food and lodging could be organized; such advance notice was essential because the court consumed gargantuan quantities of food and drink. A twelfth-century writer says that the court's daily consumption was one thousand pigs and sheep, ten barrels of wine and ten of beer, one thousand bushels of corn, eight oxen, 'and other things besides', though his report refers to the tenth century, not his own, and is probably an exaggeration. Normally the court would stay for only a short time in one place before moving on. In an average day's travel it would cover twelve to seventeen miles but there could be great variations from the average: Frederick I's best performances were a journey of fifty-five miles by land in a day and a half to two days and one of eighty-five miles by boat in a day and a half.

Until late in the high Middle Ages the Empire was a state based on personal ties. The king's power depended largely on the feudal relationship, in which a vassal received a fief in return for his services. The element of property in the relationship should not, however, be overstressed; the vassal did not owe service just because he had a fief. Lord and vassal were bound to each other in service and fidelity, and the granting of the fief followed from these obligations as well as helping to create them. The vassal's duties, the most important of which was military service, derived not only from the obedience due from a subordinate but also from the fidelity due from a comrade. He promised his lord to 'be with him' (*praesens ero*) and to give him 'advice and help' (*consilium et auxilium*) at any time. The lord, for his part, was obliged to protect the vassal's property and rights (*defensio*). The king was the suzerain lord; his kingship was no more than a noble lordship on a large scale. The danger facing the king in the feudal relationship was that he might lose all rights of ownership over a fief. If offices normally granted as fiefs became hereditary property, the king's control over them was reduced, whereas if heritability could be prevented it was much easier to preserve their character as offices. It was for this reason, though not only for this reason, that the church offered itself as an alternative body to which the king could delegate his powers of government.

The layman's influence within the church derived from his ownership of proprietary churches. According to the modern view of the proprietary church, the owner had the right to appoint priests to churches built on his land; by analogy the king made church appointments as proprietary lord of churches founded on royal land. He installed his appointees by investing them. In Germanic law, *investitura* (*gewere* in Middle High German) meant the formal act by which a landowner transferred his property to a new owner; it was done by handing over an object which symbolized the property. Feudal law adopted the notion from Germanic property law. A vassal was invested with a fief by receiving one of the secular symbols of investiture, a sword, spear or staff, while doing fealty and homage (*hominium, homagium*) to his lord. In lesser churches proprietary lords invested priests by giving them a service-book, a bell rope, or some other valuable object belonging to the church. Up to the time of Henry III the king invested bishops and abbots by handing over the pastoral staff. As this symbolized not only the church but also the office, the act of investiture made no symbolic distinction between giving the prelate his spiritual powers and giving him the secular rights and possessions which went with his church.

Moreover, Otto I (936–73) and his successors had given regalian rights to the church, thus developing the right of immunity which churches had come to enjoy by the Carolingian period. Immunity meant that every episcopal church and royal monastery enjoyed royal protection, was exempt from taxation, lay outside the jurisdiction of royal officials, and was empowered to exercise low justice, i.e. the right to impose fines as punishment for lesser offences. Because the king gave bishops and abbots the right of the ban, the royal power to command and punish, church immunity now included powers of high justice, i.e. the right to try major offences and to impose corporal and capital punishments. The result was that immunities were transformed into 'banal districts' in which ecclesiastics exercised the king's rights. At the same time, the right of immunity, which had originally covered only property owned by the church, was now extended, and could be granted over land not in church ownership. The king even gave control of some counties to bishoprics and royal monasteries, thereby drawing them into the administration of the Empire. The church received rich donations of land and grants of regalian rights, such as the right to hold a market, to mint coins, to exercise forest jurisdiction, and to collect customs dues. In this way the foundations were laid for the princely rank enjoyed by later royal bishops and abbots. This durable form of rule, the so-called 'imperial church system', traces of which survived right up to the end of the Holy Roman Empire in 1806, was possible only because the bishoprics and royal monasteries in the Empire were not mediatized, that is the king did not lose control of important ecclesiastical appointments to local magnates. In France, by contrast, more than half of these offices were controlled by secular princes, who invested candidates of their own choice. As long as the connection between the king and the major churches remained unbroken, there was no danger to his authority. When the king granted royal rights to churches, he did not have to worry about whether the rights might be lost to the crown, because he knew he could choose the men who would hold them. He knew that they would perform the various services their churches owed him, such as supplying contingents of troops for his armies and providing *servitium regis* for him and his court. Moreover, he had in the royal chapel an institution which trained and supplied him with the most important candidates for major church offices. The royal chapel, whose members were all drawn from the nobility, had originally been responsible for looking after the king's collection of relics and meeting the court's liturgical needs, but the chaplains had come more and more to be entrusted with the central administration of the Empire. Some served as scribes and notaries, headed by a chancellor (*cancellarius*). The prestige of this court officer grew: he became an archchancellor, and took over the functions of the former head of the chapel, the archchaplain, until in the twelfth century the new office of imperial chancellor emerged from the combination of these offices.

What did the 'normal' career of a clerical member of the imperial aristocracy look like? The boy would have been destined from an early age by his parents for an ecclesiastical career, perhaps being sent to a monastic school, and would then have joined the imperial chapel. He lived from a benefice attached to his duties as chaplain. At an appropriate moment the king would propose him for a bishopric; the chapter of the bishopric concerned might have expressed their wishes, but the king's will was decisive, although the procedure for canonical election required the participation of clergy and people.

Up to the eleventh century it is very difficult to distinguish between the various strata and groupings within the nobility; because of the unfavourable nature of the sources, only the high nobility are clearly visible. It should be emphasized that the nobility were 'in many ways not tied to a tribe, but had wide-ranging and fluctuating connections through their family relations and their property-holding', and it would for this reason be dangerous to 'classify nobles who appear only to have had a local range of activity as "petty" or "local" nobility' (W. Störmer). The family of the Andechser, for example, was related to the Ebersberger and the Öhninger (the name comes from Öhningen, near Stein am Rhein); these in turn were related to the ruling Ottonian house, and the 'Öhninger group' also included men like Archbishop Frederick I of Cologne (1099–1131) from the family of the lords of Schwarzenburg and Rötz (near Cham). These highly interrelated nobles were able to turn scattered land-holdings into concentrated territories, and thus create a lordly class of great economic and political importance; but there was no legally closed noble class with specific privileges.

In the first half of the eleventh century a new group of men who participated in the government of the Empire emerged, the *ministeriales* – the name may be translated as 'functionaries'. In origin they were unfree men who were drawn on by landlords for administrative and military tasks. Service in their lord's household and in the field separated them from the other dependants of the lord's *familia*, a process reflected in the household laws of the eleventh century. In the oldest surviving household law, that of Bishop Burchard I of Worms (†1025), the *ministeriales* are mentioned as a part of the *familia* without any specification of their duties, but the household laws of Cologne and Bamberg from the second half of the eleventh century treat them as a corporate group on their own: the lord's *familia* is now divided into a *familia servilis* and a *familia ministerialis*. As servants who provided their lord with armed protection, they were initially most numerous in ecclesiastical lordships, but as the king began to make use of *ministeriales* in his service a new class arose alongside the old high nobility. This turning away from the aristocracy has parallels in Italy. Conrad II (1024–39) issued an edict for imperial Italy in 1037 which laid down that the fiefs of subvassals, the *valvassores*, were heritable, something which the great lords, the *capitanei*, had refused to concede. The decision had far-reaching consequences. Up to that point the bishops, who were drawn from the high nobility, had been allied with the king, and Archbishop Aribert of Milan (†1045), the leader of the *capitanei*, was held to be the spokesman of the interests of the German king. But Aribert and his supporters did not recognize the king's decision, and the dispute ended with the deposition of Aribert at Conrad's command. Conrad's action pointed the way to future developments: against the high nobility the king supported both the rival group of subvassals, as in Italy, and the *ministeriales* who served the king and were frequently at odds with the nobility. Conrad II himself appointed a *ministerialis*, Werner, not a member of the nobility, to head the administration of the royal fisc.

The *ministeriales* were a peculiarity of Germany in this period. In England and France the king relied much more on the feudal ties with his vassals. *Ministeriales* were more controllable than vassals: they received a service tenancy, akin to a fief, but they remained unfree and were for that reason more controllable. Service as mounted warriors gave them the status of lesser nobility, a group with which they soon merged, especially as numerous impoverished *Edelfreie* became *ministeriales*. From the time of Henry III onwards the 'imperial *ministeriales*' became ever more important as instruments of royal government, until their high summer in the Staufer period.

A class of free men had also survived in Germany: admittedly there was very wide differentiation among its members, ranging from a free peasant sitting on a single smallholding to an *Edelfreier* with extensive landed property. Both, however, owned their land, and were legally on the same plane. Their ownership of land, of allods, did not prevent them from accepting fiefs, so that land held in allodial and in feudal tenure often lay side by side, patchwork fashion: this was especially common in the duchy of Bavaria. In contrast to France, the existence of extensive allodial holdings prevented the emergence of regions where all land was held as fiefs.

The majority of the population in the archaic society which came to an end in the eleventh century was the great mass of people who were incorporated as serfs and dependants into a group determined by its ties to a lord, a *familia*. This term, whose meaning is not free from ambiguities, has as its essential component some kind of servile dependence on the household of a landed lord. Such dependants could belong to the *familia regis*, like the royal *ministeriales*, or to the *familia* of a *dux* or a *nobilis*; they could also belong to a *familia abbatis* or *familia episcopi*, and in such cases the patron saint of the monastery or cathedral church often gave the *familia* its name. Bishop Burchard I of Worms refers to the dependants of his church as the *familia sancti Petri*, and in the household law which he issued there is some information about the size of the *familia* and the way of life of its members. The most extensive paragraph is that dealing with murder and manslaughter, 'which occur almost daily within the *familia sancti Petri* as if among wild beasts', often for quite trivial reasons or as a result of drunkenness. In the course of a single year, according to Burchard, thirty-five members of the *familia* had died 'innocently' – that is they had not been killed legitimately in self-defence or in order to prevent their commiting a crime – at the hands of their fellow-members. Burchard laid down punishments and penances to try to keep down the killing, which often came about in the course of blood-feuds. It is hard to estimate exactly what proportion of the population lived in dependence within such *familiae*, but Karl Bosl has suggested that up to the late eleventh and early twelfth centuries it was over 90%. From the eleventh century onwards some groups separated out from this large anonymous mass of the unfree – some burghers, peasants who achieved freedom by clearing land, and craftsmen. Those who were left were the agricultural serfs, who continued to exist as a class in some parts of Germany (Westfalia, for example) until the end of the eighteenth century.

REX ET SACERDOS – THE PRIESTLY KINGSHIP OF HENRY III (1039–56)

'If kings are good, it is a gift of God; if they are bad, it is the fault of the people, for the way of life of the ruler is dependent on the merits of his subjects.' The idea that the ruler assumes an obligation with his office had already been expressed by the church fathers, and Isidor of Seville (†636), from whose *Etymologiae* the above quotation is taken, transmitted it to the Middle Ages. No other German king of the high Middle Ages took his task with such unremitting seriousness as Henry III, a man who had 'a sense of deep subjection towards God, but at the same time a strong belief that his own divinely inspired will and command were owed unquestioning obedience', as G. Tellenbach put it. The figure of Henry III and his reign have been subjected to very varying judgements by historians. Some have seen him as the man who perfected a system of government going back to the Ottonian period, based on a harmony between the secular and the spiritual; others have depicted him as a kind of appeasement politician, a man who began the sell-out of royal rights to the church. In the 1935/6 edition of *Die Großen Deutschen (The Great Germans)*, a collection of biographical portraits which reflects contemporary attitudes very faithfully, there was no place for him, only for his son Henry IV, the man who fought against an aggressively expansionist papacy; in the post-war edition of 1956, at a time when the idea of a West based on a common tradition of Christianity was at its zenith, Henry IV was dropped and his biography replaced by that of Henry III – but even so, many critics found the assessment of Henry's statute 'problematic', in H. Grundmann's words.

No king before Henry III had showed a deeper religious feeling. After the victory over the Hungarians near Menfö in 1044 he held a thanksgiving service on the battlefield, and was the first to go down on his knees, dressed as a penitent, before the relic of the Holy Cross which had been brought with the army; he remained in penitential dress even for his triumphal entry into Regensburg for the general assembly following his victory. Reminded of the high dignity of the priesthood, he replied that he too had been anointed with holy oil. Henry III, praised by the court poet Wipo as a learned king, a *rex doctus*, was, in spite of his youth – he came to the throne at the age of twenty-two and died when he was thirty-nine – a gloomy and touchy man, who led a withdrawn and introverted life. At his marriage in 1043 to the no less pious Countess Agnes of Poitou he forbade the presence of court jesters at the marriage-feast. His father Conrad II had enjoyed crude jokes, and had had a man smeared with honey which was licked off by a bear, so that he could enjoy the sight of the man's fear; even the subsequently canonized Henry II had taken pleasure in making Bishop Meinwerk of Paderborn look ridiculous for his deficient knowledge of Latin at a public celebration of mass. Such things could not have happened with Henry III, and perhaps his attitude was determined by his wish to follow the canon law regulations for ecclesiastics to the letter: was there not a canon which forbade ecclesiastics the enjoyment of any kind of jest? For a layman to depose a bishop was contrary to canon law, yet Conrad II had deposed Archbishop Aribert of Milan; Henry III reconciled himself with the archbishop of 1040, immediately after coming to the throne, and allowed him to retain his office, although the two by no means saw eye to eye politically. Henry III also allowed Abbot Halinard of Saint-Bénigne in Dijon to refuse to take an oath of fidelity on his election as archbishop of Lyons in 1046, for ecclesiastics were not supposed to swear oaths, though few paid much heed to the prohibition; Henry himself issued an edict shortly afterwards which renewed the ban on clerics taking oaths in court proceedings. Again, simony – a crime named after the magician Simon in the Acts of the Apostles, a man who had wanted to buy from Peter the gifts of the Holy Ghost and was cursed by him for it – had always been forbidden, especially after its condemnation by Pope Gregory the Great, but the prohibition was ignored. Indeed the king, by bestowing lands and governmental rights on churches, helped to perpetuate simoniacal practices. Simony worked as a kind of equalization fund: the king would be paid a large sum for an office by a rich candidate, a sum which he would then pass on to others, or he would choose a dignitary for a not very well-endowed bishopric who disposed of substantial private means. This was undoubtedly *Simoniaca haeresis*, the heresy of simony: bestowing church offices in return for a consideration. Henry III absolutely refused to continue such practices, even against the express wish of his father Conrad II. To renounce income of this kind threatened the basis of royal government, especially since the kings were conferring not only church offices but also substantial property and rights of government. In the period from the accession of Otto III to the death of Henry III, between 983 and 1056, at least thirty-seven counties were conferred on churches, and Adam of Bremen, writing about the bishop of Würzburg in the mid eleventh century, reported that he possessed all the counties within his diocese and administered the duchy of Franconia besides.

Henry III renounced any claim to counter-gifts when conferring ecclesiastical office, but insisted on his right to invest prelates, to hand over formally the rights and properties of a see or abbey to the man elected. Besides the symbol previously used in the ceremony of investiture, the staff, Henry added the ring, the symbol of the spiritual mariage of the cleric with his church. He made up the deficit to the royal fisc which resulted from the spiritualization of election and investiture in other ways, for example by brutal confiscation of the lands of laymen. At the end of his reign, the beginning of which had been marked by the remark in a contemporary source that no one regretted Conrad II's death and all applauded Henry's accession, he had a reputation for 'greed and ruthlessness'. His attitude increasingly alienated the propertied nobility, especially as he surrounded himself with a 'secret cabinet' of *ministeriales*.

STRENGTHS AND WEAKNESSES OF SALIAN KINGSHIP

The stability of the Empire under the rule of Henry III often finds praise in modern accounts: his reign is the high-water mark of the Empire, according to A. Hauck and K. Hampe; he perfected the system founded by Otto I, according to J. Haller. The change of ruler in 1039 was the first since the accession of Otto II in 973 to pass off without a hitch. Everything was prepared. Henry had already been designated German king in 1028 and had taken part in government; on his father's death he was duke of Bavaria and Suabia, and in the same year he took over the duchy of Carinthia on the death of its duke. The dynasty was not yet secure, for in 1038 his first wife, Gunhild, the daughter of the powerful king of Denmark and England, Knut the Great, had died on the exhausting Italian expedition; the marriage had produced no children. Henry's second marriage in 1043 did not have the same political significance: Agnes was a daughter of Duke William V of Poitou and Aquitaine, and thus a member of the ducal house which had founded the Burgundian reform monastery of Cluny and had shown its religious enthusiasm in other ways – donations to monasteries, and participation in the peace movement. Agnes herself was a sternly pious lady, whose piety was in later years to turn into bigotry. It is an open question whether Henry felt himself specially drawn to the spirituality of Burgundy and of Cluny, but he had himself acknowledged as king by the magnates of Burgundy early in his reign (1041); since 1034 the kingdom had been a part of the Empire alongside Germany and Italy.

Three duchies, those of Bavaria, Suabia and Carinthia, in the hands of the king meant an unusual concentration of power. However, the king was dependent on supporters who would share the exercise of lordship with him, and he soon bestowed the duchies on others: Bavaria went in 1042 to the counts of Lützelburg; Suabia was first granted out in 1045 and came in 1048 to the Babenberger Otto of Schweinfurt; Carinthia was given in 1047 to a member of the older branch of the Welf family, Welf III. But the high nobility saw themselves in such a way as to perceive in the king a rival to their own power, and it was precisely with the dukes – besides the above-named duchies there were dukes in Lotharingia and Saxony, Franconia as a 'royal region' having no duke of its own – that Henry clashed.

Lotharingia presented the most serious danger. Unlike the other duchies it was not a tribal territory but simply an accumulation of lordships. Gozelo, the duke of all Lotharingia, had died in 1044; his son Godfrey II, the Bearded, who was already co-duke in Upper Lotharingia, demanded to be invested with the whole of Lotharingia. This was to ignore the character of the duchy as an office and assert a claim to it by hereditary right. After clashing with Henry III Godfrey had fled to Italy and succeeded in extending his power considerably. In 1054 he married Beatrix, the pious widow of Margrave Boniface I of Tuscany, who had been murdered in 1052. Beatrix was rich: she owned large allodial lands in Lotharingia, controlled the property of the house of Canossa, and held the margravate of Tuscany. The marriage meant that a powerful lord held the Empire in a pincer-grip; this would become still more dangerous should forces hostile to the king seek Godfrey's support. After the death of Henry III in 1056 Godfrey had more or less a free hand until his death in 1069. He took the king's place as the guarantor of law and order in the areas he controlled, and was the military protector of the church reformers, many of whom came from Lotharingia and were gradually becoming hostile to the king. But it was not just the Lotharingian-Tuscan complex whose ties with the Empire were weakened. Conrad of Lützelburg, duke of Bavaria, conspired with Duke Welf III of Carinthia with the aim of securing the throne. The conspiracy was exposed; both dukes were deposed from the offices they had not long before taken up, and died shortly afterwards, in 1055 and 1056 respectively. Henry III had also come into conflict with the Saxon Bernard Billung (1011–59). The Billungs were not dukes 'of' Saxony, but 'in' Saxony; there was no formal investiture with the duchy. In Saxony the Ottonian family lands had become crown lands, and Henry asserted his rights over them vigorously. He chose out the palace built by Henry II at Goslar for his principal residence, stepped up the exploitation of the silver-mines in the neighbourhood, at that time the most productive in Europe, and founded the chapter of St Simon and Jude as a *capella regia*. In general the court chaplains had been spread over the whole of the imperial church, but there was now a concentration of their canonries in the palace foundation of Simon and Jude; the king's assistants were now to be trained in Saxony. The Saxon magnates came to regard Henry as still more of an intruder when he allied with Archbishop Adalbert of Hamburg-Bremen (1043–72), the principal opponent of Billung expansion. Adalbert, who came from a Thuringian comital family and was thus also a foreigner, was intent on building up the territorial lordship of his church. He collected counties, in order to found a *ducatus*, i.e. a duchy based on a collection of lordship and property rights, modelling himself here on the bishop of Würzburg according to Adam of Bremen, who devoted a whole book of his history of the bishops of Hamburg to a biography of Adalbert, one of the earliest character-portraits of the Middle Ages worthy of the name. From Adam we learn about Adalbert's wide-ranging political activities, about his alleged refusal of the papacy, about his attempts at missionary activity as far as Finland and the Orkneys, backed by legatine privileges from the papacy, about his ostentatious court with 'flatterers, jesters, quack-doctors and actors', and about his incredible attempts to secure the rank of patriarch for his archbishopric in order not to have to let go of Denmark, which already had nine bishoprics and sought to become an independent ecclesiastical province with its own archbishop. On one occasion when Henry III was staying as a guest with this arch-enemy of the Saxon magnates, he was very nearly assassinated by Thietmar, the brother of the Saxon duke Bernard.

There is no doubt that Henry III was less and less able to keep the princes loyal to him and to the Empire. On the other hand he continued his father's policy of building up the *ministeriales* and hence of a new group capable of carrying out the government of the Empire; and he also opened up the imperial chapel for men who did not come from the highest ranks of the nobility.

HENRY III AS ROMAN *PATRICIUS* AND THE GERMAN POPES

The most notable action of Henry's reign was his deposition of three popes in 1046 and his installation of several Germans as bishops of Rome; of the seven Germans who have become pope, five reigned between 1046 and 1058. An earlier nationalistic generation of historians could claim that the German king had incorporated the papacy into the imperial church system and disposed of the Roman see 'like an imperial bishopric'. Henry's intentions have here certainly been misunderstood. The proverb that a fish stinks from its head was after all a medieval one. A man with Henry's sense of religious responsibilities will have been guided by the sincere conviction that a Christendom which conformed to God's intentions required a purified papacy, just as the king himself had to refrain from simony. If he had simply been interested in power politics he ought not to have tolerated the activities of his able cousin Leo IX (1049–54), a man he chose to be pope, or to have accepted Halinard of Dijon's refusal to take an oath of loyalty to him.

What had happened in Rome? The city, at that time with about 10,000 inhabitants, many of whom squatted rather than lived in the remains of the ceremonial buildings of antiquity, had been dominated for decades by rival aristocratic groups, headed by the families of the Crescentii and the Tusculans: the one family tended more towards a policy of autonomy for Rome, while the other sought contact outside the city, with Byzantium in particular. In 1032 the Tusculans had succeeded for the third time in succession in pushing through the election of a member of their family: Theophylact, the nephew of his predecessor, who was depicted in a sinister light by a predominantly reform-minded historiography as a man who had been at the time of his ordination as Benedict IX an immoral ten- or twelve-year-old (canon law laid down thirty as the minimum age for election to a bishopric), a man who led a wholly unpriestly way of life. If, however, we look at the few direct pieces of evidence for his pontificate, and in particular at his charters, we find clear decisions based on canon law which show him in P. F. Kehr's words as 'a politician with decisive ability'. The fact that even under the German 'ultramontane' popes much in the spheres of liturgy, administration and the organization of the clerics at the papal court remained as it had done under Benedict also does not suggest a period of complete decadence during his pontificate. His principal difficulty was with his arch-enemies, the Crescentii, who in the course of a city uprising set up their own pope, Silvester III, bishop of Sabina, the region where the family lands of the Crescentii lay. But the new pope, consecrated in January 1045, had already been forced to leave the city for his old bishopric by February. Benedict was, however, willing to resign his office, and a successor had already presented himself: Johannes Gratian, archpriest of the church S. Giovanni ad Portam Latinam, a man related distantly to the Roman and Jewish banking family of the Pierleoni. It was this family which put up the money for the transfer of office, for Benedict, obviously in political difficulties, demanded a price – allegedly 2,000 pounds of silver – for his resignation. The new pope was consecrated as Gregory VI on 1 May 1045. The Roman reformers, headed by Petrus Damiani, acclaimed him as a man wholly devoted to things spiritual and of strict morality. It was at this point that Henry III came to Italy. He was met at Piacenza by the new pope Gregory VI, but in spite of this a synod which met at Sutri held judgement over him and over Silvester III in their absence on 20 December 1046 and deposed both. Gregory's continued presence in Italy would have been dangerous because of the support he had, and Henry sent him over the Alps to Germany, following a precedent set by Otto I, *ad ripas Rheni* (presumably Cologne). He was accompanied by a monk from the monastery of S. Maria del Priorato, Hildebrand; a generation later he wrote as Pope Gregory VII 'I went unwillingly with the lord pope Gregory over the mountains.' In Rome Henry III clarified the somewhat confused position by having Benedict IX deposed at a synod on 24 December 1046, in spite of his resignation. On the same day Bishop Suidger of Bamberg was chosen from among Henry's following to become pope, a member of the imperial episcopate with a typical career behind him: he came from a Saxon noble family, had held canonries and been an imperial chaplain before becoming bishop of Bamberg in 1040. He was enthroned as Pope Clement II on Christmas Day 1046, and immediately afterwards crowned Henry III and Agnes as emperor and empress. At the same time Henry received the rank of *patricius* as a hereditary title. The name, which originally came from Byzantium, appears from the end of the tenth century in Roman sources as the title of the defender of the Roman church; Otto III received the title in 996 at his imperial coronation and after his death it was usurped by the Crescentii. After 1012 no further *patricius* is mentioned. The rights associated with the title are by no means clear, but it is certain that its holder was entitled to cast the first vote in a papal election. The fact that the German king and emperor was now the *patricius* meant essentially that the influence of the Roman nobility would be excluded in future papal elections.

In the next twelve years there were no fewer than five German popes, with remarkably short pontificates: Clement II (1046–7), Bishop Poppo of Brixen as Damasus II (1048), Bishop Bruno of Toul as Leo IX (1049–54), Bishop Gebhard of Eichstätt as Victor II (1055–7) and Frederick of Lotharingia, abbot of Montecassino, as Stephen IX (1057–9). Petrus Damiani thought that it was the burden of the papal office which shortened a man's life-span. Quite early on there were rumours that the deaths of these foreign popes were not due to natural causes, and when in 1942 the sarcophagus of Clement II was opened in Bamberg (even after becoming pope he had not given up his old bishopric, and was buried there) and a high lead content was discovered in his skeleton, the rumours appeared to be confirmed: Karl Hauck has described the poisoning of Clement II as 'a tenable supposition'. It is unlikely, however, that his successors were poisoned.

The most important of the German popes was Bruno of Toul, Leo IX, a member of the Alsatian comital family of Egisheim. He succeeded in freeing the papacy from its Roman narrowness and collected a group of supporters around him who set out and propagated the aims of church reform with clarity and force. The popes from the Crescentii and Tusculan families had remained firmly in Rome and central Italy, but Leo toured Christendom; he spent only six months out of the five years of his pontificate in the city. His itinerary is breathtaking: he journeyed three times to France, three times to Germany and no fewer than six times to southern Italy. In all he held twelve synods. His first Lateran council in 1049 set out a series of radical claims: all ordinations made by simonists were invalid, and all priests' wives and children became serfs of the church. The first claim was so extreme that it would have led to a collapse of the church as a dispenser of the sacraments, and in the end the milder provision of Clement II, who had ordained a forty-day penance for such cases, prevailed. But the reduction of priests' sons to serfs, given that serfs could not become priests, meant (quite apart from any moral consequences) an end to the custom whereby the son inherited the benefices and offices of his priestly father; this had been traditional in Italy in particular, where it was said that some canonries had been held in direct succession through several generations. Henry III did not confirm these conciliar decisions, but he accepted them, in contrast to the French king Henry I (1031–60), who summoned his prelates to a military expedition in order to keep them back from a papal council in Rheims.

Leo failed not in the ecclesiastical but in the political sphere. He had attempted to contain the expansion of the Normans north-west towards Benevento, for Benevento had appealed to the pope for protection, and Leo had gone north to Germany to seek help. He renounced income in Bamberg, Fulda and other places and received Benevento in return as a representative of the imperial government. But he got no military support; the man who led the opposition to his request was Bishop Gebhard of Eichstätt, his successor as pope. Leo proclaimed a holy war, in order to mobilize military assistance, and indeed he was followed back to Italy by a crowd of German volunteers. They were cut to pieces in June 1053 near Civitate (a now deserted settlement north-west of Foggia) by the experienced and well-armed Norman knights. Leo was a spectator of the defeat from the city walls. The Normans took him prisoner, treated him honourably, and released him after eight months. But Leo was a broken man, and died shortly after his release.

THE BEGINNINGS AND AIMS OF CHURCH REFORM

The word 'reform' is used for the period around and after the middle of the eleventh century in numerous connections: we speak of early or pre-Gregorian reform, of the reform papacy, and so on. The central figure, who gives his name to the epoch and to most of the terms used to characterize it, is Gregory VII (1073–85). The years when Hildebrand/Gregory's influence was not so strong, when the tone was set by men like Humbert of Silva Candida (†1061) and Petrus Damiani (†1072), are normally called the early or pre-Gregorian reform period. The broadest term used, 'the reform papacy', covers the period from the Council of Sutri in 1046 up to the schism of 1130 between Innocent II and Anacletus II. In many respects the reform movement led into the 'twelfth-century Renaissance', a term coined by C. H. Haskins, but the two movements must be conceptually separated: 'renaissance' or *rinascità* imply a rebirth, generally though not invariably of antiquity, and at the same time the biologically repetition of something which had already once existed, while 'reform' or *reformatio* emphasizes rather renewal through purification, and is to be understood as a conservative attitude, seeking to preserve the essence of that which is reformed. Another term which has been used for the reform movement, which was decisively backed by the papacy, is 'the papal revolution' (E. Rosenstock-Huessy), implying that Rome attempted a reordering which was to 'introduce a new principle into history once for all'. However, the reform movement certainly did not intend to introduce 'a new principle'; the idea that the wish to return to the old revealed truth would bring about something new lay outside the intentions and the consciousness of the reformers.

With Leo IX there came to Rome a group of clerics, mainly Lotharingians, whose influence was to be of great importance, though the view of A. Fliche that reform was a 'Lotharingian invention' and that its basic tenets were worked out in Lotharingia and from there spread to Rome and Italy is certainly an exaggeration. The aggressive self-confidence of the new reformers at Rome and their dismissive comments on what they had found on their arrival should not blind us to the fact that there were those in Italy and in Rome in particular who sought reform and a purified church. One such centre of reform was the monastery of S. Maria del Priorato, the house where the abbots of Cluny stayed when they visited Rome; here could be found not only Johannes Gratian (Gregory VI) but also the highly educated monk from Montecassino Archbishop Laurentius of Amalfi (†1049), Hildebrand's teacher and a friend of Odilo of Cluny. The city prefect of Rome at the time, Cencius, should also be counted among the reformers. One could also mention the numerous settlements of monks who lived together in an eremitical asceticism which owed more to the traditions of the Greek East; Petrus Damiani was deeply impressed by their seriousness, and wrote a devoted biography of one of their chief representatives, the ascetic and strict Romuald of Camaldoli (†1027). What was still absent from all these circles, however, was the concentration on the bishop of Rome, the conviction that the papacy had to take the central place in the church's spirituality.

Indications that a new clerical reform consciousness which looked away from the lay world had developed in Lotharingia can be found for example in Bishop Wazo of Liège (1047–8), who denied that the king had the right to depose a bishop and wanted all lay influence excluded from the life of the church, or the anonymous author of the treatise *On the ordination of the pope*, which sharply condemned Henry III's deposition of the pope. Among the Lotharingian newcomers in Rome one should mention Hugo Candidus, a monk from Remiremont in the diocese of Toul, who was to change sides several times in the struggles between the Gregorians and their opponents, and finally to die in 1098 an anti-Gregorian; Frederick, archdeacon of Liège and the brother of Godfrey the Bearded, who became Pope Stephen IX (†1058); and Humbert (†1061) from the monastery of Moyenmoutier, who became archbishop in Sicily in 1050 and cardinal bishop of Silva Candida in 1051. Humbert has been called the *éminence grise* behind Leo IX and his radicalism does indeed seem to have had a considerable influence. He was in charge of the chancery during Leo's absences and appears to have written the most important letters. He was also responsible for the breach with the Greek church. The differences in dogma and liturgy between the Latin West and the Greek East had grown ever greater since the ninth century, and there was already a fierce dispute in progress at the beginning of the 1050s, but Humbert of Silva Candida took the last decisive step when he laid the bull of excommunication against the then patriarch on the altar of Hagia Sophia in Constantinople on 16 July 1054, a step which was promptly answered by a counter-excommunication on the Greek side. The apostolic Greek Orthodox church, 'lacking in the moderation of faith', broke away from the papal Roman Catholic church, 'the destroyer of brotherly love', to use the phraseology of the contemporary accusations, and the withdrawal of the ban by Pope Paul VI in 1963 was little more than a declamatory gesture. Humbert pronounced the excommunication in his capacity as a papal legate; as Leo IX was already dead by this time it could be argued that Humbert's sentence was formally invalid, in spite of the consequences.

Humbert showed the same hot-headedness as he had done in his dealings with the eastern church in his treatise *Against the simonists*, written between 1054 and 1058. All reformers were against simony, but Humbert's arguments were particularly radical. Petrus Damiani, himself consecrated by a probable simonist and conscious of the fact, had argued that ordinations freely bestowed by a simonist were valid, provided the recipient was not himself a simonist; he followed Augustine's teaching that the quality of the sacrament did not depend on the quality of the priest. Humbert on the other hand argued that such ordinations were invalid, because the simonist priest had through his unworthiness not received the sacrament of ordination in the first place and hence could not himself bestow it. He also denounced as illegal and indeed heretical the receiving of a church from lay hands. Humbert's writings already indicate the main course of the later reform movement: opposition to simony and lay investiture, and insistence on priestly celibacy. This rigorism was still more a matter of theory than of practice. Humbert's arguments from canon law found little contemporary resonance, and it is for example 'very noticeable how Gregory VII ignored the rich arsenal of learned canonistic arguments in the writings of Humbert, even though he was to develop his ideas further and to put them into practice' (E. Caspar).

THE DISTANCE FROM THE REST OF EUROPE: FRANCE, ENGLAND, AND THE NORTH

The main change in France was that of the ruling dynasty: the Capetians had succeeded to the Carolingians in 987. Their rise to the kingship meant that the counts of Anjou, previously their subvassals, became tenants-in-chief and were able to extend their feudal possessions considerably. The king was cut off by his tenants-in-chief, and these in turn by their subvassals, so that it became an established principle that 'the vassal of my vassal is not my vassal'. Such anarchic feudalism led to grotesque situations, as for example when a victor forced the man he had defeated to accept his vassalage, for a lord had to give his vassal protection and military support, while the vassal could hope to escape his obligations. The crown was reduced to such straits that it had to hand over Paris as a fief and retreat to the Orléannais. The duchy of Normandy showed the possibilities of a future reorganization of the state. Among the Normans, who had become settled since the beginning of the tenth century, a much stricter feudalism had grown up, a result of their tight military discipline; independent spirits, like the family of the lords of Hautville, emigrated to southern Italy and elsewhere. In the duchy itself the centralizing principle of liege lordship became established: the feudal demands of the liege lord overrode all other claims (*dominus ligius ante omnes*). This principle was to have important consequences for the future, especially as the Normans were to found other states along similar rationalistic lines in southern Italy and in England.

Knut the Great, whose empire included England, Denmark together with Scania, and Norway, had brought about a *rapprochement* between Anglo-Saxons and Danes. His bodyguard consisted of Anglo-Saxons, and he sent Anglo-Saxon missionaries to Scandinavia, which was still largely pagan. After his death in 1035 Edward the Confessor, a member of the Anglo-Saxon royal house, was able to return to the country and ruled from 1042 to 1066; he was succeeded in turn by William, duke of Normandy, where Edward had spent the years of his exile. The victory at Hastings in 1066 gave William his name 'the Conqueror', and an English historian has described the conquest as the most important event in the history of the island since Caesar's invasion. After dealing with the bloody guerilla resistance fought by the Anglo-Saxon clans the Norman conqueror laid the foundations of a state which could almost be described as modern. The 'Domesday Book', a kind of central land register compiled in 1085–6, recorded all property-holding and the obligations owed to the king. William merely claimed to succeed to Edward's rights, but he confiscated the lands of many Anglo-Saxon nobles – it has been calculated that only 8% of the country remained in Anglo-Saxon hands – and ruthlessly doubled the lands of the crown. It was characteristic of his ideas of the relationship between church and state that he kept a close watch on communications between the English church and Rome. He bestowed numerous fiefs, even ecclesiastical fiefs, on mercenary soldiers, and secured an unrestricted suzerainty for the crown by having all those bound by vassalitic ties swear fealty to him at Salisbury in 1086. This was an important step for the future; William was the *dominus ligius*, whose summons took precedence over all other feudal claims. The German king needed *ministeriales* to secure his rights of sovereignty and his possessions; feudalism in England and Normandy produced a strong central administration, which was to become more and more institutionalized with time. The *curtis ad scaccarium* (the 'court at the chessboard', or exchequer) is mentioned for the first time in 1118 but certainly existed before then. It was at first a kind of auditing office, but developed into a real court of financial affairs. Compared with administrative developments like this the Empire was slow-moving and archaic in its institutions.

3

FROM *CHRISTUS DOMINI* TO ANTICHRIST: THE KING OF GERMANY AND THE INVESTITURE CONTEST

——— · ———

It is a widespread but mistaken belief that the expression *christus Domini* denotes the bishop. Both in the Bible and in the early and high Middle Ages it was generally the king who was denoted by the term: the 'anointed of the Lord', against whom it was a sin 'to raise one's hand'. The king was set above the profane world: after his coronation he was received as a member of a number of cathedral chapters and other foundations, after he had been, as set out in some coronation *ordines*, 'made a cleric'. Henry III in particular had laid great emphasis on the sacral character of kingship, but only a few years later the German king was to be described in the words of the pope and his supporters as an instrument of Antichrist bringing evil into the world. It was not murder but a good deed to kill this man, the plague made flesh, and exterminate his supporters; it was even beneficial for the slaughtered heretics themselves, for it was obviously 'much better ... to cut their madness short by death rather than to allow such insanity, which can only be cauterized by the eternal fire, to continue'. This shift in values took place with unusual rapidity: the key event was the deposition of the German king, Henry IV, in 1076. 'I read the history of the kings and emperors of the Romans again and again, and I cannot find anywhere that any of them before Henry IV had been excommunicated by the Roman pope and robbed of his kingdom': so wrote the Bishop Otto of Freising (†1058), Henry's grandson, in the course of his chronicle depicting the history of the world as the history of salvation.

THE REIGN OF HENRY IV AND ITS CONSEQUENCES

1 *The papacy and the regency government*

'Woe to thee, O land, when thy king is a child and thy princes eat in
the morning': among the disasters which can strike the world this
one, summed up in the words of Solomon (Ecclesiastes 10.16), is
singled out for special mention in early medieval treatises, and there
are similar allusions in the accounts of Henry III's death in the
chronicles of the high Middle Ages. At Henry's death on 5 October
1056 in the palace of Bodfeld in the Harz, his son Henry IV was six
years old. He had been designated king in 1053, and betrothed to
Bertha, a girl of his age and a daughter of the count of Turin, in
1055. On his death-bed Henry III had commended his son to the
protection of Pope Victor II, who had formerly been bishop of
Eichstätt and chancellor, and Victor had brought the princes to
accept the succession. In Germanic law even a minor could rule as
king; all he needed was a guardian. This role was taken on by his
mother Agnes, of whom it was admittedly said that she would
prefer to take the veil rather than the burdens of the imperial
regency. Victor II seems to have been a man of clear ideas and
decisions; he had been elected pope in April 1055 with Henry III's
agreement and sought with the support of the Lotharingian reformers a reasonable compromise with the military arm of the reform
party, Duke Godfrey the Bearded, who largely controlled central
Italy. By the end of 1056 Godfrey had been reinstated in the duchy of
Lotharingia, and his brother Frederick was made a cardinal in June
1057. But these efforts were rendered useless by Victor's death in
July 1057, and the papal election which followed was symptomatic
of the gradual alienation between the reform circles in Rome and the
German court. The right of the *patricius* to cast the first vote was
ignored; Frederick of Lotharingia was asked to suggest suitable
candidates, and in the end he himself was elected, taking the name of
Stephen IX after the saint on whose feast-day he was consecrated.
An embassy which included Hildebrand and Bishop Anselm I of
Lucca hurried off to secure at least an *ex post facto* consent from the
German court, but before they returned Stephen IX had already
died. The election which followed again took place immediately,
without any consideration for the rights of the German king. The
man elected was Bishop Gerhard of Florence, Nicholas II, by birth a
Burgundian from the region near Cluny. It was perhaps not just a
desire for autonomy which pushed the reformers into action, but

also the need to fend off any initiative by the Tusculans, for they had put up a pope of their own with the name of Benedict X, one often borne by popes of their family.

The reformers had been able to act independently on two separate occasions, and it is certainly no coincidence that it is in this period following the death of Victor II that the slogan *libertas ecclesiae*, 'freedom of the church', first became prominent. This concept of ecclesiastical freedom should not be confused with the later demands for absolute freedom put by groups of heretical Christians in particular, who rejected the church hierarchy absolutely. For the reformers, freedom was bound up with the duty to conform to God's plan for the world, which entailed conformity to the norms of doctrine and discipline laid down by Rome. Many sources show how much freedom to the reformers also meant a link with Rome, and Hildebrand as Gregory VII described it as 'a state of true liberty' to be subject to none apart from 'the holy and universal Roman mother', who 'treats no subjects like slaves, but receives them all as sons'. It was Hildebrand in particular whose influence grew under Nicholas II; the phrase current was that Hildebrand fed 'his Nicholas in the Lateran like a donkey in his stall'. The key event of the pontificate was the Lateran synod of 1059, which was followed by a series of further councils in the following years which often promulgated the same canons as those issued in 1059. The Lateran synod decided on new procedure for the election of the pope, and lay investiture is said to have been forbidden at the same time. The 'papal election decree' is an obviously ambivalent document: Nicholas's election was itself irregular, and this irregularity was now to be regularized. Pointing the way to the future, the decree laid down that the election of the bishop of Rome was reserved to the cardinals, and thus founded a mode of election which is still valid today. The cardinals as a body had originally had little to do with the papal election. Their concern was with the liturgical and charitable work of the church of the city of Rome. Seven cardinal bishops and twenty-eight cardinal priests performed the liturgy at the churches of S. Giovanni in Laterano (for up to the twelfth century it was the Lateran basilica and not St Peter's which was the 'mother of all churches') and at the four patriarchal basilicas of S. Pietro, S. Paolo fuori le mura, S. Lorenzo fuori le mura and S. Maria Maggiore. The cardinal deacons were in charge of alms-giving in the eighteen or nineteen city districts. These assistants of the bishop of Rome in his liturgical and charitable work became the independent electors of their papal lord, and although even today canon law lays down explicitly that 'any Catholic' may be elected pope, the historical experience is that since 1378 only cardinals have been regarded as *papabile*, as was generally the case before that date also. Apparently in order to prevent a divided election the decree of 1059 gave the cardinal bishops a kind of preferential vote by stipulating that they should nominate the candidate and laid down that the candidate should for preference be drawn from the Roman church 'saving the honour and reverence due our beloved son Henry [IV]'. This so-called 'royal clause', although it stressed that the rights of the German king and emperor-to-be in a papal election were still intact, was not precise about what they were. Future double elections with a reform pope on one side and a pope supported by the king on the other, and indeed the schism following Nicholas's death, were to show up this lack of clarity. There has been much speculation as to who formulated this decree, so full of the idea of the dignity of the Roman church and the papacy – Humbert of Silva Candida, Petrus Damiani, or even Hildebrand? The rather awkward Latin of the document suggests rather that it was composed by a group and was the result of a number of compromises.

A second decree promulgated in 1059 also affected the rights of the German king, or might do so in the future: no cleric was to receive a church from the hands of a layman, either freely or for money (*Ut per laicos nullo modo quilibet clericus aut presbyter obtineat aecclesiam nec gratis nec pretio*). This was directed not only against simony, which Henry III had also avoided, but against lay investiture of any kind. But it is possible that the prohibition was only intended to apply to lesser churches and not to the episcopal and abbatial churches which shared in the government of the Empire; in any case, it was to remain a purely theoretical provision for the next decade and a half.

The absence of the German king from Italy led to changes in the political landscape there. The Normans, previously enemies of the papacy, sought a feudal alliance with the bishop of Rome. The beginnings of Norman rule in southern Italy were seemingly harmless. The first Normans there are said to have landed on their return from a pilgrimage to Jerusalem and to have been hired as mercenaries; in 1038 Conrad II confirmed the Norman count Rainulf I of Aversa as a vassal of the prince of Salerno. In the 1040s an ever-increasing number of Norman knights came to settle there, including, allegedly, the eleven sons of Tancred of Hauteville. This family clan, which was to maintain and consolidate its position against all rivals, was always led by one of its members, and these leaders included distinguished fighters: William Ironarm (up to 1046), Drogo (1046–51), Humfred (1051–57) and finally Robert Guiscard ('sly-head'), whose career justified his name. Robert, who had grown up in a world of strict feudalism, sought protection and found it with the Roman pope. In 1059 he had himself enfeoffed by Nicholas II with Apulia, Calabria and Sicily, and at the same time Richard of Aversa, Rainulf's heir, received the lordship of Capua, which he had just taken over, as a fief from the pope. Both Normans took an oath of vassalage to the pope and promised help: Robert Guiscard's promise included the provision that he would give help when asked for it by the 'better cardinals' – a precaution against the papal schism looming on the horizon. The Normans were not yet papal mercenaries in the sense that they were simply hired troops; they had brought the feudalism they had known in their native Normandy with them to southern Italy and organized themselves along the same lines. The papal realignment, coupled with the dissolution of the feudal ties between the Normans and the emperor, was to have important consequences. The papacy renounced the protection of the German emperor, although the duty of *defensio ecclesiae* was one of the essential features of his office. The new Norman protectors were even pledged to give help against the German king and emperor. At the same time the Normans had been granted a region in which they could expand their lordship. Of the lands they had been enfeoffed with, Sicily was still held by the Saracens, while parts of Apulia were still held by the Greeks. Robert took his vassalitic oath as 'duke of Apulia and Calabria and ... future duke of Sicily'. The fact that the papacy felt entitled to treat the island of Sicily as if it were a papal possession might be an indication that the Donation of Constantine was again being studied; Humbert of Silva Candida had used it a few years earlier, with an addition directed against the Greeks, in his arguments against the eastern church. The forgery conceded to the papacy the possession of 'various islands'; and it was at this time that the popes were looking round for titles of all kinds to property and rights.

The ideas of reform secured the papacy increasing support in northern Italy. There are gloomy accounts of the way of life of the Italian clergy at this time, and the ordinary faithful laity were evidently no longer prepared to accept a state of affairs which threatened their salvation, especially as reformers like Humbert had taught that the sacraments of unworthy priests were invalid. The religious conflicts were mixed with social and political ones. The high nobility, the *capitanei*, sought to prevent the lesser nobility, the *valvassores*, from increasing their rights and their property; the *valvassores* found allies in the burghers of the north Italian cities. The church in Lombardy and Tuscany was, as in Germany, an aristocratic church; the canons in particular, living from prebends which were treated essentially as family property, led the life of aristocrats with hunting, parties and conspicuous consumption. The *valvassores* and burghers, but also craftsmen, dayworkers and the other members of the lower classes, came to oppose the rich clergy. The name 'Pataria' which was given to the movement is perhaps derived from that of the Milan market held by the junk-dealers and rag-and-bone men; the movement called itself, almost heretically, 'God's plan' (*placitum Dei*). The priests who led an unclerical life were to be systematically converted; their homes were invaded, their riches taken away, their women driven out as whores. The upper classes resisted the movement, especially as even Archbishop Wido of Milan was attacked, but could not reckon with any support from the German king. Rome had originally ignored the Pataria, but from the time of Stephen IX there were closer contacts between Roman reformers and the Patarini, whose activities, directed as they were against the high clergy and hence against the basis of imperial power in Italy, were looked on with some favour by Duke Godfrey the Bearded. After the death of Nicholas II in 1061 a friend of the Patarini, whose movement had spread to the other Lombard cities like Piacenza, Brescia and Cremona, was elected as pope: Bishop Anselm I of Lucca, a member of the prominent Milan family of the Baggio, who took the name of Alexander II as a sign of special reverence for the martyr-pope Alexander I. Alexander's election represented the final shift in the reform movement to a Roman centralism. Nicholas II had brought clerics from Florence to Rome, but Alexander relied on the reform circles already there. The leadership of these reform clerics was increasingly assumed by the archdeacon Hildebrand, evidently not without some conflicts with the ruling pope, whom he was later to accuse of slackness because of his lack of rigour.

It was to be expected that Alexander's election would not be accepted by the conservative bishops of northern Italy: they chose the worthy but colourless bishop Cadalus of Parma as Pope Honorius II and both parties sought through diplomacy to win support outside Italy. France tended towards Alexander, but the German episcopate was divided. One group around Archbishop Anno II of Cologne declared immediately for Alexander; another, which evidently included the Hamburg metropolitan Adalbert, favoured Cadalus. However, it was not possible to install Cadalus – who was the target for attacks in open letters by Petrus Damiani, a man with a high reputation – in Rome, and at the synod of Mantua in 1064, at which Anno II took part, he was rejected as a schismatic.

Compared with the purposeful energy of the reformers the position of the German government was shaky. The queen mother, who longed to enter a convent, gave away lands and offices in the hope of buying peace. Count Rudolf of Rheinfelden, a friend of monastic reform, held the duchy of Suabia from 1057 and also administered Burgundy; the powerful Otto of Northeim received the duchy of Bavaria in 1061 and in the same year the Suabian Berthold, whose family would soon come to call itself by the name of the castle of Zähringen in the Breisgau, was appointed to the duchy of Carinthia. In Saxony Bernard II Billung, who died in 1059, was succeeded by the restless Ordulf, who kept up the old conflict with Adalbert of Bremen. Characteristic of the situation is the way in which Anno II of Cologne (1056–75) was able to act. He was a brooding and ascetic man, who had been invested by Henry III; in 1057 he took on the rank of archchancellor of the Roman church – the office of archchancellor of Italy was already permanently united with the archbishopric of Cologne. In 1062 he kidnapped the young king, who vainly tried to defend himself, from the royal palace at Kaiserwerth and took him to Cologne with the royal insignia. It was pure hypocrisy when Anno justified his conduct by referring to his duty as a bishop to care for the king journeying in his diocese. The Empress Agnes resigned; she had already taken the veil, and now went to Rome, where she entrusted herself to Hildebrand as her spiritual guardian.

Anno attempted cooperation with the supporters of reform in Italy, but Adalbert of Bremen won increasing influence over Henry IV and the course of German politics, not without ensuring rich donations for himself, for example the monasteries of Lorsch and Corvey. Even after the young king had been declared of age and capable of bearing arms in 1065 Adalbert maintained his position and prevented an Italian expedition, fearing with reason that Anno as Italian chancellor would eclipse him. But at the assembly at Tribur in 1066 Henry was forced to dismiss Adalbert; this was a signal for an uprising by the Wends and Abodrites, who went so far as to plunder Hamburg. Neither of the two rival princes, Anno and Adalbert, would have a decisive influence on royal policy in future; Henry tried as far as he could to pursue his own policies and improve the position of the crown.

2 Canossa: the turning-point

Canossa is not just a ruined fortress on a cliff-top on the north-eastern slopes of the Apennines some 30 km south-west of Reggio nell'Emilia whose original form has been revealed by archaeological excavations; Canossa is also an ever-recurring symbol, and Bismarck's declaration on 14 May 1872 before the Reichstag; 'We shall not go to Canossa' is only one example among many of its use. Contemporaries were already conscious of the enormity of the events. The Gregorian Bonizo of Sutri wrote that when the news of the king's excommunication became known among the people 'our whole Roman world was shaken'. Gregory himself presented his action as the normal exercise of his office: had not a church father Ambrose of Milan acted similarly in denying the Emperor Theodosius the Great communion until he should have done penance? But Ambrose had neither deposed the emperor, nor had he announced that the priestly power stood above that of the highest layman, and his pastorally conceived action was quite different from that of Gregory, who acted as a spiritual judge standing above all laymen. The reform pope had changed the order of the world, and when Bonizo of Sutri wrote of the 'shaking Roman world' he saw the eschatological significance of the action in the same way as did Otto of Freising, who interpreted Henry' deposition in his world chronicle as a sign of the approach of the Last Days: the church had 'shaken the Empire in its final days ... when it decided not to honour the king of Rome as the lord of the world but to treat him as a mere human being formed of clay and strike him with the sword of anathema'.

(a) Gregory VII and Henry IV   The events of Canossa were shaped by the personalities of Gregory VII and Henry IV. One does not have to subscribe to the view that history is made by great men alone to have no doubt that the two brought on the crisis of Canossa, even though each was also a representative of a different world system and the incorporation of a principle; on the one hand a centralized papacy, which saw itself as carrying the ultimate responsibility for the salvation of mankind, for which it was answerable only to God, and on the other a kingship which saw itself as holding a lordship founded by God which presupposed a harmony between church and Empire. The struggle, which had a flavour of inevitability about it, was marked by the personal characteristics of the two protagonists, by Gregory's fanatical intolerance and Henry's mixture of cunning,

thoughtlessness and a sense of charismatic rulership. The excommunication of Henry was as typical of Gregory as Henry's response, the journey to Canossa, was of the king.

Gregory VII, whose baptismal name Hildebrand was interpreted not only by Luther but also by contemporaries as *Höllenbrand* ('the fires of hell'), *Prandellus* ('little fire') and so on, was born between 1020 and 1025, probably in Sovana in southern Tuscany, not far from Bolsena. His father does not seem to have been noble; about his wider family we are reduced to speculation – a connection with the Jewish banking family of the Pierleoni from the Roman ghetto or even descent from Waldrada, the concubine of King Lothar II (†869)? – but it does appear certain that his uncle was abbot of the pro-reform monastery of S. Maria del Priorato. He may have taken his monk's profession there; he certainly did not do so in Cluny in distant Burgundy, as has been suggested. After his period of exile with Gregory VI on the lower Rhine and his return in 1049 as subdeacon with Leo IX he took over the abbacy of S. Paolo fuori le mura. He undertook a number of papal legations, on one of which he preached a sermon before the Emperor Henry III: in 1054 and 1056 he went to France, and in 1058 to the Empress Agnes, to win her approval for the election of Stephen IX. As archdeacon from 1059 he was in charge of administering the property of the Roman church, and from the beginning of the 1060s he was the key figure at the papal court, as we have seen. During the funeral obsequies for Alexander II, as the procession came past the church of S. Pietro in Vincoli, Hildebrand was chosen as pope – the election was tumultuous, contrary to the provisions of the election decree of 1059, and largely brought about by the demagogy of the cardinal priest Hugo Candidus – and spontaneously enthroned in the same church. In homage to Gregory I, the exemplary pope of the early Middle Ages, Hildebrand took the name Gregory VII and adopted his motto 'For thou hadst cast me into the deep, in the midst of the seas; and the floods compassed me about.' 'They threw themselves on me as if they were mad, and left me no opportunity to speak or take advice', he wrote in the letters announcing his election which he sent to various recipients, though not to the German king. He is said to have been small, with black hair, and a facial expression described by many writers as unpleasant. His corpse, embalmed in wax, lies 'canonically authenticated' in a glass sarcophagus built into the altar of one of the side-chapels of the cathedral church of Salerno. His intolerant nature made him a mysterious figure even to his entourage, and even the peace-loving Petrus Damiani called him a 'holy

Satan', a man who would, he hoped, not come to act as a wolf to him.

The main source for Gregory's twelve-year pontificate is his register, a collection of his letters drawn up in the papal chancery containing some 360 pieces. Apart from Gregory I (590–604), no other pope before him has left so many letters and in this form, though even this represents only a fraction of the letters actually sent, whose number has been estimated by H. Hoffmann at around 1500. In spite of his importance, which was recognized by his contemporaries, he has not found an adequate biography, in contrast to the countless ordinary and comparatively unimportant medieval abbots and bishops who have had a Life lovingly devoted to them by a faithful pupil or a local chronicler; this is perhaps a sign of his almost inhuman fixity of purpose. Paul of Bernried, an Augustinian canon from Regensburg, wrote a biography some two generations later (*c.* 1128), which is, however, more informative about Gregory's subsequent reputation than about the man himself. Gregory VII was an unloved pope, in spite of the reports of miracles performed during his lifetime and at his tomb. In 1606 Paul V sanctioned the local cult in Salerno, and in 1728 this was extended to the whole of Catholic Christendom, though the Catholic absolutist states refused to allow it.

How should we view Gregory? Nationalist German historians saw him as a 'master of politics', a man for whom religion was little more than a means for the exercise of power (so Johannes Haller); more recently he has been described by G. Tellenbach as 'a religious genius'. It was his own deep conviction that as Peter's successor he alone bore the responsibility for the salvation of the whole church: 'to obey God means to obey the church, and that in turn means to obey the pope, and vice versa. Mysticism and law meet in an ecclesiology which simultaneously shows very spiritual and very legalistic and institutional traits' (Y. Congar). As Leo IX had done, Gregory used synods in order to announce principles and programmes. In his case it was the Roman councils held in Lent which served this purpose, and it was following the Lent council of 1075 that the so-called *Dictatus Papae* was entered in his register: 'Twenty-seven papal principles', as E. Caspar put it, which alongside old-established traditions made claims which were not entirely covered by existing tradition. No one, for instance, had previously claimed that the pope became 'undoubtedly holy' as a result of his ordination, or that he could depose the absent, or that he could depose emperors, or that all princes should kiss his feet alone. These principles were probably formulated before the crisis which led to Canossa broke out.

Henry IV, born in 1050, was a generation younger than Gregory VII; he lacked his father's religious seriousness, but also his joyless gloominess. He had enjoyed an excellent education by the standards of laymen of his time: he could read and write, knew Latin and enjoyed reading, as well as being interested in the arts. His childhood experiences had an influence on his later decisions which should not be underestimated: the egocentric religiosity of his mother, concerned above all with her own salvation, with whom he grew up until he was twelve; the brutal kidnapping by Archbishop Anno of Cologne at Kaiserwerth in 1062, from which he tried to rescue himself by jumping over the side of the ship on which he was being taken away into the Rhine; the constant pressure from the princes to make them grants of lands and rights; the futile appeal for peace made by the thirteen-year-old king at the Whitsun celebrations in the palace of Goslar, after a fight which led to a number of deaths had broken out between the *ministeriales* of the bishop of Hildesheim and the abbot of Fulda over which of their lords should take precedence; the magnificent and ostentatious way of life of the Hamburg metropolitan Adalbert, from whom he was forced by the princes to withdraw his grace as a formal punishment immediately after he had attained the age of majority in 1066. Having been pushed around so much in the years of his minority, Henry evidently regarded the princes as men who were in the last resort not to be relied on, and he tended to take his decisions alone. This is probably the reason why he made the unheard-of proposal in 1069 to divorce his wife Bertha of Turin, who had finally been married to him in 1065 after ten years' betrothal. No one at the court dared to point out to the young king the injustice of his proposal; this was left to the hermit Petrus Damiani, and the king withdrew his demand for a divorce. The incident shows some of the failings of which Henry's enemies were later to accuse him: thoughtlessness, unscrupulousness and a certain low cunning. On the other hand Henry was always conscious of the dignity of his office – something acknowledged even by Lampert of Hersfeld, one of his most severe critics – and as a tall and well-built man he showed this awareness in his bearing: 'That man, born and bred to be a ruler, always showed . . . whatever misfortunes befell him a royal cast of mind; he would sooner die than accept defeat.' In contrast to Gregory VII Henry had a contemporary biographer, who began his work with a quotation from the prophet Jeremiah: 'Oh that my head were waters, and mine eyes a fountain of tears, that I might weep day and night for the slain of the daughter of my people!' (Jeremiah 9.1). The moving and elegiac work, which praises the king as the protector of the poor, is anonymous, probably because its author feared 'to suffer personal consequences as a supporter of Henry IV after the latter's death' (F.-J. Schmale).

(b) Henry IV, the princes, and the Saxon opposition What a difference between the beginning of the reign of Henry III and that of his son! Henry III had had three duchies – Bavaria, Suabia and Carinthia – in his own hand; Henry IV had none. The crown lands had also been alienated to a great extent, along with the Liudolfing family lands. From about 1068 Henry began an energetic policy of recuperation of crown lands in Thuringia and eastern Saxony, without taking much account of the numerous special rights of the Saxons, which Henry II and Conrad II had confirmed. According to the Saxon view of things, property disputes should be decided by oath-helpers and if necessary by judicial duels; Henry made use of an inquisitorial procedure which established the facts. His policy was carried out largely by *ministeriales* from Suabia, men who in Saxon eyes were both unfree and foreigners. These *ministeriales* were maintained by royal castles, for whose construction the Saxon peasantry were forced to perform labour and transport services.

The king's principal opponent was Otto of Northeim, who owned rich allodial lands in the west and south of the Harz, and whom the Empress Agnes had invested with the duchy of Bavaria in 1061. Henry accused Otto of plotting to assassinate him, had him summoned before a court and then subjected to outlawry on the grounds of contumacy after Otto had refused to participate in a judicial duel under conditions which were certainly unfair. The duchy of Bavaria was taken away from Otto in 1070 and given to Welf IV, the founder of the younger branch of the Welf dynasty. Otto of Northeim allied himself with the duke of Saxony, Magnus Billung, but both were forced to submit and were placed in custody. Otto was released in 1072 but Magnus remained in captivity even after the death of his father. The Saxon magnates saw this as an injustice against one of their peers, and in 1073 refused to follow a summons to Henry's army. After Henry had also lost the support of the south German dukes, Rudolf of Suabia, Berthold of Carinthia and even of Welf IV of Bavaria, who were said to have considered deposing him, he was forced to leave his fortress of the Harzburg in secret and to seek and find protection from the burghers of Worms.

He agreed in the end to demolish his castles, but was reluctant to do this to the Harzburg, upon which it was stormed by the Saxon peasantry and destroyed; in their fury they even desecrated the graves of the members of the royal family buried there. This turned public opinion against the Saxons; the imperial army, led by the duke of Suabia, Rudolf of Rheinfelden, crushed the Saxon peasant army. The Saxon nobility under Otto of Northeim came round when Henry offered more favourable terms. Otto of Northeim received all his crown fiefs back, but not the duchy of Bavaria; instead Henry appointed him regent of Saxony, and presumably hoped for his support in future. By the end of 1075 Henry was master of the situation and had recovered the bulk of the crown lands. But he had used tactical tricks and twists: he had kept Magnus Billung over-long in custody; he had alienated the dukes still further from the imperial government and relied on unfree *ministeriales*; he had only half-heartedly carried out his promise to raze the royal castles in Saxony. Nevertheless, the king's prestige was higher in 1075 than it had been for two decades.

(c) From Tribur to Canossa In the same year, 1075, the tensions between Gregory VII and Henry IV had increased. In 1073 Gregory had excommunicated some of the counsellors *de familia regis* and urged the king to part from them. Henry, who at the time was preoccupied with events in Saxony, had sent Gregory a conciliatory letter, of which Gregory wrote that no ruler had previously sent such a deferential letter to a pope. But in 1075, after the Saxon crisis had been settled in his favour, Henry adopted a different attitude. The filling of the archbishopric of Milan became the trial of strength between the two. In 1070 the *capitaneo* Archbishop Wido, exhausted by the struggles with the Patarini, had resigned, an unusual action for the time. Henry IV had invested Godfrey, a colourless Milanese noble, in 1072; the Patarini and the burghers of Milan had set up Atto, a reformer with a good knowledge of canon law, as a rival archbishop. In Milan itself anarchy reigned: there were street battles, in the course of which the *valvassor* Erlembald, one of the Patarini leaders, was killed. Erlembald was regarded as a martyr, 'the first knightly saint in history' (C. Erdmann). Henry evidently thought that he could exploit the weakness of the Patarini, who were hostile to the Empire, and replaced Godfrey by the imperial chaplain Tedald. In response Gregory took firm steps against the royal counsellors, but also against those bishops who had been accused of disobedience or of having acquired their offices through

simony: Liemar of Bremen, Werner of Strasburg, Henry of Speyer, and Hermann of Bamberg.

Confident of the strength of his position, Henry held in Worms in 24 January 1076 an assembly which was both an imperial assembly and an imperial synod, as was the custom at that time. Two German archbishops and twenty-four bishops attended, and they were joined by the rabble-rousing cardinal Hugo Candidus, who had fallen out of favour in Rome in spite of having organized the tumultuous election of Gregory VII. Hugo Candidus made dramatic accusations against Gregory, and in the heated atmosphere two letters were drawn up, a shorter one for the pope and a longer one intended for public consumption in Germany – the first occurrence of something like official propaganda in German history. The tone of the letters was coarse, and the longer, manifesto-like letter was addressed to 'Hildebrand, no longer pope but a false monk' ('Hildebrando, non iam apostolico, sed falso monacho'); the letter ended with the words: 'We Henry, king by the grace of God, with all our bishops say to you: come down, come down!' (the often-quoted extra phrase 'to be damned through the ages' is a later addition).

The events had something of the theatrical about them, for the letters from Worms reached Gregory in February 1076, in the middle of one of the Lenten synods at which the pope was accustomed to make programmatic pronouncements. Gregory's answer was the deposition and excommunication of Henry IV, which he set out in the particularly impressive form of a prayer addressed to the Apostle Peter:

Blessed Peter, prince of the apostles, hear me, your servant ... By the powers invested in you, for the honour and defence of your church and in the name of God the Father, Son and Holy Ghost, I forbid King Henry, the son of the Emperor Henry, who has rebelled against your church with unheard-of audacity, to rule over the German kingdom and over Italy, and I release all Christians from the oaths they have sworn to him and may swear to him, and forbid anyone to serve him as king.

It must have been a bitter experience for Henry IV to find himself deserted at this critical moment by the men who had suggested the letter of deposition to him. The news that Henry had been excommunicated and deposed led immediately to the formation of a number of interest-groups: the pope, together with a part of the German episcopate, in contact with the south German and Saxon princely opposition which was being strengthened by the newly released members of the Saxon aristocracy who had previously been held in custody, and finally the weakest party, the king and his following, including especially the cities of the upper Rhine. The princes came together in Tribur in October 1076 to consult about how to treat the deposed and excommunicated king, and papal legates also appeared at the assembly. Henry IV encamped on the other side of the Rhine, in Oppenheim, and waited for the princes' decision. He agreed to abandon the city of Worms, which had supported him, and to part from the excommunicated counsellors; and he gave the pope a written promise of obedience and penance. In a separate agreement with the princes it was laid down that the princes would no longer consider Henry as their king if he had not succeeded in freeing himself from the excommunication within a year. At the same time the princes invited Gregory to appear at Augsburg on 2 February 1077 to act as mediator between themselves and Henry; it was as if they assumed that Henry would not be able to free himself from the ban.

How indeed could he do this? The three south German princes, Rudolf of Suabia, Welf of Bavaria and Berthold of Carinthia, were firmly in the enemy party and blocked the most obvious Alpine passes. Gregory set out for the meeting at Augsburg, and then the winter broke out, one of the worst that century (see above, p. 9). Henry accompanied by his wife Bertha and their two-year-old son Conrad, skirted round through Burgundy and crossed the Alps over the mountain pass of Mont Cenis, some 6,000 feet high – in January. Henry had taken on mountain guides, and the descent into the plain of Piedmont, the region ruled by Henry's mother-in-law Adelheid of Turin, became an almost suicidal undertaking:

sometimes [they] crawled forwards on hands and feet, sometimes they supported themselves on their guides, and sometimes, when they slipped on the icy ground, they fell a good way . . . The queen . . . was dragged on an ox-hide . . . The horses were lowered with special machinery, or else dragged along with their legs tied together. In spite of this many were killed on the descent, many were severely injured, and only a few survived the danger unscathed.

The rumour of Henry's coming spread through Lombardy, and royalist supporters flocked to him, assuming that he had taken up arms against the pope. Gregory made the same assumption: he had got as far as Mantua, from where he was to be escorted by a German prince to Augsburg, when he heard the news of Henry's arrival. Immediately he retraced his steps and retreated to the castle of Canossa, a fortress with a triple wall belonging to his faithful protectress, the Countess Mathilda of Tuscany. Mathilda, born in 1046 as the daughter of Beatrix and the marquis of Tuscany, had married Godfrey the Hunchback, the son of her stepfather Godfrey the Bearded of Lotharingia; since his death the previous year she had been a widow, who had inherited the allodial lands and imperial fiefs in Tuscany, Emilia and Lombardy and, praised as the 'daughter of Saint Peter', maintained a great court with panegyrists and theologians at her side. Henry appeared before Mathilda's castle as a penitent, not as a general. Gregory was to describe in a later and widely circulated letter how Henry, 'without royal vestments, barefooted and in a miserable state, dressed in sackcloth' appeared before the castle gates. Both before and during his penance there were intensive negotiations, and in spite of his ostentatious display of repentance Henry seems to have taken a calculated action as he began his penance on Wednesday 25 January 1077, the day of the conversion of St Paul, within the castle walls. After the penance Gregory could not easily refuse reconciliation, and it seems that the others present, Countess Mathilda, Henry's godfather abbot Hugh of Cluny and his mother-in-law Adelheid of Turin, convinced Gregory that he must absolve Henry. Beforehand, however, Gregory secured a written promise and an oath from Henry that he would accept the pope's judgement and allow him free passage 'across the mountains or in other parts of the world'. Following this Gregory lifted up Henry from the ground, where he was lying with arms outstretched in the shape of a cross, and gave him and his companions communion. Henry is said to have been gloomy and taciturn in the course of the reconciliation banquet which followed: he did not touch his food and drummed with his fingernails on the table-top.

The events of Canossa were judged very variedly even by contemporaries. Henry had undoubtedly scored an immediate triumph: the pope had released him from excommunication and he was king again, against the expectation of the princes. But his status as a king by the grace of God, as a divinely appointed ruler, was no longer intact: even a king was now visibly subordinate to the sovereignty of the church and could be examined and judged by the pope. Gregory VII himself laid stress on his office as judge, pointing to the example of his predecessors Zachary and Stephen, who had made Pippin king. Henry had been received back into the church, but he was no longer indispensable.

(d) Divided kingdom and divided church   The princes had set the date of 2 February 1077 for their meeting with Gregory VII in Augsburg; only a few days before this, Gregory released Henry from his

excommunication. The princes felt affronted: 'it is dishonourable to draw back', as they put it in one of their letters to Gregory. At a meeting of the princes in Forchheim in Franconia (and hence in a 'royal region') they elected, with the agreement of the papal legate who was present, the duke of Suabia, Rudolf of Rheinfelden, as king of Germany: the first German antiking and the first free royal election in German history. Admittedly, one should not overestimate the significance of Forchheim. Only ten to fifteen princes took part, and Rudolf himself was closely connected with the ruling Salian dynasty, having married a sister of Henry IV shortly before becoming duke of Suabia, though she soon died. However, Rudolf had to renounce any claim to designate his son as a successor, and to promise the pope free election of bishops and unconditional obedience; his oath to Gregory had the form of a vassal's oath of fealty.

Henry could justifiably assume that the new antiking was not a serious threat so long as he was not backed by Gregory, and Gregory adopted a neutral stance. He had, true, reissued or perhaps issued for the first time a prohibition of lay investiture in 1078 – though this did not stop Henry from disposing of church property as he wished – but he was obviously of the opinion that his cause, God's cause, was bound to triumph of its own accord. After holding back for three years he struck: at the Lenten synod of 1080 he once again excommunicated and deposed Henry. As in 1076, the sentence was clothed in the form of a prayer to St Peter. In a sermon preached at Easter he prophesied a rapid end for Henry as God's punishment, should he not immediately do penance. Gregory declared that Rudolf of Suabia was the only legitimate king, but Rudolf died in October of the same year, after losing in a battle the 'accursed' right hand with which he had once sworn fealty to Henry IV. Rudolf's downfall was interpreted as a divine judgement. Although the princes chose a successor, they avoided the choice of a powerful magnate. The Lützelburger, Count Hermann of Salm, could scarcely maintain himself as king, had to flee for a time to Denmark, and on his death in 1088 in the course of a siege of a Lotharingian castle the antikingship, insignificant and ignored by the princes, was extinguished.

Henry's second deposition and excommunication had a mixed reception; not a few regarded it as unjust. Although according to canon law any contact with Henry brought automatic excommunication with it, the greater part of the German episcopate remained loyal to Henry, including the archbishops of Cologne, Trier, Hamburg-Bremen and (after 1084) Mainz. The leaders of the

Gregorian party in the South were Gebhard of Salzburg and Altmann of Passau, who had been driven from their sees. In Saxony they were led by Archbishop Hartwig of Magdeburg and had the upper hand. Many bishoprics were occupied by both a papalist and a royalist bishop, as for instance in Paderborn, Minden, Constance and Augsburg; Altmann of Passau was able to act as bishop in the eastern part of his diocese, but the town of Passau itself was ruled by royalist cathedral canons. The Augsburg annalist bewailed this: 'What a lamentable spectacle is presented by the Empire! As the comic poet [Plautus] puts it: all are doubled; so are the popes doubled, the bishops doubled.' For Henry had responded to his renewed excommunication by having Archbishop Wibert of Ravenna chosen as Pope Clement III in Brixen in June 1080; he intended to bring him to Rome and establish him there as pope. His repeated attempts to do this in the years which followed only succeeded after Gregory had been abandoned by the Romans and by his immediate entourage; in 1084 thirteen cardinals deserted Gregory for Henry, and the Romans opened the city gates. Gregory retreated to the impregnable Castel Sant'Angelo. Only a few hundred yards away Clement III was enthroned in St Peter's at Easter 1084, and Henry IV and Bertha received the imperial coronation from him. Gregory was rescued by the Normans, who fulfilled their vassalitic duty and came to the assistance of their papal lord, but their plunderings and excesses so enraged the Roman populace that Gregory, who was held responsible, had to leave the city with his rescuers. He died on 25 May 1085 in Salerno under Norman protection. His last words, a modification of the forty-fourth Psalm, are established as authentic: 'I have loved justice and hated iniquity, therefore I die in exile.' It was the attitude of a martyr, convinced of the righteousness of his actions even on his death-bed; only a world which had turned from the path of salvation could have dealt him, God's representative, such a fate.

The hierocratic claims of the papacy appeared to have collapsed. Henry dealt with the situation in Germany; the danger from the Saxon opposition diminished after the death of Otto of Northeim in 1083 and finally vanished with the murder of the outlawed count Ekbert of Meißen in 1090. In 1085 Henry together with the imperial episcopate proclaimed a Peace of God for the whole kingdom. In 1087 he had his eldest son Conrad crowned as German king; in 1089, following Bertha's death in 1087, he married Adelheid (also known as Eupraxia or Praxedis), a daughter of a Russian prince and the widow of the marquis of the Nordmark. When Henry finally set out for Italy in 1090 he could reasonably think that he had defeated his opponents.

After the short interim pontificate of Victor III, a monk from Montecassino who had resisted election (1086–7), Urban II (1088–99) became pope. Before his election he had been the Cardinal Bishop Otto of Ostia, a man from northern France and an ex-prior of Cluny, who had had experience of Germany as a legate of Gregory VII in 1084/5 and had been among those named by Gregory as a possible successor. Urban perhaps took his name out of reverence for the martyr-pope Urban I, a pope who according to a fictitious tradition had founded the apostolic way of life (*vita apostolica, vita communis*). He was a man of tactical and political genius. Not only was he able to return to Rome in 1093, but he arranged a political marriage between the 43-year-old Mathilda of Tuscany and the seventeen-year-old Welf (V) of Bavaria, who soon left his ageing wife but had helped in the meantime to bring about a concentration of the forces opposed to the king in the decisive years after 1089. In 1093 the young Conrad renounced his father; Adelheid-Praxedis separated from Henry and spread the wildest accusations about his private life. Within a very short time the political situation had completely altered. Henry was stuck for seven years, between 1090 and 1096, in a castle near Verona, unable to leave without risking being taken prisoner. Events of epoch-making importance happened around him as if there were no longer an emperor, a German king, or a Henry IV.

3 The Libelli de lite *and the beginnings of scholastic thought*

The conflicts about investiture and church reform produced an intensive discussion which is reflected not only in polemical treatises but also in other forms of literature such as chronicles and annals; indeed, in some cases the boundaries between a pamphlet and a work of history became blurred. The party divisions cut through monasteries and religious communities. Lampert, whose annals become a history of the Empire for the period from 1069 to 1077 and were consistently anti-royalist in their attitude, lived as a monk in the generally royalist monastery of Hersfeld, until he moved in 1081 to the monastery of Hasungen, which had been converted from a canonry, to become its first abbot. Hasungen was a proprietary monastery of Archbishop Siegfried of Mainz, a prominent Gregorian. His successor Wezilo supported Henry IV and forced the monks, who had in the meantime adopted the practices of the

Hirsau monastic reform, to leave Hasungen. Very close to Lampert, who died some time after 1081 and whose annals Ranke could 'never put down without a feeling of sadness', was Bruno, a cleric in the entourage of Archbishop Werner of Magdeburg, who wrote a *Book on the Saxon war* with an anti-royalist, pro-Saxon standpoint and an Augustinian attitude of contempt for the state. The chronicle-writing around Lake Constance also favoured the opposition: both Berthold of Reichenau (†1088) and Bernold of Constance (†1100), whose chronicle still survived in the author's original manuscript and gives a unique account of many events, were Gregorians.

Henry IV's letter of deposition sent from Worms in 1076 has been called the 'beginnings of state propaganda', but its success does not seem to have been very marked, in contrast to the evidence of papal activity. Many of the letters of Gregory VII have survived in several copies, especially as they were often incorporated into treatises and chronicles, and produced a number of replies. The royalist side was here definitely weaker than the papacy, for the royal chancery was not equipped for such propagandist activity and the popes had many helpers who could disseminate their letters, such as the monks of Hirsau, who acted both as messengers and as popular preachers. They were described scornfully by the monks of Lorsch as 'vaga-bonds' (*gyrovagi*), who wandered around the countryside and seduced weaker spirits; the monks of Lorsch also expressed concern that 'the whole earth was in pain from the frequent disputes'. Gregory himself was accused of having 'destroyed unity and spread his writings over the whole of the earth'. He made use of anyone available. He instructed Count Robert of Flanders 'to read these words of ours repeatedly . . . and ensure that all clerics and laymen announce this truth'. One of the most important of his pieces of propaganda was the long letter written in March 1081 to Bishop Hermann of Metz, in which he set out at length the reasons for his second deposition of Henry IV, which had aroused some misgivings even in circles well disposed to him.

The intellectual and spiritual unrest which affected substantial sections of the population seems to have been great, but it had other effects than those which might be surmised from histories of literature and guides to historical sources. There were a small number of teachers in Germany who were not members of any ecclesiastical corporation and hence had no fixed position or income; they were the first who risked living from the profession of teaching. Benno of Osnabrück seems to have been the pupil of just such a wandering *magister*, and Manegold of Lautenbach journeyed with his wife and daughters as a teacher through France, until he came 'after many wanderings' to the Augustinian canonry of Lautenbach in Alsace. Wandering grammar-teachers who boasted of their knowledge had long been known in Italy. Moreover it became customary to seek an education not at home but abroad, and the person who had studied only in one place became almost an object of contempt. French schools took in large numbers of scholars from Germany. Adalbero of Würzburg and Gebhard of Salzburg studied in Paris, Frederick of Cologne in Angoulême. There were also exchanges of teachers: Bernard, a Saxon, taught mainly in Constance; Benno, the *scholasticus* in Hildesheim, came from Suabia; the Irishman David taught in Würzburg. Added to this restlessness was discussion of the aims of reform. Three thousand six hundred clerics from the diocese of Constance came together to a synod in 1075 after the strict Gregorian prohibition of priestly incelibacy had been announced: they rejected it, for it was above all the lesser clergy who opposed the prohibition of clerical marriage. Newsletters which dealt with current affairs circulated through the country and new doctrines were announced from the pulpit. Bruno describes how during the Easter sermon in Mainz in 1075, at which the king was present, a messenger entered with a letter from the Saxons, and demanded that it should be 'read out and interpreted to all present' from the pulpit; when this was refused, the messenger himself explained the letter's contents to the people. Some authors refer with indignation to the fact that craftsmen, merchants and women studied Latin writings, in other words that these had been translated, probably orally, into the vernacular, and Manegold of Lautenbach said accusingly of his literary opponent Wenrich of Trier that his treatise had been 'spread through all the streets and alleys in scorn of the church', whereas Manegold's own reply to Wenrich has only come down to us in a single manuscript. This is something which should always be borne in mind: terms like 'pamphlet literature', 'broadsheets' and 'public debate' are used, but the manuscript transmission of many of these works is so meagre that they can hardly have reached a wide public or had the function of a pamphlet or broadsheet in their own time. Humbert of Silva Candida's *Three books against the simonists*, Manegold of Lautenbach's works, and treatises of the so-called Norman Anonymus, have all survived only in a single manuscript, and we know of the *Liber de unitate ecclesiae conservanda,* a moderate and pro-royalist tract, only from an *incunabulum* published by the humanist Ulrich von Hutten. The diffusion of a work is no indication of its intellectual or moral quality: the works just mentioned belong to the most impressive among the literature of the Investiture Contest, without apparently having had much influence on it.

There was a leap forward in intellectual activity. It has been calculated that in the eleventh century and the period up to the Concordat of Worms in 1122 at least five times as many historical works were composed as in the previous century. There were numerous treatises on the aims of reform: some 150 are known from the pens of almost a hundred authors. Almost all were clerics, and often they dealt with isolated topics: simony, celibacy, which was often rejected by the lower clergy, lay investiture, and, most frequently, the question of whether Gregory VII was entitled to depose Henry IV. The tone was often insulting: Archbishop Anno of Cologne was described as the new high priest Annas, the father-in-law of Caiaphas, and Henry IV as a new Nero; names were perverted, so that 'Urbanus' became 'Turbanus' (meaning one who brings everything into confusion). The only layman among these authors seems to have been Petrus Crassus, who belonged to the circles around Wilbert of Ravenna, the antipope Clement III, and attempted to justify the sovereignty and irremovability from office of the king with arguments drawn from Roman law. His argumentation is a sign of an intellectual reorientation; from this time on there was a continuous and growing interest in the study of Roman law. A bridge had to be built across half a millennium; since the time of Gregory I the Digests – the part of the Corpus Iuris Civilis which contained the collected legal opinions of the Roman jurists and which was particularly suited to the discussion of legal problems – had not been quoted. They were now to become the principal item on the curriculum for the study of rhetoric in Bologna under a *magister artium* called Irnerius or Werner (*c.* 1075–1130; he was perhaps German by origin), until in the early twelfth century a separate law school was established, which was in the following decades to attract even more students.

The needs of debate meant that a weighing up of *pro* and *contra* became a standard feature of argumentation. It was no longer enough to heap up authorities; one had to deal with the various arguments in order to offer a solution. The writings of Bernold of Constance (†1100) already show the beginnings of the techniques of dialectic, long before Abaelard's *Sic et non*. The drawing of conclusions now demanded the rational weighing-up of the arguments for and against; the intellect began to experiment. The Investiture Contest, which was characterized by polemics carried out as duels between opponents, was a precondition for the rise of scholastic method. Men became conscious that faith and intellect did not exclude one another, that on the contrary the tradition of the church could be grasped more deeply by the intellect and hence the faith strengthened. The priority remained the same, however: *Credo ut intelligam* ('I believe so that I may understand'), or, in a still more precise description of the approach, *Fides quaerens intellectum* ('belief seeking understanding'). Both axioms are taken from the writings of the first great representative of early scholasticism, Anselm of Canterbury (†1109), whose declared aim it was to convince the unbelieving opponent that the truth of the faith could be demonstrated by rational argument: hence his question 'Why did God become man?' (*Cur Deus homo*) and his proof for the existence of God, the first in a long series. He tried to show by ontology that God's existence could be demonstrated from the concept of perfection which is essential to him.

It cannot be said that the Germans did not take part in this intellectual renewal, but political polarization prevented intellectual life from unfolding fully.

4 The expansion of the West and the First Crusade

Towards the end of the eleventh century changes were taking place in Europe and in the Mediterranean region which left Germany and its kingdom remarkably untouched: the first signs of the future separate development of Germany. Something like a system of states began to come into existence; the reform papacy helped in the setting up of new states and saw itself as a centre of political integration. In Spain the *reconquista* began, the reconquest of the lands controlled by the Moors. The brutal King Ferdinand I (1035–65) brought about a union of the kingdoms of Leon, Navarre, Aragon and Castile, and their united military strength was turned southwards by his son Alfonso VI (1065–1109). The model Christian knight of the frontier was the Cid (1045–99), known as *el Campeador* (the fighter), whose main sense of obligation was towards his knightly code of honour (which also allowed him to fight on the side of the Moors). His aim was to build up a lordship, an immunity of his own, but these shifting petty states of the *reconquista* soon disintegrated.

The most remarkable of the new states was the Norman kingdom in southern Italy; the Normans exploited the complicated territorial position there, with Greek enclaves alongside areas settled by the

Saracens, old Lombard principalities and papal territories, and from
their bridgehead around Naples conquered the region bit by bit. The
last Byzantine stronghold in Italy, Bari, fell in 1071, and after fierce
fighting Saracen Sicily was also conquered. It was from Sicily that
the well-known and tightly organized feudal state of the Normans
was built up, which was to have a feature regarded as an essential
characteristic of a state by later political theorists: in 1098 Pope
Urban II conferred the spiritual rights of a papal legate on the ruler
of Sicily, thus laying the foundations of the *monarchia Sicula* which
united temporal and spiritual leadership in one hand. The Byzantines checked further Norman expansion in the Mediterranean, and
Robert Guiscard, with characteristic energy, had carried the fight
from Italy to the Balkans. The campaign began well in 1080 with the
Norman conquest of Dyrrachium/Durazzo, but their fleet was
annihilated by the combined fleets of Venice and Byzantium. Robert
Guiscard died in 1085 in the middle of a new campaign on the island
of Kephallenia. The fact that the Normans did not find the Byzantines such an easy prey as might have been expected was due to the
reorganization in Byzantium which had been carried through by the
military aristocracy; Alexios Comnenos (1081–1118) had assumed
the throne as their representative. In order to increase his military
strength Alexios sought a *rapprochement* with the West and opened
negotiations with Pope Urban II for a reunion of the churches. He
evidently planned that western mercenaries should fight for the
Byzantines, and in 1095 a Byzantine embassy appeared at the papal
synod of Piacenza with a request for help. The Byzantines do not
seem to have intended that this should have been transformed by
papal initiative into a crusade to Jerusalem.

From the early days of the reform the popes had seen themselves
as leading the struggle against the pagans. Alexander II had granted
indulgences to the knights who fought against the Moors in Spain,
and Gregory VII, whom Carl Erdmann called the most warlike
pope (at least in intention) who ever sat on the throne of St Peter,
had planned in all seriousness in December 1074 to lead an army to
the East to fight against the Arabs. It is no coincidence that the
reform popes combined a religious claim with a political one. As in
the case of the Normans in southern Italy, so also elsewhere the
papacy sought to establish new ties of feudal suzerainty, sometimes
using brutal methods to do so. Gregory VII, who had declared a
Spanish campaign to be a holy war, wrote to French knights who
were going to fight there: 'if you will not pledge yourselves to
maintain the rights of St. Peter, we would sooner forbid you to go

to Spain at all'. At first the papacy only succeeded in bringing a few scattered counties into vassalitic dependence, but under Paschal II (1099–1118) the county of Barcelona and Catalonia became a papal fief, with the result that the whole of north-eastern Spain had the pope as its feudal lord. The papacy had no success with William the Conqueror, even though a papal banner had been conferred on him before the conquest of England; William rejected the subsequent attempt to give this a feudal significance. If the antikings had won in Germany then this kingdom too would have become feudally dependent on the pope, for both antikings, Rudolf of Rheinfelden and Hermann of Salm, had promised to become vassals of the pope, and from the papal point of view the German king was simply a *rex Teutonicorum*, one king among others. Seen as a whole the efforts made by the popes in this direction were greater than their successes: only a few counties submitted in France; attempts to subordinate Denmark and Hungary were unsuccessful. In eastern Europe only a few lesser princes accepted papal overlordship: in 1076, King Demetrius of Croatia and Dalmatia received his kingdom back as a fief and it is possible that there were feudal ties between the papacy and Prince Isjaslav of Kiev. Apart from its attempts to establish feudal overlordships, the Roman church, which up to the beginning of the twelfth century had been poor, succeeded in acquiring very substantial lands – the most important gain being the so-called Mathildine lands. The Countess Mathilda was the sole heiress to a huge complex of imperial fiefs and allodial lands in Tuscany, Emilia and Lombardy, which she made over to the Roman church in 1079, reserving only a right of usufruct for her own lifetime and ignoring possible royal rights.

The numerous new financial and organizational tasks taken on by the papacy demanded the expansion of the central administration. The expression *Curia* occurs for the first time under Pope Urban II in 1089 to describe the papal court, and the *Curia Romana* was a counterpart to the secular court of a king, the *curia regis*. The papal chancery was reorganized in order to cope with the increased correspondence; a financial administration was established – Urban II demanded payment of court fees in advance, for example – and the management of papal property was set on a new footing under the papal *camera*, whose first head, significantly, was a monk called Peter from the monastery of Cluny. The satires on the greed and corruptibility of the Roman *Curia* began almost simultaneously. The administration was so arranged that particular tasks were delegated to cardinals – curial cardinals, as they would later be called

– and the consistory of the cardinals began to function as a permanent advisory body for the papacy. Compared with the rationalistic bureaucracy of the papal central administration the itinerant kingship of Germany looks very primitive.

Although the German emperor regarded himself as the 'defender of Christianity', Latin Christendom achieved its greatest military success without him. The First Crusade, proclaimed by Pope Urban II in 1095 at the synod of Clermont, was largely carried out by French and Norman knights under papal leadership; Otto of Freising saw clearly that the absence of the Germans from the crusade was the result of 'the hostility which existed at that time between the king and the pope'. Godfrey of Bouillon, widely admired for his unselfishness and bravery, was as duke of Lower Lotharingia a German vassal and indeed a supporter of Henry IV, but when a crusader state was set up in 1099 after the conquest of Jerusalem and Godfrey became its first head – he called himself 'advocate of the Holy Sepulchre' and it was left to his brother and successor Baldwin I (1100–18) to take the title of king – his feudal connection with the German king played no part.

The new crusader states had a tightly-organized feudal structure. This was all the more necessary because the initial flood of settlers into the new states rapidly dried up. The anarchical People's Crusade under the leadership of the hermit Peter of Amiens, who claimed to have been called to the leadership by a letter sent from heaven, had ended in disaster: his bands of adventurers had began by organizing bloody pogroms against the Jews of the Rhineland and were largely wiped out in Hungary in 1096 after they had begun plundering. Further large-scale pilgrimages had equally little success. In 1101 a crusade which is said to have had the incredible number of 150,000 participants from Lombardy, southern France, and Germany failed to get through, and a little later a group of pilgrims led by William IX of Poitiers and Welf IV of Bavaria with about 60,000 participants was wiped out. The defence of Christianity depended on the 'Franks', who regarded themselves so highly that the 'deeds of the Franks' (*gesta Francorum*) could become 'the deeds of God through the Franks' (*gesta Dei per Francos*) in the title of one history of the crusades. The western neighbours of the Germans were on the way to becoming the 'most Christian nation'.

The crusades did not just expand the political and economic sphere of influence of the West; the knights and pilgrims from the West were able to encounter new experiences and ways of life outside the Christian world. Islam became more familiar; we meet

for the first time the idea of the 'noble pagan', and William of Tyre
(†1186), who was born in Jerusalem, said of his contemporary the
Sultan Saladin that 'he was an extraordinarily generous man'.

5 The town as an institution and a way of life

The crusades brought a boom for the Italian maritime cities, which
transported many of the crusaders to the Holy Land and maintained
the communications between it and the West. Genoa and Pisa in
particular secured concessions for themselves; Venice acquired the
privilege of trading without customs duties and other taxes within
the Byzantine empire, and extended its trade to the Holy Land only
somewhat later. The inland cities of nothern Italy also profited from
maritime trade, and in the newly rich communes, whose pride and
independence was frequently symbolized in a standard-wagon,
there were often tensions and struggles over questions of town
government. The lower orders demanded participation in the
administration alongside the higher nobility and the lesser nobility,
which tended to side with the bourgeoisie. New offices and officials
were set up, in particular *consules*, who appear at first as military
leaders, as in Lucca in 1080, in Pisa in 1084, in Milan in 1097 and in
Genoa in 1099, but later took on administrative roles. Urban
law-codes evolved, based on Roman law, which aimed at equality
for all citizens. But the community of the burghers was not a
corporation: every burgher was responsible for himself, and the
oath of a city consisted of the sum of all the individual oaths of its
citizens. Both in their size and in their legal organization the cities of
northern Italy were considerably in advance of other cities in
Europe, though movements towards urban autonomy can also be
observed at about this time within the kingdom of Germany. The
first surviving charter of liberties for a north European town was
issued for the Flemish town of Huy in the diocese of Liège. The
count of Flanders, an opponent of the bishop of Liège, had destroyed the place in the course of a feud; in order to encourage the
inhabitants to return, the bishop issued the charter of liberties as lord
of the town in 1066. The dues owed the lord were considerably
reduced, and the burghers – it is the first occurrence of the word
burgenses – were allowed a limited independent jurisdiction: anyone
who committed a felony outside the town and fled into it was
protected by the town's peace, so long as he was prepared to accept
the town's judgement. The cities in the heartland of the German
kingdom were still far from achieving such a degree of autonomy,

especially as the first attempts to secure independence from the lords of towns had often ended in failure. There were, however, signs of change: in 1066 the leading families of Trier had chosen a candidate as archbishop who was rejected by Archbishop Anno of Cologne. He wanted to appoint his own nephew Kuno, but the latter was captured by the advocate of Trier on his way to the city and murdered. Here it was the self-confidence of the inhabitants of Trier which refused to tolerate the foreign candidate (whose election was also contrary to the provisions of canon law).

The struggles between king and princes, which sucked in the German episcopate, gave many towns the opportunity of freeing themselves from their episcopal lord. When Henry IV had to flee from Saxony in 1073 he found sanctuary with the citizens of Worms, who drove out their Bishop Adalbert with his *ministeriales* and received the king into the city with cheers. The king rewarded this by issuing a privilege in Worms in 1074 for the 'inhabitants of the town of Worms', who were freed from royal tolls at the royal toll-stations of Frankfurt, Boppard, Hammerstein, Dortmund, Goslar and Enger (near Herford). It was not the town or the burghers who lived in it who were thus privileged, but the merchants who lived there; the rights of the bishop as lord of the city were evidently not to be infringed. A long preamble promises 'the inhabitants of all towns' the royal generosity 'which has here been shown to the inhabitants of Worms'. The 'evil example' of Worms, as the anti-royalist historian Lampert of Hersfeld described it, was not without consequences. In April 1074 the ruthless Archbishop Anno II of Cologne (1056–75) confiscated the ship of a Cologne merchant as it was already loaded and about to cast off. He wanted it to set at the disposal of his suffragan Frederick of Münster, who was staying with him as his guest; but confiscation was something he was only entitled to do when on the king's service, and there was an uprising. The archbishop's residence was stormed; Anno fled in disguise through a tunnel under the wall. As in Worms, it was primarily the merchants who opposed their episcopal lord. Anno, a 'foreigner' from a Suabian family of *Edelfreie*, had succeeded in making enemies both among the citizens and among the clergy. He had brought Cluniac reform monks from the monastery of Fruttuaria in Piedmont and established them in the old city monastery of St Pantaleon after having simply driven out the old convent; the monasteries of Grafschaft and Siegburg were also stocked with monks from Fruttuaria. It is said that the reform monks barely escaped with their lives from the uprising. Anno's unrestrained policies of reform and expansion, which extended to the filling of offices as well as to monastery and property, had made him a hated man; even his own *ministeriales* planned to murder him. Had they succeeded he would have suffered the same fate as several of his relatives, for it was not only his nephew, whom he tried to install in Trier, who was murdered: his brother Werner, who had been promoted to the archbishopric of Magdeburg in 1063 after Anno had secured control of the court by kidnapping Henry IV at Kaiserwerth, died violently in 1078, and his nephew Bishop Burchard of Halberstadt was fatally wounded in 1088 by burghers from his own diocese in the course of an uprising at Goslar. Anno dealt out a harsh punishment to the unrecalcitrant burghers of Cologne; the city was recaptured in April 1074 and he allowed it to be sacked. Around six hundred burghers of Cologne are said to have fled to the king and begged him for help. Henry persuaded Anno to pardon the city in June 1074, but did not issue a privilege as he had for the inhabitants of Worms. Anno lifted the excommunications and sentences of exile, and retired to his favourite monastery of Siegburg, which he had chosen as his burial place; he died at the end of 1075. It was the grateful recollection of the monks of Siegburg, not of the burghers of Cologne, which kept Anno's memory alive with reports of miracles and of the holiness of his way of life, and in 1183 the abbot of Siegberg secured Anno's canonization from Rome.

A further attempt at securing city liberties has been ascribed to the burghers of Cologne for the year 1112: a report of a *coniuratio pro libertate* has been interpreted as having been directed against the episcopal lord of the city. But the dating of the conspiracy and its purpose are somewhat uncertain: it could equally well have been intended to preserve the independence of the city against the emperor. However, the citizens of Cologne did acquire some rights in the first decades of the twelfth century: the city had its own seal, there was a group of jurymen who formed a separate court independent of the archbishop, and the *Schreinsbücher*, which had a similar function to that of a modern land register, came into existence.

Towns often sought help from the king against their bishop; the king in turn expected assistance from the burghers. In 1102 the burghers of Cambrai, who had formed a commune, took an oath to their bishop which was to be valid only so long as he remained loyal to the emperor, and they themselves promised loyalty to the emperor so long as he should help them against the count of

Flanders. There is eloquent testimony to the community of interests between towns and Henry IV in a letter sent to him by the citizens of Mainz after they had driven out their archbishop in 1105: they will remain loyal to him, for they have common enemies: 'If God grants us victory we shall both be secure, you on your throne and we in our town.' Cologne and Liège behaved similarly

It was not just some of the old episcopal cities, with a history which often went back to Roman times, which found themselves on the way to urban liberty. New towns founded in open country generally had certain liberties conceded them from the beginning by their lord and founder. The oldest surviving example of such a foundation is probably the town law of Freiburg im Breisgau from the year 1120. In 1091 the Zähringer had built a castle with a *suburbium*, a surrounding settlement, on their allodial lands, called Vriburg. In 1120 messengers were sent out to summon merchants to the town, and the Zähringer reached a 'sworn agreement' (*coniuratio*) with them about the foundation of a market. This process of settlement and organization, which will certainly have taken some time, was completed by a ratification in 1122, at which twelve *ministeriales* of the Zähringer swore oaths. The rights conceded in this early phase included the granting to each merchant of a piece of land on which he could build his own house. The founder promised peace and safe conduct to all who visited the market and guaranteed to ransom back stolen goods; the merchants and citizens were freed from customs duties and inheritance restrictions; they were to decide disputes according to their own law or that of the merchants, 'especially those of Cologne'; in case of need they could sell their urban property freely. The core of the citizenry, who are sometimes called *mercatores* (merchants) and sometimes *burgenses*, was a group of twenty-four *coniuratores fori*, men who had taken an oath to the market; it was these men who for example administered the inheritance of a man who had died without heirs for a year before dividing it into three parts, to be devoted to a benefaction for the memory of the deceased, to the buildings of the city and to the lord of the city respectively. They chose the mayor, called *rector* or *causidicus* (thus indicating his judicial functions), from among themselves. The town law of Freiburg was adopted by a whole number of other towns, for example Diessenhofen in 1178, Freiburg im Üchtland between 1170 and 1180, and Berne in 1191. Such 'families' of town law sometimes, though not always, provided for the court of the original town to act as a court of appeal.

The rise of the autonomous town brought with it the notion of urban freedom, that is, freedom from any of the characteristics of serfdom. Even serfs who had escaped from their lords and fled into the town could acquire such freedom if their lord did not succeed in reclaiming them within a certain period. Royal charters of liberty guaranteed their position as burghers (so at Worms in 1111 and at Speyer in 1114). The legal maxim 'town air enfrees' is first found in lower Franconia. Unfreedom here is not the same as it had been in antiquity, for instance. Then a lordless slave was still a slave, a thing without an owner, and his owner could reclaim him at any time. In medieval law serfdom lapsed when the lord failed or forgot to enforce it.

The towns of the eleventh and even of the twelfth century must have looked pretty shabby. Almost all houses had only one room and were built of wood, much like peasant huts; even those artisans who needed fire for their work like bakers and smiths only had a stone fireplace or a separate stone furnace-house. The plots of land which were to tempt the merchants to Freiburg were about thirty metres by fifteen. Fortifications around the town – generally earth ramparts with wooden palisades – could only be built with the permission of the lord of the market or town or on his instructions. Big cities had rather better fortifications, though if a siege threatened the fortifications generally had to be put into order. When Henry IV fled to Cologne in 1106 he ordered that the city should be surrounded by a wall, a ditch and gates with arches, and after this it was indeed possible to defend the city; thirty years earlier, in the course of the uprising of 1074, a defensive fortification had evidently scarcely presented any obstacle to the troops of the archbishop. Aachen, Soest, Brunswick and a small number of other towns had a stone ring-wall, but only towards the end of the twelfth century.

THE RISE OF THE SECULAR STATE AND THE PRIESTLY CHURCH

1 *The Investiture Contest in France and England*

Simony and lay investiture were of course practised not only in the German church, and elsewhere there was a trade in offices unknown in Germany. The archbishopric of Narbonne was to be had in 1016 for 100,000 gold shillings; Albi cost 5,000 shillings when it was sold with a sitting tenant in 1038, and the rich Pavian father of Petrus Mezzabarba, bishop of Florence, groaned in 1062: 'My son's bishopric has cost me 3,000 gold pieces.' Seen in this context Benedict IX's sale of the papacy to Gregory VI in 1045 does not seem so extraordinary. Although the abuses were probably much worse in France and Italy, the struggle between Roman church reform and lay control over the church was nowhere else so destructive as in Germany. The king of Germany was as emperor or emperor-to-be the leading lay ruler, and the intermingling of secular rights and spiritual office in the so-called 'imperial church system' of the Ottonian and Salian rulers did not allow a painless disentangling.

The reformers did not shrink from prohibiting lay investiture in France, but this affected magnates almost more than it did the king. The main struggle between the papacy and the French crown fell in the reign of Philip I (1060–1108); it did not have the drama of the German Investiture Contest, tending to break up into a series of little disputes, often confused by being mixed up with disagreements over other things. Philip was certainly not a friend or propagator of Gregorian reform or Roman centralism, but still less were a number of French prelates, Manasses I of Rheims for example. He had a reputation for preferring warfare to ecclesiastical matters, and is said to have made the statement that being an archbishop would be a fine thing if one did not have to read mass, which should not blind us to the fact that Manasses was a man of considerable education who had a good knowledge of canon law and was not ill-disposed towards church reform. What brought him into conflict with Rome was his refusal to accept the jurisdiction of a papal legate in France; he demanded a Roman tribunal. After much toing and froing Manasses was finally declared deposed in 1081; his case did not lead to any display of solidarity from the rest of the French episcopate, in spite of its Gallicanistic aspects. Gregory wrote repeatedly in sharp tones to Philip I, but never took such severe measures against him as he did against Henry IV. In 1092 Philip repudiated his wife Bertha of Holland after being married to her for twenty years and from then on lived in concubinage (according to the church's standpoint) with the Countess Bertrada of Montfort. After ecclesiastical censures, including repeated excommunications, had had no effect, he was anathematized at the great reform and crusading council of Clermont in 1095; it was at this synod also that bishops were forbidden to take an oath of fealty to a layman.

The problem appeared to be turning into an issue of principle, but Urban II, a Frenchman by birth who referred to France as the *filia specialis* of the Roman church, did not display Gregory's intolerant severity. Philip was not prevented from ruling, although he did not part from Bertrada and continued to invest bishops. Even before the council of Clermont there were signs in the contemporary pamphlet literature that people were looking for an acceptable compromise on the question of investitures. There was in any case a tradition in France of separating ecclesiastical office and temporal possessions conceptually – as early as Abbo of Fleury (†1004) we find reflections on the distinction between the two spheres. The most important proposal for dealing with the problem of investiture came from the learned bishop Ivo of Chartres (†1116), who had been a pupil of Lanfranc of Bec and had learnt how to make distinctions both in theology and in canon law. After 1097, when Ivo had already written a number of important works on canon law, one can observe the distinction in his writings between the ecclesiastical office and the temporal endowment which can be bestowed by a layman: the distinction between *temporalia* and *spiritualia*. Pope Urban II took up the proposal made by Ivo and approved by Philip I; it was put into practice for the first time in May 1098 with the election of Archbishop Daimbert of Sens. Philip refrained from investing Daimbert (who had been elected with his approval) with the ecclesiastical symbols of ring and staff, and was content with an oath of fealty without homage. After taking this the bishop received the temporalities of his office. This was to be the model for the normal sequence of events: canonical election; no royal investiture, but simply an oath of fealty taken to the king by the elect; finally the elect took possession of the lands and rights attached to his church. It was in the last resort a milder version of investiture without the provocative use of ecclesiastical symbols; the compromise was reached without any formal agreement.

The Anglo-Norman kingdom was a special case. To the duchy of Normandy, which was a fief under the French crown, William the Conqueror had added the kingdom of England, where he had been able to establish new structures of government. Just as the 'Domesday Book' regarded the king as the ultimate owner of all land, so also William regarded himself as the head and protector of the English church. He brought French prelates to the island, led by the learned and subtle Lanfranc of Bec, who as archbishop of Canterbury (1070–89) reorganized the canon law of the English church along the principles laid down in the decretals of Pseudo-Isidore. William's relations with the reform papacy were distinctly cool, and Gregory VII was for a time uncertain whether William would not declare for the imperial antipope Wibert of Ravenna (Clement III). William accepted that the church had a sphere of its own, and established a new separate system of church courts, but he was not prepared to tolerate any deviation from his centralism: synods had to be summoned by him; he nominated the bishops and did not allow them to go to Rome without his permission. After William's death in 1087 the Anglo-Norman empire threatened to fall apart. William Rufus, king of England, was an opponent of church reform; he refused at first to recognize Pope Urban II and insisted on his right to enjoy the *spolia*, which meant that the king confiscated the movable property of a dead bishop and administered the see until a successor had been chosen, drawing on its income in the mean time. It is not surprising that a man like Anselm of Canterbury (1093–1109), who moved in the rarified atmosphere of scholastic theology, was driven into exile under William. On Rufus's death as a result of a hunting accident in 1100 the English crown was taken over by his youngest brother Henry I, a man of energy and flexibility. He took his elder brother Robert Curthose, duke of Normandy and one of the heroes of the First Crusade who had helped to conquer Jerusalem, captive in 1107 and reunited England with Normandy. He sought a compromise with the papacy and with his primate Anselm of Canterbury, but when Anselm would still not tolerate any feudal tie between the dispensers of sacraments and lay rulers he sent him into exile again in 1103. In the Norman monastery of Bec, where Lanfranc and Anselm had taught, a compromise was worked out in 1106 which was the basis of the so-called Concordat of London agreed the following year. Prelates were to be elected by canonical election in the presence of the king; there was to be no investiture after the election but the elect had to do homage for the temporalities (not just to take an oath of fealty as in France) – a clear breach of the prohibition by Urban II and the Council of Clermont in 1095 of homage to laymen by ecclesiastics.

2 *The beginnings of Henry V's reign*

Urban II had checkmated Henry IV; the fact that Henry was able to make a political recovery was not due to his own actions but to changed circumstances. In 1095 the 23-year-old Welf V separated from his wife Mathilda of Tuscany, who was almost thirty years older than he was; Welf IV, his father, one of the leaders of the opposition, was reconciled with Henry IV and was again granted the duchy of Bavaria. Henry was also able to secure Suabia, for the Zähringer, who had succeeded to the inheritance of Rudolf of Rheinfelden as supporters of the antikings, were prepared to renounce their claims to the duchy in favour of Henry's son-in-law

Frederick I of Staufen, who moved his family seat to the castle of Stauf near Göppingen. The Zähringer retained the title of duke, which was no empty one, for their lordships consisted of almost territorial complexes of land and rights, notably in the Breisgau, in Switzerland and in upper Suabia, where the Staufer dukes had no power.

In 1098 Henry had recovered sufficiently to be able to hold an assembly in Mainz and regulate the succession anew. King Conrad, his oldest son, who had gone over to Urban II, was excluded from the succession and declared deposed (he died in 1101); the new heir was Conrad's younger brother Henry V, who at the time was perhaps twelve or thirteen years old. The new king had to take an oath not to interfere in the government of the kingdom during his father's lifetime. The relations with the church and the papacy also improved: Urban II had apparently refrained from renewing the emperor's excommunication, and on the death of the imperial antipope Clement III in 1100 Henry IV in turn refrained from setting up a new pope, though Roman aristocratic cliques elected three antipopes in succession. But Urban's successor Paschal II (1099–1118), a gloomily serious Cluniac, who was devoted to the ideals of monasticism and had the kind of all-or-nothing temperament which led him to have the corpses of excommunicates exhumed from consecrated ground and the ashes of Clement III thrown into the Tiber, renewed the excommunication of Henry IV in 1102; even Henry's promise to go on a pilgrimage to Jerusalem did not free him from the ban. Henry continued to act as king as though nothing had happened. At a general assembly held in Mainz in 1103 a peace was proclaimed for the Empire which was to be valid for four years. 'For the first time an emperor took up the peace movement and extended it to the whole of the Empire' (E. Wadle). Henry, who had perhaps been influenced by the revived study of Roman law in Lombardy, took the peace very seriously: the ordinance laid down mutilations and death sentences for those who broke the peace, regardless of their rank, and specifically included the Jews, who had suffered badly in pogroms at the beginning of the First Crusade, under its protection. There had already been hints at a renewed clash between Henry IV and the high nobility, especially as Henry had begun to confer the right of blood justice on royal advocates in order to maintain law and order; the conflict became an open one after an incident in 1104. The *ministeriales* and burghers of Regensburg, dissatisfied with an arbitration by a royal advocate, the count of Burghausen, took the count prisoner almost under Henry's nose and beheaded him. Henry did not intervene. Henry V exploited the indignation of the princes and the nobility, and at the beginning of 1105 broke with his father; the pope dispensed him from the oath of non-intervention he had taken in 1098. Henry V summoned a general assembly to Mainz at the end of 1105, with the support of the high nobility. The emperor was promised safe conduct, and Henry IV wanted to appear, especially as his chief supporter, Duke Frederick of Suabia, had died; he might hope to make up for this loss of support by a personal appearance. But he was taken prisoner by treachery and forced to hand over the royal insignia in the palace of Ingelheim. Henry agreed in the presence of the princes and of a papal legate to do penance, but he refused to make a public confession of his sins, for such a confession would probably have led to a permanent deposition. The young Henry V regarded his father's handing over of the royal insignia as a resignation, and at the beginning of 1106 he had himself acknowledged as sole and legitimate king at the Mainz assembly. But Henry IV was able to escape and found support from the Rhenish cities. Cologne, fortified on his instructions, was able to drive off the troops of Henry V, and as the latter was travelling with his court through Rufach in upper Alsace the burghers attacked him, seized the imperial insignia and only returned them after having received extensive promises. Numerous *ministeriales* joined the camp of the old emperor, who based himself at Liège in lower Lotharingia. 'In these places [Cologne and Liège] I have always found devoted supporters, unshakeable in their loyalty to the crown', wrote Henry IV, and Henry V's army was crushingly defeated before the walls of Liège. Henry IV prepared for a counter-attack, and a civil war seemed inevitable.

A number of letters written by Henry IV have survived from this period – to his godfather Hugh of Cluny, to King Philip of France, to his son Henry V, to the princes of the Empire – which show both the active propaganda carried out by the ageing king and his determination not to accept defeat. But in the middle of his preparations Henry died at the age of fifty-six on 7 August 1106 in Liège. From his death-bed he had sent his sword and ring to his son and asked him for forgiveness for his followers; for himself he requested burial in the cathedral at Speyer, whose rebuilding he had personally supported. When his corpse was laid to rest in an unconsecrated chapel, widows, orphans and 'all the poor', in the words of the *Vita Heinrici IV*, flocked to the spot in order to bewail the death of the merciful king, and even on the journey between Liège and Speyer peasants had placed earth on the coffin so that they could recover it and spread it, charged with the fruitfulness spread by the king, on their fields. Henry IV had always known how to exercise his charisma on the lower classes, although his character defects had alienated the members of his immediate family – his second wife Praxedis, and his two sons Conrad and Henry. He probably did not grasp the nature of the reform movement or of the changes which accompanied it; his support for burghers and towns and the support he received from the lower orders were scarcely due to any policy on his part, but simply to the tactical consideration that help should be taken wherever it was offered

3 The road to the Concordat of Worms (1122)

Henry V had secured an ecclesiastical dispensation from the oath which he had taken to his father and found support from the princes. But it was clear as soon as he began to rule alone that he was not prepared to be the creature of either papacy or princes. He continued to practise investiture. A papal synod in Guastalla in Emilia renewed the prohibition of lay investiture in early 1106; Henry's representative at the synod, Archbishop Bruno of Trier, continued to claim the right of investiture for the king in spite of this. Both sides upheld their principles, but tolerated the differences, and the pope recognized almost all the prelates whom the king had invested and began negotiations with Henry. In 1107 the *regalia* were defined for the first time in the course of these negotiations, but Henry was preoccupied with war in the East and with the princely opposition, and could not continue the dialogue.

Abruptly, as was his wont, he announced an expedition to Rome in 1110. It was not only a politically favourable situation which had led to his decision, but also the substantial dowry of 10,000 marks of silver which his betrothed, Mathilda, the daughter of King Henry I of England, had brought him. Henry passed over the Great St Bernard with a large army. In 1109 royal negotiators had put a treatise before the *Curia* which explicitly acknowledged the right of the German ruler to invest prelates; it relied for its argumentation on a number of documents which had been forged only a few decades previously. This treatise *On the investiture of bishops*, which has survived anonymously, was in fact the work of a royalist monk, Sigebert of Gembloux (†1112), who had already clashed with Paschal II after the pope had incited the returning crusader Count Robert II of Flanders to attack the imperialist towns of Liège and Cambrai: Sigebert accused the pope of being worse than Alaric, for the Gothic barbarian had at least spared the churches of Rome after conquering it. Sigebert knew how to point to practical realities and legal principles which were embarrassing for the pope. The preliminary negotiations with the *Curia* had not made any progress when Henry V, who had been able to rebuild the machinery of imperial government in Lombardy on his way to Rome, began the decisive negotiations at the beginning of 1111.

His representatives declared to the pope that the king could under no circumstances renounce the right of investiture, which they claimed had been exercised since the time of Charlemagne. Paschal's counter-offer was at least in theory a reasonable one: the king should renounce his rights of investiture, and in return the royal lands and rights of sovereignty which had been made over to the church should return to the king; the church could perfectly well live from tithes and donations. There has been much speculation about why Paschal should have made such an unrealistic proposal – perhaps the hopelessness of his military position (his appeals both to the Lombard towns and to the papal vassals, the Normans, had been ignored), or his monastic unworldliness. In any case he had underestimated the extent to which ecclesiastical offices and secular possessions were intermingled in Germany. The papal proposal was turned into a kind of treaty in the course of secret negotiations on 11 February 1111 in the church of S. Maria in Turri (a small church which was demolished in the sixteenth century to make way for the new St Peter's). The king was to renounce all claims to investiture in the course of his coronation as emperor and to confirm this renunciation for the future with an oath; the pope would in return compel the prelates to return the *regalia* under threat of excommunication. The coronation and the announcements were planned for the following day, 12 February 1111. Henry was escorted into St Peter's with great ceremony. The two documents were read out before the coronation ceremony began. Even during the reading out of the royal promise there was unrest, which grew to a storm of protest when the decisive passage in the papal document was read out: 'We forbid and prohibit any bishop or abbot, either now or in the future, to hold *regalia*, that is, towns, duchies, marches, counties, rights of mint or toll, imperial advocacies, rights of low justice, royal manors with their appurtenances, armed followings or imperial castles.' The bishops and abbots protested because they would have to give up their fiefs from the Empire, and the lay princes because they held fiefs from the church which they would also have to return. The agreement was denounced as a forgery, as invalid, as heresy, and the tumult was so great that the imperial coronation could not go ahead. As the pope had not fulfilled his side of the treaty, Henry returned to his earlier demand of the unrestricted right of investiture; Paschal in turn refused to crown Henry as emperor. Henry responded by taking Paschal and the cardinals prisoner, breaking through the armed lines of Romans surrounding St Peter's and withdrew, wounded, to a fortified stronghold near Rome. The following weeks in royal captivity wore Paschal down. On 4 April 1111 a new agreement was made in Ponte Mammolo near Tivoli. The pope conceded the right of investiture with ring and staff to the German king throughout the Empire, provided that the election had taken place without simony. Paschal promised not to excommunicate Henry for transgressing the prohibition of lay investiture and promised him imperial coronation. Henry in return agreed to release the pope and the cardinals. On 13 April, an ordinary Thursday (a sign of haste), the extorted imperial coronation was carried out. Both sides issued justifications which only served to increase the tension. Paschal, released, declared at a Lateran synod in 1112 that he had not deviated from the path followed by his predecessors Gregory VII and Urban II. The extorted privilege of Ponte Mammolo was soon denounced as a 'pravilege', a distortion of right. Paschal's hands were bound by the oath he had taken, but a synod held in southern France by Archbishop Guy of Vienne anathematized the emperor as a 'second Judas', and Paschal confirmed the sentence.

Henry V had returned to Germany, where a new opposition had developed with its centre in Saxony. In 1106 the Billung dynasty had become extinct in the male line with the death of Magnus Billung, and Henry had conferred the duchy on Lothar of Supplinburg, ignoring the expectations of other candidates. However Henry acted, he was bound to offend the interests of princes and dynasts, and he began to turn to the groups on which his father had relied for support: *ministeriales* and towns. It was not just tradition that made Saxony the centre of opposition; Henry had brutally overridden rights of inheritance, and the new duke of Saxony, Lothar, sought to build up his lordship. In 1111 he conferred the counties of Holstein and Stormarn on Count Adolf of Schauenburg. Holstein and Stormarn were still organized as they had been in pre-Frankish Saxony, as regions with legal and governmental structures in which all free men participated, without *ministeriales* or feudalism and hence with a certain degree of autonomy from the Empire. After Henry, the Christian prince of the Abodrites – he was the son of the king Gottschalk who had died in the Wendish uprising of 1066, and a grandson of the Danish king Sven Estridsen – had established a new lordship with its centre in Old Lübeck, north-east of present-day Lübeck, he found support from Lothar, who saw in the lordship a base for missionary work. Saxony was already hostile when Henry V decided in 1112 to intervene and consolidate royal power there.

The leader of the princely and Saxon opposition was Archbishop Adalbert I of Mainz (1109–37), who had been Henry's first chancellor in 1106 and later negotiated on his behalf with the *Curia* as one of his principal advisers. He was pushed into opposition mainly because the king turned away from the high aristocracy. Henry imprisoned him out of hand in 1112, and this decisive step had initial success; even Lothar of Supplinburg had to submit in 1114. But resistance flared up again when Henry planned to introduce a general tax along English lines; it was evidently impossible to transfer such a 'modern' form of taxation from a state which was tightly organized and centralized to a polity which depended principally on the cumulation of individual rights and the precarious exploitation of royal and family lands. In 1115 the imperial general Count Hoyer of Mansfeld suffered an annihilating defeat at the hands of the Saxons at Welfesholz, north of Eisleben. Count Hoyer was killed; Henry V, who lacked military ability, had to flee from Saxony.

Henry was saved from further defeats through the death of Countess Mathilda of Tuscany on 24 July 1115. He set out for Italy without an imperial army, accompanied only by his entourage. His main aim was to secure the so-called 'Mathildine lands'. Mathilda had altered her plans for these several times in the course of her seventy-year life. In 1079 she had made them over to the Roman church, but later rescinded the gift, only to renew it in 1102. In 1111 she had made Henry V her heir; he was to inherit not only the imperial fiefs but also her allodial lands. Henry's Italian expedition of 1116 showed his mastery of political tactics. He handed out urban privileges with great generosity *en route*, and made contact early on with the urban opposition in Rome, with which Mathilda had also been in touch at the end of her life. After negotiations with the *Curia* had ended without result – the *Curia* insisted on the withdrawal of the 'pravilege' and the renunciation of all rights of investiture – Henry exploited the situation created by the death of Pope Paschal on 21 January 1118 to set up a pope of his own, Archbishop Mauritius of Braga, who regarded the rights of his church as having been diminished by Paschal. The new pope, who was backed by the Frangipani in Rome and by the Bolognese jurist Irnerius, took the name of Gregory VIII, so regarding himself as a reformer. The former chancellor of the Roman church, Johannes of Gaeta, was chosen by Paschal's entourage as Pope Gelasius II; he was forced to leave the city. But Gregory VIII, whose opponents christened him 'Burdinus' ('Spanish donkey'), soon found himself abandoned, especially after the cardinals had elected Guido of Vienne as Calixtus II in January 1119 at Cluny, following Gelasius' death there in exile. This was the same Guido of Vienne who had excommunicated Henry V in 1112 on behalf of the pope but without explicit papal instructions. Calixtus' election was significant in a number of ways. He came from the high nobility of Burgundy, and was distantly related to the Salian dynasty; he was the first secular cleric to become pope since Alexander II; although not a monk, he was elected within the walls of the most rich and powerful monastery of the time. If he was expected to achieve a reasonable compromise after decades of uncompromising politics then the electors had made the right choice; his pragmatism is best demonstrated by the fact that he confirmed as Pope Calixtus II privileges which he had had forged as the metropolitan of Vienne.

Henry V could not overlook the fact that the treaty of Ponte Mammolo of 1111 had been a failure; he could neither enforce it nor come to an agreement. Soon after the beginning of Calixtus' pontificate, while he still remained in France, negotiations were begun, led on the papal side by Abbot Pontius of Cluny and Bishop William of Champeaux. William had been famed as a teacher of dialectic and rhetoric – Peter Abaelard was his pupil for several years – before his election as bishop of Châlons-sur-Marne in 1113. He was one of the founders of the school of Saint-Victor, and one of the earliest authors of *quaestiones*, a form of scholarly writing which sought to treat theological questions with finely nuanced distinctions; his writings still give *auctoritas* priority, but allow *ratio*, rational argument, a considerable part. The papal negotiator's ability to make distinctions became apparent right from the beginning of the discussions in Strasburg: he argued that Henry as the German king did not have to lose the services of the imperial church if he renounced the right of investiture of a spiritual office. A meeting was arranged between pope and emperor to be held in Mouzon, near Rheims, where a council was being held, for 24 October 1119. The show of ecclesiastical strength at the council may have made the *Curia* more self-confident; in the end the negotiators demanded that

Henry should renounce all rights of investiture. Henry withdrew from the planned meeting, and the pope renewed his prohibition of lay investiture of bishops and abbots under threat of excommunication; the secular possessions of these churches, the *temporalia*, were not mentioned.

A group of princes had gradually emerged as a third party between the king and the implacable princely opposition led by the papal legate Archbishop Adalbert of Mainz. In autumn 1121 this group arranged a peace conference in Würzburg, which produced a 'princely law-finding' recommending a meeting. This took place in Worms, where Henry V held a general assembly in 1122. A papal embassy with very wide-ranging powers, led by the Cardinal Bishop Lambert of Ostia, the later Pope Honorius II (1124–30), negotiated with the emperor. On 23 September 1122 the so-called Concordat of Worms was made public on the Laubwiese, a section of the town common which can no longer be identified; 'the oldest concordat in German history' as Leibniz put it in 1693, 'an international treaty between the papacy and a state concerning their relations in the ecclesiastical sphere'. Formally, the Concordat consists of two privileges, known as the Heinricianum and the Calixtinum after the names of their issuers. Henry's privilege still exists in the original in the archives of the recipient in the Vatican, but the Calixtinum has only survived in copies.

What do these two documents say, whose every word seems to be the result of difficult negotiations? Henry renounced investiture with ring and staff, the symbols of spiritual office; this made it clear that a spiritual office was not the subject of lay investiture. The symbol to be used for investiture in future was the neutral sceptre (in contrast to the banners used for investiture of laymen with fiefs); the king promised to allow canonical elections and free consecration, and at the same time promised the return of lands alienated both from the Roman and from other churches. In conformity with his duties as emperor Henry promised the pope and his followers help. For his part Calixtus agreed that 'the elections of bishops and abbots of the German kingdom' should take place in Henry's presence 'without simony or violence'. If the election was divided, he was to give his help and agreement to 'the better part' (*sanior pars*, a term drawn from canon law). The elected candidate was to receive the *regalia* by investiture with a sceptre – in Germany this was to take place before consecration, in Italy and Burgundy within six months of consecration. The papal state was excluded from the agreement.

The Calixtinum is addressed to Henry as recipient, whereas the Heinricianum is made out to 'God, the holy apostles Peter and Paul and the Roman church'; nevertheless, the Calixtinum was probably also intended to be a permanent concession.

Both parties felt that they had done well out of the agreement of Worms. The king still had a number of ways of influencing the process by which a prelate took office – through the election in the king's presence and through his control of the *regalia* through investiture. The procedure agreed on was similar to that reached in the so-called Concordat of London of 1107. The key features were canonical election, and no investiture with the old spiritual symbols, but an investiture of the *regalia* before consecration with the sceptre – in England accompanied by homage, not just fealty, from the elected prelate. The term *hominium*, 'homage', seems to have been deliberately avoided in Worms; the Calixtinum says somewhat circumstantially that the elected prelate should 'perform that which he owes to you (i.e. the king) by right'. The *Curia* on the other hand certainly regarded the Concordat as a victory; Calixtus had a mural erected in the secret council-chamber of the Lateran which depicted both texts. There is said to have been some opposition to the agreement in ecclesiastical circles, however, especially among the Roman clergy. The German princes who had not been present at Worms gave their agreement to the Concordat at a general assembly at Bamberg in 1122, but at the Lateran Council of 1123, later recognized as an ecumenical council, there was a disturbance when the Calixtinum was read out. There were shouts of disapproval, and it was only when it was pointed out that much had had to be accepted for the sake of peace that the atmosphere quietened. The papacy had after all managed to ensure that the spiritual office of an abbot or a bishop was seen as such in the course of election and consecration, and did not appear to be a mere appendix to the material possessions or the governmental rights associated with the office.

The Concordat of Worms brought the system of government known as the 'imperial church system of the Ottonians and Salians' to an end. 'The immediate control over the imperial church was transformed into an indirect one through feudal ties on the basis of the concordat', in the words of H. Mitteis. The king was excluded from the sacramental aspects of election, and ceased to be the lord of the imperial bishoprics and monasteries in a proprietary sense, for he could no longer install candidates in the spiritual office, even though his influence over the election remained so extensive that Elpe von Repgow could still write a hundred years later in the *Sachsenspiegel* that the king nominated the bishops. The prelates remained bound to the king through the *regalia*, for which they performed *hominium*, and formed a group of princes found only in Germany, the 'ecclesiastical princes of the Empire', a group which was to be of long-term importance in German history.

The Concordat of Worms was Henry V's last substantial political achievement. Another chance for Henry came to nothing in the end; when in 1120 Henry I's only son was drowned in the English Channel there seemed for a time to be the possibility of a union of the German and English kingdoms, for Henry V was married to the English king's only daughter. Added to this, Henry I had taken possession of the duchy of Normandy, which he held of the French crown as a fief; the union of the two empires would have brought about a far-reaching shift in the European balance of power in favour of the German emperor. But such a calculation ignored the changed situation in France. Philip I's son Louis VI (1108–37), known as 'the Fat', had Suger, abbot of Saint-Denis (1122–51) as his counsellor, and he managed to bring about something like a revival of national consciousness. When in 1124 a German army was poised to invade France in support of Henry I, there was a wave of patriotic feeling in response: the shroud of St Denis, the Oriflamme, was taken from the altar of Saint-Denis to be borne as a banner before the army. Henry V had not reckoned with such determined opposition. He gave up the invasion and retreated; shortly afterwards he fell dangerously ill, probably of cancer, and died in Utrecht on 23 May 1125, aged only thirty-nine and leaving no children.

With Henry V's death the Salian dynasty became extinct in the direct male line, and it also meant if not the end of an age at least the end of a form of government which went back to archaic times, based on the participation of ecclesiastics in politics and government and the active participation of the laity in the life of the church. State and church were from now on to be divided; the king only bestowed the *regalia* on the prelates without affecting their office. Henry V probably failed to understand many of the new developments which had come about in his time: scholastic thought and the new spirituality. He had even less interest in new currents of thought and feeling than his father had had. The contemporary chronicles give only a blurred picture of Henry's personality, and the characteristics they do mention are almost all negative ones. He stood out by his perfidiousness and his greed, and he often succeeded in uniting his opponents by his injustices. He certainly had a sense of his own dignity, but he lacked warmth; no one wrote an elegy on his death as the author of the *Vita Heinrici IV* had done for his father.

4

POLITICAL REORIENTATION AND EMERGENT DIVERSITY: FROM SALIAN IMPERIAL CHURCH SYSTEM TO STAUFER KINGSHIP

Hereditary monarchy had managed to survive for about two centuries; a candidate for the throne had to be a member of or closely related to the royal house. The elective kingship of Rudolf of Rheinfelden (elected in 1077 but himself agnatically related to the Salians) and Hermann of Salm (elected in 1081) had not been able to prevail against the hereditary kingship of Henry IV, but the elective idea had certainly been strengthened. It was supported by the papacy and by the supporters of Gregorian reform, for its own internal structures made the church sympathetic to the idea of election. Rudolf of Rheinfelden had had to take a vassalitic oath to the pope and to swear to the princes that he would renounce any claim to found a dynasty or to his son's succession. Henry V came to the throne in 1106 on condition that he 'ruled rightly'. 'If you are not a just judge and a protector of the church', said Archbishop Ruthard of Mainz, 'may the same fate which befell your father befall you.' After Henry V's death the princes twice exercised their right to elect, in 1125 with Lothar III and in 1138 with Conrad III, before the election of Frederick I gave new strength to the dynastic element in royal succession. But it was not simply a matter of deciding between elective or hereditary kingship, especially as even elective kingship was restricted to a comparatively small group of candidates. A king who was chosen by the princes had to be prepared to make concessions. Elective kingship was a well-tried means of getting usurped rights legitimized: alienated advocacies and counties, adulterine castles. It is perhaps no coincidence that in this period of radical change in Europe the principle that might creates right is found elsewhere. Roger II of Sicily expressed the view openly, and Catalonian charters of the period say explicitly that the validity of rights of ownership is not affected by whether or not they were legitimately acquired. The Investiture Contest and the struggle with the papacy, the division of the Empire into rival camps, formally ended in 1122. But the reigns of the kings who followed the last Salians, Lothar III (1125–38) and Conrad III (1138–52), allowed the imbalance in favour of the princes, already begun with Henry V's election in 1106, to continue. The reigns of Lothar III and Conrad III were in each case a kind of legalized antikingship: the princes chose, not the candidate closest to the deceased ruler, but the one who suited them. As a result, the period up to the accession of Frederick I in 1152 saw an extension and consolidation of the new social and legal conditions which had emerged from the Investiture Contest.

THE RESULTS OF THE INVESTITURE CONTEST

1 The kingdom of Germany

The Concordat of Worms changed the nature of royal rule.

By a strict separation of the *regalia* and *spiritualia* in legal theory and symbolism, the Concordat of Worms made it possible to treat all the *temporalia* of the church from the point of view of purely secular law, which meant in this case feudal law, and to interpret the relationship between the king or emperor and the ecclesiastical princes who held *regalia* as a feudal one. In place of the direct royal lordship over the church exercised by the Ottonians and Salians we find the feudal suzerainty of the Empire over the *regalia* of the ecclesiastical princes. (P. Classen)

But it was not only the character of royal government which changed as a consequence of the Investiture Contest; it was at this time that the political and social transformations of later German history had their beginnings.

We can say least about the group which formed the largest part – perhaps over 90% – of the population: the unfree. They were the least likely to experience social change. But the new *Hofrechte* (manorial laws) laid down rights and duties of the dependent peasantry and by doing so gave them a certain protection against arbitrary exploitation. Their daily labour services and often their weekly obligations as well, their payments, on succeeding to their tenancy for example, and the restrictions on their freedom to marry were all recorded in writing. Other groups in the lowest levels of society suffered a reduction in their rights and status. In the poem

Unibos (One-ox), which is set in a peasant milieu in what is now Holland, probably in the eleventh century, there is a reference to the gentle-born (*nobilis*) lady brought back by the priest of the village as his wife, and a confraternity-roll from Tours dating from around the middle of the eleventh century includes among some 150 names the daughter of a bishop and two wives of clerics; in both cases the references are matter-of-fact and there is no sign that these women enjoyed any lower social standing than their fathers and husbands. But the reform was pushed through, and priests' wives came to be regarded as concubines with a reduced legal status. It is understandable that it was members of the lower clergy who repeatedly protested against the new edicts enforcing celibacy. And priests' children soon came, as a result of their doubly sinful origin, to be especially severely handicapped in law: they were serfs of the church (*servi ecclesiae*) and hence a form of ecclesiastical property. The later Middle Ages were largely to ignore the married cleric (*clericus uxoratus*) and the legal status of his children.

Social mobility could take a variety of forms for the members of the lowest strata of society. It could be horizontal: with the break-up of the traditional patrimonial organization of great estates, it was possible for members of a *familia* to pass into another through marriage, or for a lord to make them (or their labour-power) over to a church or to another secular lord. In the disturbances and fighting of the Investiture Contest large numbers of the unfree probably abandoned their lord, or rather their manor, or were driven away by want or violence. There are increasing numbers of references in the sources to wandering gangs of paupers, who hung around the gates of churches and monasteries, and around roads and market places. They were mainly cared for by ecclesiastics, but from the twelfth century on also by lay confraternities devoted to the charitable care of the poor. But upward social mobility was also possible. By going to a town, villeins could acquire the legal status of burghers. From the beginning of the twelfth century onwards it became more and more easy to escape the domination of one's lord by moving to new areas of clearance either on the frontiers or in regions of 'internal colonization'. The most important avenue of advance, however, was the rise of the *ministerialis* from an originally unfree status to that of a professional warrior and administrator. The fiercer the civil war which had begun in 1073 became, the more demand there was for trained and permanently available soldiers. The constant fighting wore out the independent peasantry: the weaker of them sank to the status of the unfree, while the stronger ones rose to become mercenary soldiers or *ministeriales* by entering the service of a great lord. Many free peasants and small landholders seem to have lost their lives on the battlefield through lack of military experience, both in hand-to-hand fighting and in tactics. Not only was the peasant militarily inferior; he was also unable to organize his farming while away in the army, so that he lost out both as warrior and as landholder. *Bauer* ('farmer' or 'peasant') had up until this time simply been a word for anyone who tilled the fields: it now came to denote a caste separate from that of the professional warriors, with its own legal and social characteristics.

The *ministeriales* on the other hand were able to go on improving their social and legal position. They tried to free themselves from the personal legal ties which went with the services they performed, an attempt which found expression in their slogan 'a *ministerialis* is not a serf'. In the end they were able to shake off their restrictions and become capable of holding fiefs. In the legal codes of the thirteenth century, the *Sachsenspiegel* and *Schwabenspiegel*, they are included in the feudal pyramid. In spite of their origins, they soon came to be regarded as part of the nobility, a development favoured by fluctuations within the aristocracy: the nobility lost its dynastic exclusiveness, and old houses died out. Saxony, where the Investiture Contest had had particularly marked social effects, may serve as an example. Here numerous families prominent in the Ottonian and early Salian period can no longer be found after the end of the eleventh century: the Immedings, the Ekkehardines, the Walbecker or the counts of Haldensleben. Other families of the high nobility like the Northeimer, the Billungs, the Katlenburger, the Brunonids or the counts of Weimar-Orlamünde became extinct in the male line; their lands were taken over by other powerful families without any particular regard for legal rights of inheritance. Lothar, a member of the Supplinburg family, which had recently risen to prominence, was one of the most ruthless exploiters of this technique. The son of a Saxon noble who had fallen in the struggle against Henry IV, Lothar was elevated to the rank of duke by Henry V after the death of Magnus, the last Billung. Magnus's two daughters were married to powerful princes – Wulfhild to the duke of Bavaria, the Welf Henry the Black, and Eilika to Count Otto of Ballenstedt, a member of the Askanian dynasty – and Henry V obviously wanted to stop either of these families acquiring too great a power in Saxony. But Lothar himself soon achieved a prominent position by marrying Richenza, the granddaughter of Otto of Northeim. In the south-west of Germany as well, new and previously insignificant noble familes came to power and influence: the Staufer, for example, who owed their rise to the support they received from the legitimate kings, or the Zähringer, who were backed by the antikings. Many rising *ministeriales* joined up with this new aristocracy, and thus the new nobility characteristic of the Staufer period was created, with its many fine gradations from prince – lay and ecclesiastical – through counts to *ministeriales* and ordinary mercenary knights. Hand in hand with the transformation of landlordship and the differentiation within the feudal system went a decline of the means of lordship at the king's disposal. Already in the Ottonian period the county was broken up by immunities and franchises, even though these did not at this point present any real threat to royal lordship. The Salians had not, however, succeeded in building up areas of concentrated royal power such as the Capetians, for example, had managed to do in the Île-de-France. Henry IV tried it in the Harz region, but in so doing provoked an avalanche of resistance. If the royal bishoprics and abbeys were to refuse to render *servitium regis*, the material basis of royal lordship throughout the kingdom would come under threat.

The feudal lords who were rising to power at this time, on the other hand, were building up the administration of their territories, often basing it on a central castle. It was precisely the insecurity and instability produced by the Investiture Contest which led to the building of a large number of castles: small and well-fortified buildings which were extremely difficult to capture with the siege-machinery then available. It was an obvious action for a noble family to build on their own allodial lands a castle which provided both protection and the ability to defy one's enemies, without paying any attention to the royal right to license fortifications which existed in theory, and to use it as a base from which to control the land around at a time of semi-anarchy. Newly powerful lords like the Staufer sought to protect their possessions with a large number of castles. It was said of Duke Frederick of Suabia (†1147), whose claim to the throne was rejected by the princes in 1125, that 'he dragged a castle around with him at his horse's tail'. It was all the more necessary for the nobility to organize and protect their property because the old tribal groupings which had previously functioned as communities offering protection and law – like Bavaria and Suabia and, still earlier, Franconia – began to disintegrate; the individual noble was thrown back on his own resources and had to defend his rights himself. It was an almost inevitable consequence that the aristocratic member of a caste was transformed into a lord over a territory; to some extent the process was accelerated by the weakness and failure of royal government. At the same time, the sense of family began to change. The principle of leading-names, which meant that a family showed a preference for particular names and through these displayed its descent from a prominent and possible distant ancestor, was extended by references to a territory or castle owned by the family, e.g. 'of Staufen', 'of Habsburg', 'of Luxemburg', until these themselves in the course of the thirteenth century became family names: Staufer, Habsburger, Luxemburger. These new names appeared in all the old tribal territories: in Suabia, for example, with the families of the Zähringer and Staufer. In the case of the Staufer, the fact that they were named after the castle Stauf near Göppingen did not accurately indicate where their main possessions lay. Their widely scattered lands lay around a number of centres. including the small town of Waiblingen, from which their Italian supporters took the name 'Ghibellines'. Rivals of the Staufer in their attempt to build up a great lordship in Suabia were the Welfs, whose territory centred on the town of Ravensburg, and the dukes of Zähringen, who had a compact territory in the valley of the Upper Rhine around the newly founded town of Freiburg im Breisgau and the monastery of St Peter in the Black Forest. The rights thus acquired – lawfully or otherwise – were very various, including comital powers and advocacies and rights of landlordship and rights over proprietary churches; in Saxony many nobles even managed to acquire control of the powers of the old popular courts. Out of such heterogeneous collections of powers and property the dynastic lord would attempt to form a homogeneous lordship. Such lordships were often called counties, and in some cases may have included comital rights; but the 'counties' which emerged as a result of territorialization were radically different from the counties of the period before the Investiture Contest. These were defined by the possession of public powers of government, which were conferred by the king and could be taken back by him. In the twelfth century a county could exist without any royal confirmation, as a feudal lordship based on large-scale land-holding coupled with assorted rights of government. This new constitutional element, the territory, found its expression in a phrase used increasingly in the course of the twelfth century: *dominus terrae*, the lord of the land, in which the lord's own landed possessions and the area over which he exercised power were taken together as a principality, a *terra*. In 1111 Count Robert of Flanders issued a peace ordinance *per totam terram suam*, throughout the whole of his land, and in so doing clearly displayed the new territorial form of lordship. One of the main sources of such jurisdiction was the advocacy, which meant the exercise of secular powers of jurisdiction over monasteries and monastic lands. Many nobles collected such advocacies, and as these often had rights of high justice (i.e. the right to punish by death or maiming, not just by imposing fines) attached, they were able to accumulate powers of government. If the monasteries whose advocates they were colonized new lands, their advocacy covered these as well. Sometimes the nobles themselves initiated such colonization. The enthusiasm of many dynasts for founding monasteries often had quite practical origins besides religious zeal. It meant a real breakthrough for the principles of the reform movement if the founders of new monasteries or priories renounced their rights of advocacy. In theory, newly colonized land was royal land, but with the decline in royal power such land came to be treated as allodial. Clearance and colonization helped to stimulate territorialization and in consequence to weaken royal power. If the power of the kings should ever revive, there was bound to be a conflict with the forces of particularism and territorialism.

2 The rest of Europe

Just how much damage the Investiture Contest did to the German kingdom can be seen by comparing it with other European countries. In France, for example, there were no antikings and no conflicts which shattered the fabric of society. A further consideration is that between 1060 and 1270 only six kings, all from the house of Capet, ruled in France, and with long reigns; they all exerted themselves to extend the crown domain. If in the tenth and to some extent in the eleventh century the *rex Francorum* had not ruled directly over some nine-tenths of his kingdom, the crown now succeeded in expanding its own territory and in absorbing a number of principalities. The absence of royal power in the late Carolingian period and the period immediately following did not lead to the formation of small territories but of large principalities with an incipient bureaucratic administration. When the French kings took some of these principalities over, as happened in Normandy or in Champagne, they took over the organization which had been built up as well. The re-establishing of central authority had been favoured by the First Crusade: numerous magnates, including some of the most powerful, had gone to the Holy Land

and expended their energies there. Under these circumstances the French kings were able to establish the Île-de-France as the central crown domain. In the period of weak kingship a number of castellans had established themselves. Louis VI (the Fat) (1108–37) succeeded in a series of lengthy struggles in reducing these intransigent lords to obedience, often with the support of the surrounding population; whole parishes, led by their priests, joined up with the royal hosts led against the hated robber-barons. Since these feud-happy lords had often appropriated church property, such campaigns frequently took on the character of a crusade. While the Île-de-France slowly turned into an island of peace under royal protection the king was able to cement his alliance with the church. In 1119 Louis VI took Cluny and all its dependent priories under his protection; in return he acquired the right to build castles on Cluny's lands with the agreement of the abbot of Cluny. In contrast to the position in the German church, high offices in the French church were more readily open to non-aristocrats. Such leading figures as Bishop Ivo of Chartres and Abbot Suger of Saint-Denis were not noble. Paris, the centre of the Capetian lands, from which the kings had for a time had to withdraw, became a capital city, and the name 'Francia', which had until then denoted the land between the Meuse and the Loire, became the term for the French kingdom as a whole. To secure his succession Louis VI had his son crowned king in Rheims; in Rheims, because Remigius of Rheims had crowned the Frankish king Clovis there, and because the archbishops possessed a vial of chrism allegedly brought from heaven by an angel which was used to anoint kings. From the time of the French pope Urban II (1088–99) up to the middle of the twelfth century almost all the popes visited France or took refuge there: Paschal II (1099–1118), Galasius II (1118–19), Calixtus II (1119–24), Innocent II (1130–43) and Eugenius III (1145–53). No pope after Leo IX (1049–54) visited Germany, apart from occasional stays in Lotharingia. One might wonder whether the Germans had abandoned the leading role in Europe which they had played up until the time of the Investiture Contest.

Henry I, king of England and duke of Normandy, had managed, in spite of the family ties between the aristocracies of the two countries, to preserve the feudal obligations of his English vassals, so important for the king. While tenants-in-chief in Normandy only had to supply the king with a small number of soldiers, their English counterparts had much heavier obligations. Virtually no ducal vassal in Normandy had a military obligation (*servitium debitum*) of more than ten knights, whereas in England before 1135 no fewer than eleven lords owed sixty or more knights, twenty-seven owed twenty-five or more, and six bishoprics and three abbeys owed forty knights or more. The bishop of Bayeux, by comparison, owed twenty knights, though he had a hundred and twenty in his service. It was difficult to pursue private feuds in England, especially as William the Conqueror was swift to dispossess in such cases, whereas in Normandy it was part of a knight's duties to support his lord in the event of feud. However, both English and Norman feudalism had in common the important advantage that the vassal held his fief in a kind of hereditary tenure, which descended to the oldest son. The obligations of a vassal were precisely defined; they consisted mainly of military service, which could under some circumstances be commuted for payment, and in membership of the *curia* of one's lord. Henry I created dynastic arrangements which were to be of great importance for the English crown. His daughter Mathilda, the widow of the German king Henry V and his only surviving child after the death of his son in 1120, was acknowledged as his successor in England and Normandy in 1127. In 1128 he married her to Geoffrey Plantagenet, son of the count of Anjou, Maine and Touraine. The threat of a 'super-vassal' of the French crown, which was to become reality in the second half of the twelfth century, here appeared on the horizon.

The creator of the much-admired Norman kingdom of Sicily was Roger II (1101–54). Roger did not fit into the pattern of the swashbuckling Norman leader like William Iron-Arm or Robert Guiscard; he was no great hero, nor was he particularly keen on or good at fighting battles. In this he followed his father, Count Roger I of Sicily, who had taken part neither in the First Crusade nor in the raids on the Byzantine empire organized by his brother Robert Guiscard, although he had received Sicily as a fief from him in 1061. He devoted most of his attention to integrating the various elements of the Sicilian population. While the Norman princes on the mainland had to deal with unruly barons and rebellious Lombard subjects, the Norman count of Sicily was a guarantor of peace and justice for the large Greek colony on the island and even for the Saracens there. The native Greeks soon attracted Byzantine immigrants, and the Norman rulers were so confident of the loyalty of the Arabs that they moved the central administration from Messina to the city of Palermo, whose population was almost wholly Muslim. Greek and Arabic were official languages just as much as Latin or Norman French, and the young Count Roger II, who grew up and was educated in the Greek colony in Palermo, was able to subscribe Latin diplomata for distant western recipients with his own name in Greek, at a time when the German kings Lothar III and Conrad III were scarcely able to do more than make the small line completing the royal monogram as a mark of authentication. Roger II had acquired a number of footholds in southern Italy through inheritance, forfeiture of pledged lands and plain violence, but the breakthrough came with his succession to Duke William of Apulia, the grandson and last direct descendant of Robert Guiscard, in 1127. Roger II, now calling himself 'prince and duke of Apulia, count of Calabria and Sicily', was not deterred by papal excommunication from expanding northwards. In 1128 Honorius II was forced to invest him with Apulia, Calabria and Sicily, and had to recognize shortly afterwards that the oath taken by Roger not to attack Capua and Benevento was worthless; he succeeded in persuading them to submit voluntarily to his rule. Roger was lucky that Anacletus II was elected in opposition to the anti-Norman Innocent II in 1130, for the Pierleoni pope was forced to turn to him for support, and Roger probably himself dictated the terms of the general privilege which in September 1130 turned his principality into the 'Kingdom of Sicily, Calabria and Apulia'. When Anacletus' party got into difficulties and the Pierleoni appealed to him for help Roger took the opportunity to make them his liege vassals and to garrison his troops in their fortresses. Neither Lothar III's march on southern Italy in 1137 nor Anacletus' death in 1138 nor the excommunication by the Lateran council in 1139 had any lasting effect; in the end a generally recognized pope, Innocent II, acknowledged Roger's royal title and not only that but also enfeoffed him and his heirs with the entire territory of the kingdom of Sicily, the duchy of Apulia and the principality of Capua. The Norman principle of the heritability of fiefs prevailed over the papal policy, which was that they were freely disposable on their holder's death.

After decades of fighting Roger II was finally able to turn to the peaceful consolidation of his government. He had already enforced a general homage-taking in Melfi in 1129; now he issued a comprehensive legal code in Ariano, in the province of Avellino. This code, which was heavily dependent on Roman law, respected the laws of the various groups in the population, Greeks, Arabs, Jew, Lombards and Normans; however, the new royal law was to prevail in cases of conflict. The code strongly emphasizes the divine responsibility of the monarch: to disobey his edicts is blasphemy and *lèse-majesté*, punished as high treason by death. With great care and

constant attention to the sensibilities of a multi-racial state Roger
built up a sophisticated bureaucracy. The incomes from customs
and leasing of state lands were controlled by an office staffed almost
exclusively by Saracens; the *camera*, another part of the financial
administration, was run by Greeks; a kind of exchequer was
organized on Anglo-Norman lines, and so on. The officials bore
impressive titles – 'emir', 'admiral', *archon, logothetes, protonotarius*.
The criminal law was enforced by itinerant justices. All subjects
were to have access to the king; in spite of this, Roger surrounded
himself with an aura of unapproachability. His biographer wrote
that he never allowed himself to become too jovial, friendly or
confiding, 'lest the people should cease to fear him'.

Italy can be divided roughly into three spheres of influence: the
Norman kingdom in the South, Rome and the papal state in the
centre, and in the North imperial Italy with Lombardy, the march of
Verona, the margravate of Tuscany and the great trading cities:
Milan, Genoa, Pisa, and Venice. The grip of the German kings on
imperial Italy had slackened. In the last years of Henry IV's reign
and under Henry V there are hardly any references to royal envoys
(*missi dominici*) or to royal jurisdiction. Possession of the Mathildine
lands was still uncertain, even though Henry V had established his
claims as heir. It was in this period that northern Italy became a land
of city-states. The landed aristocracy could not maintain its
independence and had to submit to the cities. According to Otto of
Freising the margrave of Montferrat was the only noble who was
not under city jurisdiction: 'almost all the land belongs to the cities,
who compel all the inhabitants of their territories to acknowledge
their rule, and there is hardly a man of rank or standing who does
not recognize the authority of his city. They surpass all other cities
in the world in wealth and power, and the long absence of the ruler
from north of the Alps has contributed to their independence.' Otto
of Freising's description should be taken at face value. The cities
claimed lordship over the land around them, the *contado* (from the
Latin *comitatus*, 'comital district'). Smaller settlements within the
contado were swallowed up; larger ones, especially if they threatened
to become unwelcome competitors, were often simply destroyed.
This was what Florence did to Fiesole in 1125, as did Viterbo to
Ferento, and Rome to Tusculum. The cities relied heavily for their
military strength on the nobles who lived within their walls. The
nobility behaved here as elsewhere like feudal lords, building town
houses like small fortified castles and pursuing their feuds within the
city walls. For their defence they built fortified towers, which they

extended ever higher in rivalry with other families. The Jewish traveller Benjamin ben Jona from Tudela in Navarre, who travelled through Italy in 1160, wrote of a 'forest of ten thousand towers' in Pisa and Genoa. As the cities extended their rule over the *contadi* and the rural population who lived there, the *contadini*, they took over the right to tax together with the right of lordship. The rule of the communes was backed up by fortified settlements, whose inhabitants were often of very doubtful origins. Such *borghe franci* ('adulterine castles') grew up along the main routes and especially in the open countryside in Lombardy, Piedmont, Romagna and Emilia.

From the end of the eleventh century onwards the population of the Italian cities grew rapidly. The population of Bergamo has been estimated at 6,000 in the third quarter of the twelfth century, and that of neighbouring Brescia at 15,000; these were not particularly large towns compared with Milan, Florence or Venice, which were among the largest cities of medieval Europe, or with Pisa and Genoa. For comparison, Cologne, the largest city in Germany, a land with few towns, was not much bigger than a medium-sized Italian town like Brescia. Under the pressure and influence of such rapid urban growth the economy altered: the economy of barter was eclipsed by the money economy driven by the Mediterranean trade, which itself had been boosted by the crusades and was creating a new consumer demand among the elite. Trade and craftwork flourished and attracted further immigrants into the towns to work in service industries. Such *contadini* and serfs who arrived in the city were governed by special rules issued by the communes. According to a Sienese by-law probably already valid in the twelfth century, the serf of a non-Sienese lord became free and capable of becoming a citizen after four months' residence in the city, whereas the serf of a Sienese lord who moved into the city had to hand over almost all his possessions to the lord and only acquired free status and citizenship after ten years' residence.

Rome was an exception; it was not a trading city, and not so large as the great cities of northern Italy. In theory the emperor was the lord of the city, but in practice the pope and the aristocratic factions in the city struggled for control. The highest official was the prefect, who was elected by the people, that is the militia organized in city districts; he received the imperial eagle and sword from an imperial representative and was considered the emperor's deputy in Rome, though the pope was held to have the right to confirm his appointment. There were fierce struggles among the leading families of Rome for the office, and the papal reform party put heavy pressure on the prefect. There were also old tensions between the citizens of Rome and the nobility of the Campagna with its fortresses in the surrounding countryside as well as in the city. The long-held sense of grievance among the town population came to a head in 1143 when Pope Innocent II, a member of the Papareschi family from Trastevere, refused to yield to the demand of the citizens that the rival and neighbouring town of Tivoli should be destroyed. Tivoli had submitted to the pope when besieged by the Romans, and had been able to negotiate favourable terms. The Romans felt cheated of the fruits of their labours and occupied the Capitol. In an action which may have been inspired both by the example of other Italian cities and by memories of Rome's former greatness, a senate was proclaimed. The name was not really very appropriate for the newly created offices; it was meant to apply both to the city council, to which citizens were elected for a period of time, and to the highest city officials, who were otherwise known as consuls. The echo of the Rome of antiquity turned thoughts to the emperor, and one group among the citizens considered setting up an imperial title independent of the papacy. Innocent II is said to have died of rage at the Roman rebellion.

Let us turn from the centre of Europe to the regions on the fringes. The *reconquista* in Spain had produced independent lordships, 'autogenous immunities' on the frontiers with the Moors, but these did not last. The future belonged to the larger Christian kingdoms: Aragon, Navarre, Castile and later Portugal. The most powerful of these was Aragon, which held Catalonia as a fief from the French crown and so had access to southern France and the Mediterranean. The Aragonese were to become the great opponents of the French crown. The fact that the Aragonese crown survived the great attacks by the fanatical Almohads from 1147 on was due not least to its centralized constitution. The laws on fortifications and passes were strictly enforced; fiefs held by tenants-in-chief passed undivided to the eldest son, but younger sons had to do homage, even if they were subvassals of other lords.

The *basileus* of Byzantium, Alexis I (1081–1118), had unleashed the First Crusade with his appeal for help, and skilfully fended off Norman attacks. The struggle against the Normans was again and again to bring the Greek and German emperors together. Alexis' son John II (1118–43) allied with Lothar against Roger II, and the political alliance was accompanied by exchanges of culture and institutions. The old system of military peasant-colonists and mercenaries had not functioned well, and the Comneni tried a version of feudalism. Estates were given out to people who were pledged to do military service and homage for them. The estates were not supposed to be heritable, but heritability crept in on a customary basis. The westernization of the Byzantine empire's internal structures made the subsequent alliance between Comneni and Staufer possible.

In Palestine four crusader states had been set up by the First Crusade: the county of Edessa, the principality of Antioch, the county of Tripoli and the kingdom of Jerusalem. After a number of parties of pilgrims had been wiped out it became clear that the mainly French nobility of the country, the *Franci*, would have to depend on its own resources. There was some intermarriage with the Arab population; the *pullani*, children of unions between crusaders and Syrian women, soon came to form a stabilizing element in the population. The main problem standing in the way of a *modus vivendi* between crusaders and Muslims was the tourist crusaders, men who came for a season with the desire to kill as many infidels as possible and then go home. The feudal law of the country, codified in the Assizes of Jerusalem (1130/40), shows definite French and Norman influence. The vassal's obligations were strictly defined, but so were those of the king, against whom a right of resistance was allowed if he should fail to respond to a vassal's call for help. At this stage there were few links between Germany and the Holy Land; the histories of the two countries would later come to be more closely interwoven.

'THE LOVE OF LEARNING AND THE DESIRE FOR GOD': CHURCH
AND SPIRITUALITY IN THE AGE OF BERNARD OF CLAIRVAUX

The discussion about the nature of the church is as old as the church itself. It is closely connected with the answer to the question how best to live a just life and one which will lead to salvation. Up to the time of the Investiture Contest the church included all Christians, priests and laymen: there was no clear demarcation between those in orders and those not. In the course of the Investiture Contest the clergy of the reform party increasingly adopted the view that the church consisted of all those in orders, through whose mediation the sinful layman could participate in the means of grace dispensed by God and the church. For centuries the formula of Gelasius I (492–6) had defined the relationship between spiritual and secular power: there were two powers in the world, the *potestas regalis* and the *sacra pontificum auctoritas*. Vocabulary and definition suggested that the priestly power was higher both in its scope and in the responsibility it carried, but at the same time it was conceded that the secular power had an autonomous sphere of activity. The early reformers gave this theory of two powers a new twist in the allegory of the two swords. According to this interpretation of Luke 22.38, Christ had given two swords to the church, the *gladius materialis* and the *gladius spiritualis*; the worldly sword was passed on to the secular power, but was to be used on the instructions of the priesthood, according to the influential interpretation of Bernard of Clairvaux. The doctrine of the two swords was soon to offer an important argument for the view that the secular power had no autonomous existence but was a mere *potestas indirecta*, an indirect power, derived from and subject to the priesthood. The cooperation of a previous age, the 'harmonious synergy', was over. Laity and priesthood, Empire and papacy were worlds apart, both in their nature and in their value.

But within the spiritual world there was also differentiation. There was first of all the great difference between the monk, who lived in a monastery and prayed for his own salvation and that of the world, and the secular priest, whose most important duties were pastoral, the *cura animarum*. It is true that some monks ordained as priests were active in baptismal churches and otherwise beyond the gates of the monasteries, but they were not numerous and the monastic ideal was not endangered by their existence. But new and more intensive forms of spiritual community were coming into being. The order of canons, those who followed the Rule of Augustine, flourished anew, promoted by popes from Gregory VII on as a form of religiosity which relived the early Christian life, and given special privileges by Urban II, who because of their way of life – at once communal and open to the world – probably saw in them an effective means of spreading reform ideas. They were something between monks and secular priests; their way of life was not strictly enclosed, but it was communal, and they were not scattered like secular priests in the manses of individual parishes. They held property in common and followed the Rule of Augustine. It was above all in the time around 1100 that new orders were founded: Cistercians, Carthusians, Premonstratensians, Templars.

Until the reform period the monastic world of the West had been remarkably homogeneous, since the Rule of Benedict was the basis both for the foundation of new monasteries and the reform of existing ones. Cluniac monasticism had provided a particularly influential and widespread version of Benedictine monasticism. On the death of Abbot Hugh in 1109 the Cluniac 'family' consisted of some 1,450 monasteries, all subject under a kind of monarchic constitution to the abbot-primate of Cluny. Admittedly, Cluny had passed the peak of its influence by the beginning of the twelfth century. Many factors contributed to the decline in its attractiveness, which culminated in the spectacular deposition of Abbot Pontius in 1126. Cluny had placed one-sided emphasis on the liturgical and contemplative side of monastic life. Prayer, in the form of intercessory prayers, masses for the dead and the commemoration of anniversaries, took up the greater part of the day of a Cluniac monk, while manual labour, the *opus manuum*, was little in evidence, even though Benedict had specifically prescribed it in his rule. Cluny's protective prayer attracted the laity, and Cluniac monasteries, with Cluny at the top of the list, were richly endowed by nobles who sought to secure their salvation. The abbey church at Cluny, consecrated by Pope Urban II, was the largest church in western Christendom, almost half as large again as St Peter's in Rome. A further reason for the decline in Cluny's reputation, it has been suggested, was its strong connections with the wealthy feudal aristocracy and its failure to reach the new movement of apostolic poverty and the rising bourgeoisie. It diverted the 'classes' in revolt against their exploitation by the feudal aristocracy 'with liturgical pomp' (E. Werner); 'exhausted by its wealth and prestige', it moved 'ever further from the original monastic ideal' (F.-J. Schmale); and indeed contemporaries made the charge that Cluniac monasticism had degenerated into 'eating, drinking and [monastic] customs'. Cluniac monasticism found only a late entry into Germany through the monastery of Hirsau; one of the reasons why the Germans were reluctant to adopt it lay in the constitutional peculiarity of Cluniac monasteries, which were exempt from the authority of their diocesan bishop. As long as monastic popes sat on the throne of St Peter such enclaves within an otherwise strictly organized church hierarchy were tolerated, even encouraged, but with the change to a more pro-episcopal attitude in Rome which took place in the 1120s the Cluniac constitution could come to seem dangerous.

In contrast to the Cluniacs the new order of the Cistercians experienced its peak in the twelfth and thirteenth centuries. German kings and emperors entrusted the imperial insignia to the Cistercians for safe-keeping, and Frederick II took the Cistercian habit on his death-bed. Cîteaux (*Cistercium*) near Dijon, the founding house, was founded in 1098 with the slogan 'purity of the Rule, correctness of the Rule' (*puritas regulae, rectitudo regulae*). The Rule to which they

intended to return was the Rule of Benedict. Founded on the allodial
lands of the viscount of Beaune (who waived his proprietary rights)
some eighty kilometres north of Cluny, Cîteaux enjoyed an undisturbed development. The *charta caritatis*, composed around 1110,
was confirmed by Calixtus II in 1119, so that the order could depend
on support from the official church. In contrast to Cluniac foundations the daughter monasteries were separate and autonomous
monasteries, which were not, moreover, exempt from the power of
their diocesan. Annual general chapters – the meetings of all the
abbots – enforced the observance of the pure Rule. The *charta caritatis*
insisted that the monks should live by the work of their hands. The
Cistercians were in consequence great colonizers, at first in internal
colonization but later on in the settlement of the East. The economic
base of Cistercian monasteries was strengthened by the institution
of the grange, which was run by lay brothers, *conversi* of a new kind,
and thus represented a first step away from older forms of manorial
organization based on serf labour. Their influence over the lands
around their monasteries was further strengthened by the leasing
out of farms to peasants. It took a century and a half after the
foundation of Cluny in 910 for Cluniac monasticism to reach
Germany, whereas only a few years after the papal confirmation of
the order the first German Cistercian monastery was founded:
Altenkamp near Rheinberg on the lower Rhine. Altenkamp, the
third daughter monastery of Morimond, which was particularly
active in Germany, was herself the 'fruitful mother' of at least
fourteen 'daughters' and of about fifty 'granddaughters'. Among
these were Walkenried in the southern Harz and Pforta in Thuringia, later famous as Schulpforta. They played a major part in
eastern colonization: Lehnin, Chorin and Zinna in Brandenburg,
Leubus in Silesia, Reinfeld in Holstein. In accordance with their
notion of a life of service, the Cistercians developed their own
architecture, very different from that of the Cluniac churches with
their high towers and multiple aisles: hall churches of a deliberate
simplicity and harmony, with no tower, only a ridge turret. The
way of life of the Cistercians, who often chose remote valleys for
their foundations, had a great appeal; by the mid twelfth century
there were about 300 monasteries, fifty of them in Germany. Here it
should also be borne in mind that their attraction as centres of
economic activity and colonization was considerably greater than
that of the more contemplative Cluniacs.

   The most outstanding figure of early Cistercian history was
Bernard of Clairvaux. Born around 1090 in Burgundy, he entered

Cîteaux in 1112, and as early as 1115 became abbot of the newly founded house of Clairvaux in the diocese of Troyes. Under him Clairvaux flourished and was responsible for the foundation of no fewer than sixty-eight daughter monasteries. Since the Cistercians did not have a monarchic constitution with an abbot-primate at its head, the influence of an individual abbot within the order depended on his reputation, and Bernard came to be something like the leader of the Cistercians, though his reputation declined somewhat towards the end of his life (†1153). The second quarter of the twelfth century is often called the 'age of St Bernard', a time when a 'monastic humanism' was practised, the union of the 'love of learning and the desire for God', in Jean Leclercq's phrase. Bernard of Clairvaux saw in the increasingly influential rational and dialectical habits of thought of early scholasticism a danger for the faith, and advanced against it a mystical and contemplative theology. God is not to be experienced with the intellect: 'one knows God, in so far as one loves Him'. His contemplation centres round the relationship of the soul to Christ, and he was the founder of the Christocentric mysticism of the high Middle Ages, which was to be renewed as late as the fifteenth century by the *devotio moderna*.

Bernard, with his mystical longing for God, was the natural opponent of Abaelard. Abaelard, born in Brittany in 1079 as the son of a pious knightly family (both his parents entered monasteries in their old age), came to theology through the study of the arts, adopted a position of moderate realism in the then controversial question of universals and was throughout his life an enthusiastic supporter of dialectic and its methods of argument, to which he devoted his book *Yes and no* (*Sic et non*). His brilliance as a logician and rhetorician brought him many pupils from different countries: John of Salisbury and Arnold of Brescia, for example, but also Otto of Freising and possibly Rainald of Dassel. In his autobiography, the work of a restless and arrogant intellectual superiority, Abaelard describes how William of Champeaux, his logic teacher in Paris, was an intriguer and envious of his success, but was forced to correct his views on universals in public in the face of the objections made by Abaelard; the 'greybeard' Anselm of Laon, whom he sought out around 1113, and 'whose reputation depended more on long routine than on ability or power of memory', had 'a remarkable command of words', which, however, were 'contemptible as to their content and quite without sense' – Abaelard was soon able to show to Anselm's pupils that he was better able to gloss biblical texts than their masters; and so on. Abaelard came into conflict with Bernard, who had a number of his doctrines condemned at a synod in 1140 without giving Abaelard a chance to defend himself or even to speak. Through letters Bernard tried to stop Rome and the *Curia* from dealing with the case themselves and Abaelard had not been able to justify himself by the time of his death shortly afterwards in 1142.

But it was not his role as defender of the faith but his gift of preaching which made Bernard's reputation so great: he was the 'honied teacher', *doctor melifluus*. His writings, which have survived in nearly a thousand manuscripts, included some hundred sermons, some of which are recorded as transcripts, with all the freshness and spontaneity of a direct address to the public ('pray, while I receive guests') and of his positions on burning contemporary problems, which are also found in his five hundred-odd surviving letters. His pupil Pope Eugenius III (1145–53), a Cistercian who was in Clairvaux for a time, was the recipient of a 'mirror for popes', the *De consideratione*, in which the two swords allegory, mentioned earlier, is set out. It would thus be far too narrowing to see in Bernard only the leading exponent of monasticism of his day. He called himself the 'chimera of the age': not quite a monk, not quite a knight, for besides his proclamation of the monastic ideal as a form of the apostolic life we find him setting religious goals for the Christian knight, and it is certainly no coincidence that the foundation of the knightly orders fell in this period as well.

Other newly founded orders besides the Cistercians came to flower in this period. After a comfortable career as a cathedral canon the aristocratic Norbert of Zanten had a conversion 'on the road to Damascus' – a bolt of lightning threw him from his horse – and entered the monastery of Siegburg as a penitent. He then travelled through northern France and the Rhineland as a wandering preacher, and in 1120 founded Prémontré (*Pratum monstratum*; Dép. Aisne, near Laon), which gave its name to the Premonstratensian order. It was an order of preachers resulting from Norbert's own experiences, based on the way of life of the canons, with a communal life and communal property. As archbishop of Magdeburg (1126–32) Norbert remained in touch with the world, enjoyed the trust of Lothar III and became chancellor of Italy. Cappenberg, in the diocese of Münster, was the first Premonstratensian priory in Germany (founded in 1122) and in 1129 Norbert founded one in Magdeburg. Some cathedral chapters adopted the Premonstratensian constitution; the order devoted itself with energy to missionary and preaching activity in the period of colonization which followed and was encouraged by great missionaries like Bishop Otto of Bamberg.

A further German who founded an order was Bruno, born in Cologne, who after a normal career as a cathedral canon in Cologne and Rheims founded an eremitical settlement near Grenoble in the rocky district of Cartusia, which was to give a pattern and a name to further settlements; they offered a unique combination of eremitical and coenobitical monasticism. His *Consuetudines*, which took definitive form after his death in 1101 and laid particular stress on the contemplative life of the individual, were adopted by the Carthusians, whose numbers rose to some forty settlements by the end of the twelfth century.

In the face of such monastic diversity, all of which reflected the search for a life pleasing to God, it is not surprising that people disagreed about where the Christian life was best realized. A whole literature grew up in which these controversies were worked through, in fictive disputes between a Cluniac and a Cistercian or in pamphlets in defence of the communal life of the canons regular. Even an author like Rupert of Deutz (†1129/30), in essence a theologian concerned with the interpretation of history as the record of God's plan for man's salvation and a reactionary late Gregorian in his spirituality, defended the Benedictine monasticism of his monasteries, Siegburg and Deutz, and claimed the right of pastoral work for monks as well. In spite of the shared desire to please God, the disputes over the best form of monastic life were often marked by hatred and vicious polemic.

The flourishing of the life of the soul was accompanied by a flourishing of the life of the intellect, which occurred in all orders. Whatever their origins, the various forms of the monastic life gave people an opportunity to develop their minds. Honorius Augustodunensis (†*c.* 1156) probably taught in Regensburg – there is a strikingly large number of manuscripts of his works surviving from Bavarian and Austrian monasteries – but it is uncertain where he came from (the Celtic regions of England are one possibility) and which schools he had attended. Hugo of Saint-Victor's birthplace has been given as northern France or Lotharingia, but most frequently as Saxony. His work was done in Saint-Victor in Paris, a house of canons regular where he lived a withdrawn life without holding any monastic office, surrounded by pupils who spread his teachings. He was concerned to reconcile the critical teaching of scholasticism with contemplative mysticism, and he made much use of the writings of the fathers, particularly those of Augustine. His doctrine of perception is a mixture of philosophical and theological elements. Man perceives in three ways: with the eyes of the body, with those of reason, and those of contemplation. The fact that Master Gratian, who taught pastoral theology in the Bolognese monastery of St Felix and Nabor, was a Benedictine monk from the order of Camaldoli, in other words a member of an eremitical order, did not prevent him from composing around 1140 his *Concordia discordantium canonum*, which, although a private work, soon became a quasi-official collection of canon law texts and received the name *Decretum Gratiani*.

Women thinkers, who had previously – not least because they could not become priests – not studied theological questions, also concerned themselves with the understanding of the world. Hildegard of Bingen (†1179) conducted an extensive correspondence with emperors and popes among others, in spite of her deficient Latinity which meant that she needed an assistant. Her prophetic revelations, which owed much to the Apocalypse and her discussion of scientific questions in a mystic-allegorical style are impressive not least because of the self-confidence of their author, whose thinking was characteristically aristocratic: asked why only noble nuns were found in her monastery she answered, 'What man collects his whole herd in a single stall – oxen, asses, sheep and goats?' The differences of birth were laid down by God and should be respected. Herrad of Landsberg (†1195), like Hildegard a Benedictine nun, created a huge encyclopaedic work in her 'garden of delights' (*hortus deliciarum*), which displays surprisingly modern traits. The work includes portraits of all seventy nuns in the convent of which she was abbess, and the portrait medallions clearly display an attempt of realistic depiction of the portraitees. Heloise (†1164), lover and for a time wife of Abaelard, could almost be called emancipated, though the genuineness of the correspondence between the two is not so above suspicion as it is usually treated in popular French literature and even in scholarly writing.

LOTHAR III: KINGSHIP WITHOUT A FUTURE

From the point of view of imperial history the period between 1125 and 1152, that is the reigns of Lothar III (1125–37) and of Conrad III (1138–52), seems like an interlude between two dynastic epochs, the Salian era and the time when Staufer rule had definitively established itself.

1 Lothar as a 'legal antiking'

The Salian king Henry V was succeeded on his death at the age of thirty-nine by the Saxon duke Lothar of Supplinburg, then aged well over fifty. Lothar III founded no dynasty; the fact that he had no male heirs recommended him to his princely electors. Another factor in Lothar's favour was his family: he was not a Staufer and was related neither agnatically nor cognatically to the Salian dynasty. Henry V had considered Duke Frederick II of Suabia, then aged about thirty-five as his successor – he was the eldest son of Henry's only sister Agnes – and had also designated him heir of the Salian family lands, in other words as his private heir. Other families were as closely related to the Salians as the Staufer; after the death of Duke Frederick I of Suabia, the man who built Stauf, Agnes married the Babenberger margrave Leopold III of Austria, and Conrad, the son of this marriage, was Henry V's nephew just as much as the two Staufer, Frederick II and his younger brother Conrad. But the Babenberger had not emphasized their Salian ancestry, so that the Staufer were generally considered as the heirs to the Salians. They thought of themselves as a continuation of the Salian dynasty; the Babenberger Otto of Freising referred to them as the 'Henrys of Waiblingen', using the Salian leading-name and the centre of the Staufer possessions to define them dynastically.

Archbishop Adalbert I of Mainz (1109–37) acted as the spokesman of the princes' claim to elect the king against the Staufer claim to succeed by blood-right. After breaking with Henry V in 1112 he had been a determined exponent of the princely cause and had ruthlessly extended the territory of the archbishopric of Mainz. Not only did he persuade the dowager empress to hand over the imperial insignia, which played an ever more important role in determining the succession, he succeeded in securing the agreement of the representatives of the tribes to meet at Mainz for the election. We have an extraordinarily detailed account of the election proceedings from the pen of a pro-Welf monk from the monastery of Göttweig in Lower Austria. The papacy was represented by a legate at the election, as it had been at the elections of Rudolf of Rheinfelden and Henry V as antikings; there was even a French observer in the person of Abbot Suger of Saint-Denis, who had just successfully led the defence of the French kingdom against Henry V's attack. The electoral procedure revealed the shifts which had taken place in the political structures of the Empire. From the tenth century onwards the participation of the people had been regarded as constitutive at royal elections, even if the *populus* was in practice only represented by the *principes*. In Mainz in 1125 even this representation was reduced; an electoral college of forty was formed from among the magnates present, consisting of ten representatives from each of the four main tribes: Franconians and Lotharingians together, Suabians, Saxons and Bavarians. There was a candidate from each tribe, but only three had serious chances: the Bavarian margrave Leopold III of Austria from the Babenberg house; Duke Frederick II of Suabia; and the Saxon Lothar of Supplinburg. Each of the candidates was confronted by Adalbert of Mainz with a catch-question: was he prepared to recognize another candidate as king, if he were elected? Frederick asked for a pause for deliberation; the assembly, without waiting for his answer, elected Lothar of Supplinburg *per inspirationem*. The idea of suitability propagated by the church had triumphed over the ties with the previous dynasty favoured by German law. When Adalbert proclaimed Lothar king the Bavarians at first protested, but surprisingly quickly declared themselves in agreement with the result of the election. It is probable that their duke, the Welf Henry the Black, was won over by the promise of a marriage between his son and Lothar's daughter Gertrude, which took place two years later. Gertrude, as Lothar's only child, inherited the immense family possessions of the Supplinburger. On 13 September 1125 Lothar was crowned king by Archbishop Frederick of Cologne in the correct place, Aachen. The influence of the ecclesiastical princes at the election and the request to Pope Honorius II to give his approval (*confirmatio*) to the election gave Lothar the reputation of being a *Pfaffenkönig*, a priest's king. But it was not so much his particularly compliant attitude towards the church which recommended him as his record of opposition to the Salians and the fact that he had no male heirs. His reign was characterized by the struggle with the Staufer, who maintained the Salian tradition, and by his partnership with the papacy.

The struggle with the Staufer became unavoidable when Duke Frederick II of Suabia refused to hand over the crown lands to the new king; under the Salians royal and family lands had become difficult to distinguish. Before the end of the year Frederick had been outlawed and a campaign against him proclaimed. Lothar tried to encircle the Staufer. He conferred the county of Upper Burgundy (the lands around Besançon) west of the Staufer territories on Conrad of Zähringen, while to the east of the Staufer lay the lands of Lothar's Welf son-in-law, Henry the Proud, duke of Bavaria, whose family possessions around Ravensburg also threatened the Staufer from the south. But the expedition of 1127 which was to compel the Staufer to submit got bogged down with the siege of Nürnberg. The Staufer now made the breach complete; in December 1127 they had Frederick's younger brother Conrad elected as antiking. Conrad sought support in Italy, had himself crowned in Monza as king of Italy by the archbishop of Milan, and attempted to seize the Mathildine lands. But the coup was unsuccessful. Conrad was forced to flee from Italy, and the Staufer would certainly have had to admit defeat if Lothar had not soon had to face other problems. Once again the papacy was threatened by schism. Already in 1124 there had been the threat of a divided election on the death of Calixtus II, and the families of the Frangipani and the Pierleoni, rivals for almost a century, had each put up candidates. Only the political skill of the papal chancellor Haimerich, cardinal-deacon of S. Maria Nova, a Burgundian by birth and a friend of Bernard of Clairvaux, secured the undisputed election of the Frangipani candidate, Honorius II, who was not, however, himself a Frangipani. Lambert of Ostia, who had been one of the negotiators at Worms, was of humble birth, so that the abbot of Montecassino could say to his monks on the news of the election, 'I do not know whose son he is, but I know one thing for certain: he is filled from head to foot with learning.' On Honorius' death in 1130 there was a similar division, and again Haimerich tried to push through the Frangipani candidate, Innocent II. But the majority of the college of cardinals favoured Petrus Pierleone, who called himself Anacletus II after the martyr-pope of the early church.

The schism was not just an expression of family feuding within the Roman nobility, and now that recent research has established Anacletus' integrity and rehabilitated his reputation from the accusations heaped on him by the victorious party – the official Annuario Pontificio now places Innocent and Anacletus as equals in the papal lists – the question of other possible origins for the schism must be answered. The double election was also the outcome of parties within the *Curia*. Innocent was mainly supported by the younger cardinals, most of whom came from northern Italy, while Anacletus drew his following from the older cardinals, mostly of south Italian or Roman origins. Innocent, like Haimerich, favoured the new orders: Cistercians, Premonstratensians, canons regular. Anacletus was more drawn to older Gregorian conceptions of reform and to the spirit of Cluny, where he had for a time been a monk. He did not favour the tendency recently shown by the papacy to support the episcopate against monasteries. Although Innocent II was a colourless mediocrity, and although he could not maintain his position in Rome, it was foreseeable that his cause would be successful. He was supported by Bernard of Clairvaux and Norbert of Magdeburg and their circles, who represented a more modern form of monasticism and one with increasing influence on the lay world. It was a victory of the Cistercians and the episcopate over the Cluniacs. Bernard's eloquence won over Louis VI of France and Henry I of England, who both recognized Innocent. Anacletus' main support came from Roger II of Sicily; to secure this he turned Apulia, Calabria and Sicily into a kingdom in 1130 and enfeoffed Roger with it.

It would be important how the German king and future emperor decided. Both popes notified him of their election, and after initial indecision Lothar declared for Innocent. But more than a declaration was expected of him. Bernard of Clairvaux and Innocent sought him out in Liège and Lothar was willing to make a gesture which throws a revealing light on the position: he agreed to perform the symbolic service of a groom and marshal as laid down by the Donation of Constantine, that is he led the pope's horse a short distance and held the pope's stirrup while he mounted. What Lothar considered merely a gesture of respect and reverence could easily be construed as a recognition of feudal submission. On the other hand Lothar claimed the full right of investiture from the pope; in other words, he wanted to turn the clock back to the time before the Concordat of Worms, no doubt as a result of his experiences in Saxony. Only in return for this was he willing to escort Innocent back to Rome. It needed all Bernard's skill in persuasion to get Lothar to back down from his demand for the right of investiture and accept the imperial coronation as an adequate return for his services.

In the late summer of 1132 Lothar fulfilled his promise. He marched on Rome with an army of 1,500 knights – several times smaller than that with which Henry V had undertaken his coronation expedition twenty years before. Anacletus II had dug himself in in the Leonine city around St Peter, so that Lothar had to be crowned in the Lateran. It was here that Lothar and Richenza were crowned emperor and empress on 4 June 1133. After renewed negotiations on the subject of the royal right of investiture Lothar was at least able to secure a papal privilege which forbade the bishops to take possession of the *regalia* without being enfeoffed with them by the king. He took an unfortunate position in the matter of the Mathildine lands, for he implicitly recognized the Roman church's rights of ownership by agreeing to hold them in usufruct – in return, moreover, for an annual rent of a thousand pounds of silver. Lothar invested his son-in-law Henry the Proud with the lands; Henry was to do homage to the pope for them. The *Curia* ran both these things together, as if Lothar, who two years previously had done marshal service, had become a papal vassal for the Mathildine lands. In the Lateran a wall-painting showed the pope sitting on the throne while crowning Lothar as emperor, with a distich as inscription: the king 'becomes the pope's vassal' by accepting the crown being offered him.

Soon after Lothar left Rome Roger II drove Innocent II out of the city, and Bernard began to remind Lothar of his duty as an emperor to protect the church. A new Italian expedition became possible when the Staufer Frederick II and Conrad III submitted to Lothar in 1135. They had to hand over the crown lands, but Frederick remained duke of Suabia and Conrad was even honoured with the title of imperial standard-bearer. For the Italian expedition of 1136 a large army was assembled. Henry the Proud alone led 1,500 knights, and Lothar was this time able to assert imperial rights in Italy in full. 'Following the customs of the ancient emperors' he held an imperial assembly at Roncaglia (near Lodi) and issued an edict which was strongly influenced by Roman law: all *valvassores* (sub-vassals) were forbidden to subinfeudate or alienate their fiefs without their lord's consent, as these would not otherwise be able to undertake 'a felicitous expedition' for the good of the Empire. Lothar made a real attempt to make the imperial presence in Italy felt once more. The expedition, continued through into 1137, promised to be a success: Benevento and Bari were taken, Roger II offered peace negotiations and was even prepared to offer his sons as hostages. But there was opposition within the army, and there were differences of opinion between emperor and pope. When Count Rainulf of Alife was to be invested with the duchy of Apulia Lothar and Innocent were unable to agree on who was to be the suzerain; the result was a grotesque piece of theatre in which the two lords of the world together held the lance and handed over the symbol of investiture to Rainulf. The expedition was broken off; on the return march, after he had handed over the imperial insignia to the newly invested margrave of Tuscany, Henry the Proud, Lothar died near Reutte in Tirol on 4 December 1137. Most of what he had achieved in Italy was at once nullified. Roger advanced, but his suzerain Anacletus II died on January 1138. The schism was effectively over, and Innocent felt strong enough to summon a Lateran council in 1139, which was later to count among the general councils. The assembly excommunicated Roger II, but an expedition against him ended, as Leo IX's war against the Normans had done, in a fiasco. The papal army was annihilated; Innocent II was taken captive, and was only released after he had agreed to recognize Roger's kingship and enfeoff him with the kingdom of Sicily.

2 Lothar III and the position on the eastern frontier

Lothar III's achievement has been assessed very variedly by modern historians. The church historian A. Hauck (†1918) called him an insignificant man, while a distinctly ideologically coloured book by F. Lüdtke which appeared in 1937 praised him as a representative of the best traditions of imperial politics, because of his eastern policy. Lothar was twice a second-best candidate, as duke in 1106 and as king in 1125. However unfortunate his request for papal confirmation of his kingship, his acceptance of the papal view of the imperial title and his indirect homage for the Mathildine lands were, he gave a new emphasis to eastern expansion and so continued as king what he had begun as duke.

A man who bore witness to this from his own experience was the priest Helmold from Bosau in Wagrien, on Lake Plön; although he only came there around 1143, after Lothar's death, he wrote 'In the days of the emperor Lothar a new star arose, not just over Saxony but over the whole of the Empire', for Lothar had worked in cooperation with the church. Without question missionary and colonizing activity had received new impulses around the beginning of the twelfth century. Already in his time as duke of Saxony Lothar had defended the borders energetically, and had taken the field numerous times against the heathen Slavs, for example in the Rügen expedition of 1114. He installed Adolf I of Schauenburg as count of Holstein and Stormarn in 1111, and in 1123, in usurpation of royal rights and against the will of Henry V, he appointed Albert the Bear to the march of Lausitz and Conrad of Wettin to the march of Meißen. The energy of these three marcher lords admittedly created its own problems. When Count Henry of Stade died in 1128, Albert the Bear wanted to succeed to the Nordmark, and indeed – after his temporary deposition and rehabilitation on the Italian expedition in 1133 – he was invested with it. He had early established contact with the Christian prince of the Hevelli, Pribislav-Henry, who gave him flanking support in his conquest of parts of the march beyond the Prignitz. Pribislav made Albert his heir in Brandenburg, and after Albert had been able to defend this inheritance, which fell to him in

1150, against the heathen prince Jaxa of Köpenick in 1157, he was lord of a large if in places somewhat patchy territorial complex. The later fate of the Nordmark – the territory between Stendal and Salzwedel, known from the fourteenth century onwards as the Altmark – is bound up with that of the Brandenburg march, the colonization of which was begun by Lothar. Albert's expansion in the Nordmark led him to renounce the Lausitz march; it was conferred on the margrave of Meißen, Conrad of Wettin, in 1136, an event which marks the beginning of the 'Wettin State'.

Lothar's reach extended across the borders. The Danish count of Schleswig, Knut Laward, who called himself duke, was invested by Lothar with Wagrien in 1127, since Knut had a quasi-regal position over the Abodrites of Wagrien and was thus in a position to support missionary activity there. The Danish king Niels, Knut's uncle, will scarcely have looked favourably on his nephew's being incorporated into the German feudal pyramid, and when Magnus, Niels's son, who saw his succession endangered by Knut, had Knut treacherously murdered in 1131, Niels came under suspicion of complicity. The result was a family feud, in which Knut's kin were victorious; Knut himself had his reputation posthumously enhanced to that of a Christian martyr. Lothar had undertaken a revenge expedition as soon as he heard the news of the death of his vassal; this compelled Niels to do Lothar homage and to pay a fine of four thousand marks of silver. In 1134 Knut's brother Erich Emune was able to drive Niels out, and in 1135 he formally did homage to Lothar at the assembly of Magdeburg. The Danish king had become the vassal of the German king.

The border warfare in the East offered no permanent security; in the first decades of the twelfth century there began an intensive colonization of the Slav lands. We still have the eloquent appeal of a Flemish cleric writing on behalf of the archbishop of Magdeburg from the Altmark in 1108: 'The cruellest pagans have attacked us . . . men without mercy, who boast their inhumanity . . . These [Slav] heathens are terrible men, but their land is rich in meat, honey, flour, birds, and if properly cultivated would be so fruitful that no other land could be compared to it.' The mixture of crusading appeal and economic opportunity is very significant, for where internal colonization was virtually complete people were willing to undertake the colonization of border and virgin lands. Regions in which internal colonization had already largely been completed were for example the lower Rhine area, Flanders and Holland. At about the same time as the appeal was written – 1106, or 1113 at the

latest – Archbishop Frederick of Hamburg-Bremen had called
Flemish settlers in to colonize the lands around the mouth of the
Weser, and allowed them to live according to the law of Holland.
Cleared land was in theory royal land, but in a period of weak
kingship it was the nobility who were most active in colonization,
an activity which enabled them to extend their power. Count
Wiprecht of Groitzsch (near Leipzig) is the first territorial lord
whom we know to have attracted colonists to new lands in the East
by offering contracts of settlement; in this way he settled Franconian
peasants on new lands between the rivers Mulde and Pleiße. The
flood of settlers into the mid Elbe regions must have been considerable throughout the twelfth and thirteenth centuries; east of the Elbe
the colonization movement began rather later. The German kings
played only a limited role in this, and Lothar's activities were
confined to the North-East. Adolf II of Schauenburg, whom Lothar
had invested with Holstein and Stormarn like his father before him
in 1130, colonized on a large scale. The Slavs who remained among
the new German colonists became dependent tenants on their lands
and gradually merged with the immigrants. As Helmold of Bosau
reports, Adolf II, because Holstein and Stormarn were unpeopled,
sent 'messengers to all countries, that is to Flanders and Holland,
Utrecht, Westfalia and Frisia, to announce that all who had too little
land should come with their families to the finest and most fruitful
fields rich in fish and meat and with good pasture'. The tone of the
appeal is similar to that written by the Magdeburg cleric quoted
earlier. Lothar's death in 1137 meant a crisis for eastern colonization,
which stood under the duke of Saxony's protection. Shortly before
his death Lothar had conferred the duchy on his son-in-law Henry
the Proud, and in this way Saxony was drawn into the conflict
between Welfs and Staufer. Conrad III, elected king in 1138,
deprived the Welf Henry the Proud of the Saxon duchy and gave it
to Albert the Bear, who in his turn deposed Adolf II of Schauenburg
as count of Holstein and Stormarn and named Henry of Badwide in
his place. It has been claimed that this led to a setback in colonization
which was only reversed with the re-establishing of the status quo in
1142/3.

Ecclesiastical colonization and mission complemented the settlement organized by secular lords. Cistercians and Premonstratensians provided support. Lothar III was on good terms with a
number of the great missionaries of the period. He had appointed
Norbert of Xanten, the mainstay of the Premonstratensian mission
in the North-East, as archbishop of Magdeburg, and Bishop Otto of

Bamberg (1102–39) carried out his Pomeranian mission, which ended with mass baptisms, under Lothar's protection. Admittedly a proper course of religious instruction could not be provided by Otto, who had to run his mission from Bamberg; this was left to the priests in the newly converted districts. As in the tenth century, when the mid German bishoprics were founded, there were conflicts over whose diocesan jurisdiction these regions belonged to: that of Magdeburg or that of Gnesen? Reports of the great successes achieved by missionaries like Otto of Bamberg, who is said to have achieved a mass baptism of 22,000 heathens, should not deceive us about the everyday reality of missionary work: more typical is the career of the Wagrian missionary Vicelin, recorded by Helmold. Born around 1090, perhaps in Hameln, he received Wagrien as his missionary territory after a career as a schoolteacher in Bremen and after studies in France. He wandered preaching from place to place, and acted as parish priest in a small settlement near Neumünster. At the suggestion of Vicelin, whose mission was supported sympathetically by Adolf II of Schauenburg, himself once destined for an ecclesiastical career, Lothar built a protective castle in Segeburg. In spite of the uncertain position after Lothar's death Vicelin was able to begin the foundation of the priory of Neumünster in 1141/2. Often he found himself caught up in political conflicts. On his election as bishop of Oldenburg in Holstein in 1149 Henry the Lion as duke of Saxony cut off his payments of tithes, because he claimed the right as duke to invest the bishops of the newly converted Slav regions. Vicelin gave way; he received investiture from Henry the Lion and was able to continue with his mission for the few years until his death in 1154. In a retrospective charter Vicelin's missionary years are described as follows: 'a time of tiring and unsuccessful work, and of continual trials . . . pillage, arson, imprisonment of his companions, wounds and death – that was the picture of his life' (A. Hauck).

CONRAD III: KINGSHIP WITHOUT IMPERIAL GLORY

1 *Conrad's election and the Welf opposition*

Just as in the election of 1125, so in 1138 the candidate whose election would have strengthened the idea of hereditary monarchy was excluded. Lothar's son-in-law, Henry the Proud, the husband of Lothar's only daughter Gertrude and the man to whom Lothar had handed over the imperial insignia, thought he had good chances of the succession. He was duke of Bavaria, margrave of Tuscany, and papal vassal for the Mathildine lands; shortly before Lothar's death he had become duke of Saxony, and he disposed of rich allodial possessions. But the Welf's arrogance was expressed in his name alone. According to Otto of Freising he boasted that his *auctoritas* extended from sea to sea, that is from Denmark to Sicily; and what was worse, he had crossed the pope's plans for Norman Italy. The *Curia* and the princes between them saw to it that Henry's plans were not realized.

Memories were still alive of how close the Staufer had come to the throne in 1125, especially since Conrad had been able to maintain himself as antiking until 1135, two years before Lothar's death. Both the Staufer party, who favoured hereditary succession, and those princes who wanted a free election could agree on the election of Conrad III. The circumstances favoured a rapid election. Mainz, the archbishopric of the previous kingmaker Adalbert, was vacant; the archbishop of Cologne had only just been elected and was not yet consecrated. Albero of Trier, a friend of Bernard of Clairvaux who had excellent connections with the *Curia* under Innocent II, had no rivals among the Rhenish archbishops. In a coup, without waiting for the meeting arranged by the princes, Albero had Conrad III elected at Coblenz on 7 March 1138, and a papal legate was ready to crown him a few days later at Aachen. Like Lothar, Conrad has become known as a priest's king, and certainly he owed his election to the rapid action of the archbishop of Trier and the intervention of the *Curia*. Conrad, who had a reputation for bravery and immense physical strength, was about forty-five years old on his election. Many sources talk of his aimlessness, and his uncritical and credulous nature. He, the 'simple man' (*simplex*) was impressed by the dialectical argumentation of an Abaelard, and it is recorded that he found enjoyment in syllogistic jokes. Asked whether he had one eye, he agreed; asked whether he had two eyes, he agreed again; told that since one and two made three he had three eyes, he was vastly amused. Chief among Conrad's advisers, who enjoyed not inconsiderable influence, was Wibald (†1158), abbot of Stavelot from 1130 and of Corvey from 1146; his surviving letter-collection contains some 450 items from the period 1147–57.

In spite of his hurried election Conrad was generally recognized and Henry the Proud handed over the imperial insignia. However, there was soon a clash with the Welf when Conrad laid down as a constitutional principle that no prince was to hold two duchies.

Henry the Proud refused to do homage, for Conrad had demanded that he should give up either his family duchy of Bavaria or Saxony, which he had only recently acquired in 1137. Henry the Proud was outlawed and deprived of both his duchies. Saxony was given to Albert the Bear, and Bavaria to the Babenberger Leopold IV of Austria, a half-brother of Conrad's. At the height of the crisis in October 1139 Henry the Proud died. The Welfs continued to insist on their right to both duchies, but their resistance was divided. In Saxony it was led not by the ten-year-old Henry the Lion, son of Henry the Proud, but by his grandmother Richenza, Lothar III's widow, who as a Northeimer by birth had a substantial following in her own right. In Bavaria the leader was Welf VI, Henry the Proud's brother. Conrad tried at first to drive the Welfs from their allods and family castles in Suabia; to this stage of the campaign belongs the anecdote about the conquest of the castle of Weinsberg, near Heilbronn. When the castle surrendered Conrad allowed the women to depart with as much of their possessions as they could carry on their backs – so they carried their husbands piggyback through the castle gate. It is said that the chancellor wanted to claim this as a breach of the terms of surrender, but Conrad waved his objections aside:

> The royal word is given, the royal word shall stand,
> not twisted bent or broken by lawyers' scheming hand,

to quote the nineteenth century ballad by A. von Chamisso. It was here also that the battle-cry *Hie Welf, hie Waibling* ('here Welf, here Staufer') is said to have been used first.

In spite of this victory and in spite of the death of Richenza in 1141 the Welf resistance continued, and it was only in 1142 that a compromise was reached. Albert gave the duchy of Saxony and returned to the Nordmark. Saxony was given to Henry the Lion, who in return had formally to renounce his claim to Bavaria, following the principle laid down by Conrad III. The agreement was sealed by a marriage between Gertrude, widow of Henry the Proud and mother of Henry the Lion, and the new duke of Bavaria, the Babenberger Henry Jasomirgott, who had succeeded his brother Leopold IV on his death in 1141. But Gertrude herself died in the following year, 1143, and Henry the Lion and the Welf party demanded that Bavaria should be handed over. The Welfs found considerable support even among the Staufer party; it is said that Frederick of Suabia, the later King Frederick Barbarossa, did not

back his uncle's policy. King Roger II gave financial assistance to the
Welfs as part of his defence against a Byzantine-Staufer alliance, and
until Barbarossa came to the throne the Welf claims remained an
unsolved problem.

2 European alliances and the Second Crusade

Since the coronation of Otto the Great as Roman emperor in 962
every German king had been crowned as emperor; Conrad III never
went to Rome and never achieved the imperial title. In spite of this
his chancery used the title *Romanorum rex Augustus* or *semper
Augustus* off and on from 1139, even though the title of Augustus
was essentially an imperial attribute. It was perhaps the negotiations
with Byzantium which showed up the lack of an imperial title.
Conrad and the *basileus* of Constantinople were pushed together by
their common enemy the Normans, who in turn were allied with
the Welfs. Roger II seemed particularly dangerous to the Greek
emperor Manuel I Comnenos (1143–80) because of his close connections with the crusader states. A marriage alliance between Staufer
and Comneni was arranged; Manuel I married a sister-in-law of
Conrad III, Bertha of Sulzbach, whose choice of the Greek name
Irene ('peace') was probably not just coincidental. For the Byzantine
emperor to take a foreign wife who was not of royal blood was a
revolutionary act. Contact with the West, especially with western
crusaders, had brought about a transformation in the Byzantines'
understanding of themselves. The feudalization of society had
created a new chivalrous ideal, which embraced the emperor just as
much as the ordinary knight. Manuel I had helped this process along
by doing away with much of the traditional court ceremonial,
which had with oriental pomp set a distance between the emperor
and his subjects. The emperor took part in public life, and Manuel
could be seen taking part in tournaments against other knights in the
palace of the Comneni on the Golden Horn.

Imperial intervention was called for by the new position which
had arisen in Rome. The middle classes – *plebei* and *negotiatores* – had
revolted and set up a *sacer senatus* in 1143, aiming at freeing Rome
from papal control. The unrest continued in the following pontificates of Celestine II and Lucius II (1143–5); Lucius is said to have
died as the result of being hit by a stone in the course of street-
fighting. In 1145 Abbot Bernard of the Roman monastery of
S. Anastasio became pope. Eugenius III, a friend and pupil of
Bernard of Clairvaux, himself of an unworldly and misanthropic

disposition, refused to recognize the new communal organization and had to live outside Rome. Both Bernard of Clairvaux and Eugenius, who soon fled from Italy to France, appealed to the German king and future emperor for assistance, for the situation in Rome had become even more anti-papal; what was originally a normal communal movement threatened to be transformed into a more radical religious and social movement under the influence of Arnold of Brescia. Arnold had been deposed by his bishop from the office of prior of a house of canons regular in his home town of Brescia for his sermons attacking the church hierarchy. He went to France, was taught dialectic and rhetoric by Abaelard, was driven out of France, and came to Rome, where he did penance in the catacombs. By 1147 at the latest he had begun preaching again. His general theme was the absolute poverty of the church, and he was assisted by the general increase in contemporary criticism of the unevangelical wealth and greed of the church. It is in this period that the bitter parody 'The gospel according to the mark' (*Evangelium secundum marcam* instead of *Marcum*) was composed; in it a petitioner knocking at the door of the *Curia* is told in pure biblical language: 'Friend, may thy poverty perish with thee; get thee behind me, Satan, for thou savourest not of the things which are of gold. Verily, verily I say unto thee, thou shallst not enter the kingdom of heaven until thou hast paid thy uttermost farthing.' After Arnold had made contact with the communal movement in Rome, which rejected the local lordship of the pope, he took on more and more the role of the leader of a Roman popular movement with a nebulous anticlericalism as its programme. Without holding any particular office he played the part of a tribune of the people, persuaded the populace that they were the source of imperial law, and rejected the Donation of Constantine as a lie. Pope Eugenius III tried a number of different methods of dealing with him: in 1148 he excommunicated him and deposed the clerics who supported him. The fact that more energetic measures were not taken at the time was the result of an event of European importance, the Second Crusade.

The immediate occasion for a new military campaign in the Holy Land was the final loss of the easternmost of the four crusader states, the county of Edessa, which had been taken in 1146 by Nur-ed-Din, the 'holy Emir', as he is known in Islamic historiography. However, it was due to Bernard Clairvaux, whom Eugenius III had entrusted with the task of preaching a crusade, that such distant events produced a new European crusading movement. Under the spell of his overpowering rhetoric first the French king Louis VII and then at

Christmas the German king Conrad III took the cross, and with Conrad many German princes. Among the hasty preparations were the proclamation of a peace ordinance for the Empire in March 1147 and the election of Conrad's ten-year-old son Henry as German king: a crusader had to put his affairs in order, as Bernard of Clairvaux had preached. 'Life is good, victory brings fame, but it is still better to die as a martyr. Blessed are those who die in the Lord; but those who die for him are still more blessed.' Many of the German participants in the Second Crusade were indeed not to see their homes again. From Constantinople the German army marched in divided columns, supported not entirely whole-heartedly by Emperor Manuel I. The main army under Conrad followed the footsteps of the victorious First Crusade across Asia Minor and, deserted by its Byzantine guides, suffered an annihilating defeat at Dorylaeum, survived by a quarter of its number at most. The other group, mostly pilgrims, led by Bishop Otto of Freising, proceeded along the coast, but had to turn back after suffering heavy losses. The crusade, the first which had consisted principally of German knights, had turned into a catastrophe. Conrad returned to Byzantium and travelled to Jerusalem, where Louis VII and his army had already arrived, via Antioch. In order to fulfil the terms of the crusading vow the crusaders agreed, quite in the fashion of the crusading tourist, to undertake an expedition against the neighbouring Arabs. The chosen target was the Emir of Damascus, the one Arab ruler who was on friendly terms with the Franks and an embittered enemy of the taker of Edessa, Nur-ed-Din. But this expedition also ended in failure and disunity before the walls of Damascus, a failure made worse by the fact that the local knights appeared to take part only half-heartedly. In the end the whole crusade was called off; Edessa was not recaptured. Conrad III returned to Germany in early 1149, followed only a little later by Louis VII. The consequences of the crusade were disastrous. In spite of very heavy losses nothing had been achieved. Previously Islam had lived in fear of a new crusade, of the arrival from the West of an unconquerable Frankish army. The aura of invincibility was gone; Nur-ed-Din gathered the forces of the Islamic counter-attack to him. The peaceful *modus vivendi* which had begun between Franks and Arabs was destroyed, the belief in integration or at least in coexistence shattered. The following crusades were no more successful and brought no change for the better; the Holy Land depended for its extent and its reputation entirely on the great success of the First Crusade.

A crusading vow was being fulfilled at the same time in other places. A fleet of crusaders from England, Frisia and the Lower Rhine conquered Lisbon on their way to the Holy Land and thus ushered in the rise of Portugal as an independent state. North German crusaders undertook a crusade against the Wends in two campaigns in 1147. In the North a small army moved against the leader of the Abodrites, Niklot, the ancestor of the house of Mecklenburg which ruled until 1918; he had conducted a pre-emptive strike against Old Lübeck in 1143 and on the approach of the army under the leadership of Henry the Lion and Conrad of Zähringen retreated to his castle of Dobin on Lake Schwerin; in the end he agreed to accept baptism. The southern contingent under Albert the Bear and Conrad of Meißen advanced from the Elbe on Stettin and joined up there with Polish crusaders. Once Prince Ratibor of Stettin had agreed to accept Christianity, the southern army returned home, as the northern had done. Many contemporaries thought of the Wendish crusade as a failure: 'so this great undertaking ended with little success', wrote Helmold, and indeed the military and missionary gain was small. But the appeal of Bernard of Clairvaux and Eugenius III talks of *Christiani religioni subiungere*, as the goal, which one should perhaps interpret as a purely external Christianization: baptism, possibly under duress, the sacrament and the immanent Word of God were to have their effects without any catechismal training. This was the view of Bernard, the contemplative theologian; Helmold, writing on the missionary front, thought that 'many [of the Slavs] were wrongfully baptized ... for immediately after their baptism they behaved even worse than before'.

The outcome of the Second Crusade had seriously damaged Bernard's reputation, especially as his visionary enthusiasm had been accompanied by quite evident calculation on the part of others. The older western idea of a Christian *imperium* under an emperor gave way to a system of international politics in which the individual countries simply pursued their own egotistical ends. Roger, king of Sicily, was not mesmerized by the general enthusiasm for achieving remission of sins through crusading. When he heard that Manuel Comnenos had pulled troops out of the west of Greece at the time of the Crusade, he conquered Corfu and crossed over into the Peloponnese. The pillaging of towns and destruction of settlements were part of the normal techniques of contemporary warfare, but Roger was careful to preserve the Greek silk-weaving industry of the area, in order to be able to transport it to Sicily. Roger II's attack during the Second Crusade led to a polarization of the European powers. Manuel won over Conrad III, whom he proposed to support with troops and subsidies in the event of an Italian expedition, while reserving Byzantine sovereignty for any regions won back from the Normans. The Welfs naturally joined up with the anti–Staufer coalition; Welf VI, Henry the Lion's uncle, promised Roger II to fight against the Staufer and Babenberger. Louis VII of France also joined Roger's coalition, and a European war seemed imminent.

In 1149 Manuel I began the reconquest. Corfu was won back and a bridgehead formed at Ancona. Pope Eugenius III looked in danger of being drawn into the hostilities; he had approached his Norman vassal with an appeal for help, for the Roman communal movement had taken a dangerous turn under the influence of Arnold of Brescia. The *sacer senatus* offered Conrad III the imperial crown from the Roman people in 1149; the senate and the Germans together would restore the *imperium* which had been held by Constantine and Justinian. Conrad turned the offer down, since the acceptance of a secular Roman imperial title would have meant an open breach with the pope. After much toing and froing Eugenius III found himself in the end driven from Rome and unable to reach agreement with the Romans; he invited Conrad to come to Rome and promised him imperial coronation. However, Conrad III died on 15 February 1152 while still preparing for the forthcoming expedition in Bamberg, where he was buried. His last action was to regulate the succession; his son Henry, who had been elected German king, had predeceased him in 1150. Conrad designated his nephew, Duke Frederick of Suabia, as his successor. Compared with Frederick Barbarossa and even with Lothar III Conrad and his reign seem remarkably pale and uninspiring: 'this king's times were very sad ones ... through ill-fortune the state began to decay under his rule', as the later author of the Royal Chronicle of Cologne wrote. Conrad, not in any case politically a strong or imaginative personality, belonged to the generation which had had first-hand experience of the period before the Concordat of Worms and was unable to develop new forms of royal government.

It was not only the history of the kingdom of Germany which was to enter on a new era on Conrad's death. A whole number of deaths of important figures occurred at round about the same time, with significant consequences. Bernard of Clairvaux died in 1153, almost at the same time as 'his' Cistercian pope Eugenius III, the last monk for a long time to sit on St Peter's throne. Before this Suger of

Saint-Denis, the principal adviser of Louis VII of France, had died in
1151. He had been a leading figure in the cultural and political life of
France right up to the end of his life; he had had the abbey church of
Saint-Denis rebuilt in the style later known as Gothic, following
new ideas on the architectural form appropriate for the house of
God, in 1144; between 1147 and 1149, during Louis's crusading
expedition in the Holy Land, he had acted as regent. The year after
Abbot Suger's death Louis committed an act of political stupidity;
he divorced his wife Eleanor in 1152 and a synod explicitly confirmed the divorce as lawful. Louis had married the last representative
of the ducal house of Aquitaine in 1137; her dowry consisted of rich
lands in central and southern France. Louis had taken his flirtatious
wife, whose courtly patronage had inspired troubadours, with him
on crusade, and evidently she had been in her husband's opinion all
too obviously attracted by the exotic brilliance of the Franko-Syrian
magnates. Louis pushed through his divorce with so much energy
that it seemed as if he feared for his salvation should the marriage
continue; he was even prepared to renounce Eleanor's dowry,
which she thus brought to her new husband. This was Henry, son of
Geoffrey Plantagenet and Mathilda, the daughter of Henry I of
England and widow of the Salian Henry V. Geoffrey Plantagenet,
already count of Anjou, Maine and Touraine, had taken advantage
of the French king's absence to secure Normandy for himself.
Geoffrey died in 1151 and his son married the vivacious Eleanor a
year later, almost immediately following her divorce from Louis
VII. The latter was now in a precarious position, in danger of being
encircled by the Angevin empire. Henry Plantagenet held Normandy, Maine, Anjou, Touraine in the North, and in the South, as
Eleanor's dowry, Poitou and Aquitaine. Louis VII was cut off from
the sea by his tenant-in-chief Henry Plantagenet. But worse was to
come. With support from the *Curia* Henry Plantagenet was able to
establish himself in England in 1153 and in 1154 became king: Henry
II began the rule of the house of Plantagenet, which was to continue,
if we include cadet branches of the family, until 1485. Henry II of
England was at the same time the most powerful tenant-in-chief of
the French king, and when he conquered Brittany shortly afterwards the whole of western France was in his hands. But he was
intelligent enough not to try to depose the French king, and to
respect him as his suzerain.

There was also a change of rule in the Norman kingdom of Sicily.
Roger II died in 1154, still at war with Byzantium. Manuel had
already established a bridgehead in Italy and won over the dis-

enchanted opposition in southern Italy, not difficult in view of the harshness of Roger's rule and the racial diversity of the kingdom. Roger's son William I tried to hold up the Byzantine advance by allying himself with the leading sea-power in the Adriatic, Venice; then, in 1156, he succeeded in a remarkable effort in defeating the Byzantines and the rebels. In the same year, 1156, he did homage to the pope, was confirmed as king, and received as a fief in return for the payment of an annual *census* a lordship which reached far into the Abruzzi mountains. In 1158 Manuel I admitted defeat in a treaty which gave up plans for a Byzantine reconquest of Italy.

5

THE CENTRE-POINT OF THE GERMAN MIDDLE AGES: FREDERICK BARBAROSSA AND HIS AGE

Without belonging to those who have radically transformed the world, Frederick Barbarossa has always enjoyed a high reputation; after Charlemagne he is probably the most popular medieval German ruler. It is characteristic that the legend of the emperor who sleeps in the mountains and waits for the reunification of Germany and the imperial apotheosis should have been transferred to Frederick I. Originally the legend had concerned Frederick II, whose sudden death in a remote south Italian castle had aroused contemporary fantasies; he was supposed to have disappeared in Etna, whence he would reappear as the Last Emperor before the Last Judgement. The confusion of Frederick I with Frederick II first occurred in a chap-book of 1519.

Barbarossa had one advantage over all previous German kings and emperors: none lived to be as old as he did – probably he was sixty-eight when in 1190 he died an accidental death (again, the first German ruler to do so) – and none, apart from Henry IV, who was declared of age at fifteen, ruled for so long as he did, around thirty-eight years. Barbarossa had better chances of realizing his plans and building up the Empire according to his conceptions than his predecessors. He was also the first ruler to have grown up after the Concordat of Worms and not to have been hampered by nostalgic ideas of a time of harmony between church and state.

There is a great increase in the volume of historical evidence in Frederick's time: he issued diplomata at nearly twice the annual rate of his two predecessors; the new intensity of diplomatic relations is marked by the survival of far more peace treaties and alliances than for previous eras; and the court circle produced literary writings of high quality. The most important writer of the mid twelfth century was Otto of Freising, whose work reflects contemporary attitudes very strongly. His work of historical philosophy belongs to the reign of Conrad III, that of straight history to the reign of Frederick I. Otto was the son of Margrave Leopold III of Austria and Agnes, daughter of Henry IV, whose first husband had been Frederick I of Staufen, duke of Suabia (†1105). Conrad III was his half-brother, Frederick his nephew. Otto was born around 1112, and already as a child was provost of the house of canons regular founded by his father at Klosterneuburg near Vienna. At the age of about fifteen he went to France to study, and was taught by Hugo of Saint-Victor and probably Abaelard. In 1133 he made the surprising decision to transfer with fifteen of his companions to a 'stricter piety', and became a monk in the Cistercian monastery of Morimond, in the diocese of Langres. He was elected bishop of Freising in 1138, before the canonically prescribed age, took part in the Second Crusade (1147–9) and died in 1158 in Morimond on his way to the Cistercian general chapter, wearing the Cistercian habit which he had worn even as a bishop.

His work of historical theology, the *Chronicle or history of the two cities* (*Chronica sive Historia de duabus civitatibus*) was written between 1143 and 1146; it is a world chronicle. The title shows Otto's dependence on Augustine's *City of God* and of its conception of two intermingled empires, or perhaps better communities of thought, which determine the Christian perception of the world: the *civitas caelestis* and the *civitas terrena*, the one ruled by *amor Dei*, love of God, which also includes the love of one's neighbour, the other ruled by the *amor sui*, love of oneself and of the world rather than of salvation. But while Augustine's theology was timeless, Otto's was an interpretation of the twelfth century. The relationship of the history of salvation to the present can be seen in the division of the work into seven books corresponding to the Week of the World; the seventh and last Day deals with Otto's own time and is followed by an eighth book devoted to eschatology, that is the future until the Last Judgement. Otto perceived a sequence in the history of the various empires, a *translatio imperii*. The lordship of the world had been taken from the Greeks and transferred definitively to the West. Otto was convinced that the *civitas Dei* could be realized in the true *imperium Christianum*, an idea which has been described as 'imperial metaphysics'; but faced with the collapse of the Empire during the Investiture Contest and under Conrad III his assessment of the chances of this happening was not high. For Otto, those who realized the City of God on earth through seeking their own salvation were the monks, and it is with praise of monks that the seventh book ends and the transition to the eighth, dealing with the Last Things, begins.

Otto's pessimism was evidently dispelled by Frederick's accession in 1152. In 1157–8 he wrote the first two books of the *Gesta Friderici*. The first deals with the period from Henry IV to Conrad III as one of preparation for the coming era of peace, while the second deals with Frederick I and his reign up to 1156. After Otto's death the Freising notary Rahewin (†1177) continued the *Gesta* to 1160, in part using Otto's drafts, and sent a dedication edition decorated with a cycle of miniatures to Frederick. The special importance of the *Gesta Friderici* lies in its semi-official character; both authors used official documents as well as an *aide-mémoire* prepared by Frederick, and they offer a tendentious court historiography. Only at the beginning of the thirteenth century was a continuation of Otto's and Rahewin's work attempted: Otto, monk and briefly before his death abbot of St Blasien in the Black Forest (†1223), wrote a chronicle which is a conscious continuation of the *Gesta Friderici* to 1209.

The *Gesta* is not the only work which was produced in the court circle: a native of Bergamo close to events described Frederick's struggles with the Lombard cities, especially Milan, in a poem, the *Carmen de gestis Friderici*; Gottfried of Viterbo (†1200), who had studied in the cathedral school at Bamberg and was a member of the royal chapel under Conrad III, Frederick I and even Henry VI in the course of a long life, wrote a number of works which dealt with Frederick's reign, including his *Liber universalis*, in which the *Gesta Friderici* plays a central part. The poet Gunther turned Otto's and Rahewin's work into elegant hexameters for an epic poem *Ligurinus*, which treats of Frederick's struggle for the *urbs Ligurina* (Milan); there is little new information in the work, but the use made of the material is interesting and so is the form, an epic poem intended to please the court.

THE ELECTION OF FREDERICK I AND THE NEW POLICY OF BALANCE

'Emperor' Conrad III was survived by an eight-year-old son, Frederick of Rothenburg. So as not to endanger his family's hold on the throne, however, he had designated his nephew, Duke Frederick III of Suabia, as his successor, the man who according to Germanic conceptions was the nearest male relative of his young son. Only two and a half weeks after Conrad's death, on 4 March 1152, Frederick I was chosen as king by an 'electorate organized on a tribal basis' (H. Mitteis) and was crowned king on 9 March in Aachen. If Lothar and Conrad had been 'priests' kings' Frederick was a 'princes' king'. Neither the papal *Curia* nor an archbishop acted as kingmaker; the princely electors, divided into two parties (Staufer and Babenberger and their following on the one side, Welfs and their following on the other) agreed to compromise on Frederick. What made him attractive was his political and above all his dynastic position between the two camps. Although he was a Staufer he had shown himself favourably disposed to the Welf claims to lordship and property, and through his mother Judith, a daughter of Henry the Black, he was as closely related to Henry the Lion and Welf VI as to Conrad III; both the latter were his uncles. Otto of Freising wrote:

There were two families in those parts of the Roman Empire which lie in Gaul and Germany: the Henrys of Waiblingen and the Welfs of Altdorf. The one produced emperors, the other great dukes. As often happens among great men hungry for glory, they had frequently disturbed the peace of the realm by their rivalry ... The princes were thus guided in their choice not only by the energy and qualities of the young prince, but also by the fact that as he belonged by blood to both houses he could act as it were as the cornerstone and reconcile the enmity between the two houses.

Otto's Christological language is characteristic: the metaphor for the peace-bringing Saviour as the cornerstone of the building is taken from the Letter to the Ephesians and applied to Frederick. Otto's comparison glosses over the tough and quite secular negotiations with the Welfs which must have preceded Frederick's election.

Frederick, who was about thirty at the time of his election, was one of the few German rulers of the high Middle Ages about whose appearance we know something, and in spite of all the conventional elements in the various accounts, some of which go back to the descriptions of emperors in late antiquity, we can definitely sense an element of individuality here, a sign of the extraordinary impression which Frederick made, and also of the tendency of the period to seek the particular among the general. A number of accounts agree in describing him as being slim, not particularly tall, and with well-proportioned limbs like Charlemagne. He had reddish-blond hair, which gave him his Italian name of Barbaròssa, from the colour of his beard. His extroversion and friendliness – one is tempted to say his charm – are repeatedly mentioned: 'His face was cheerful', wrote the imperial palace justice Acerbus Morena (†1167), 'so that one constantly had the impression that he wanted to smile.' This impression is confirmed by 'the first independent portraitistic representation in western art since the Carolingian period' (H. Fill-itz), the so-called Barbarossa-head of Cappenberg; Frederick presented what in a contemporary description is called a 'silvered head formed after the appearance of the emperor' around 1160 to his godfather, Otto of Cappenberg (†1171), who used it as a reliquary. H. Grundmann describes it as 'a conscious, controlled and calculated presentation of joyfulness and cheerfulness, more a pose than a feeling'. Barbarossa's education was that of a high aristocrat of the period, in other words confined essentially to training in arms. However, his achievement was to be a political, not a military one. Barbarossa was said to be of great eloquence in his mother tongue, and the root of his success lay in his gift for handling people. His contemporaries admired his equanimity (*constantia animi*), which corresponded to the knightly virtue of *mâze*. His preferred road to success was the compromise which could act as a starting-point for further progress, and he was in this way often able to turn a military defeat into a political advantage, or at least to avoid the worst of the consequences.

What impressed his contemporaries as soon as he came to power was his purposefulness. While still in Aachen he wrote to the pope that he wished to restore the glory of the Roman empire, while preserving the privileges of the Roman church. The letter made it clear that Frederick was only informing the pope of his election; he was not making a request for confirmation as Lothar III had done. He thus deprived the *Curia* of the chance to turn a confirmation into a right of approval of the newly elected German king. He was also careful to install Frederick of Rothenburg, the eight-year-old son of Conrad III who had been passed over for the succession, in the vacant duchy of Suabia; as the young duke's nearest male relative Frederick acted as regent for him in any case. In a series of general assemblies and courts in the course of 1152 Frederick dealt energetically with the difficult inheritance he had received from Conrad III. It was not only the Welfs and Staufer among the princes who were in a state of feud. Mostly it was a question of rights of property and lordship to which different families had rivalling claims. It was often difficult to decide which claim was the better, and political clout was often the deciding factor. If there was a strong king such questions could be settled in court according to tribal law, but if there was not the conflicts could often turn into feuds. The Welfs, Henry the Lion in particular, had ruthlessly extended their lordship in Saxony. At the time of Barbarossa's accession there was a dispute between Henry and Albert the Bear over the inheritance of the counts of Plötzkau and of Hermann of Winzenburg. Frederick assigned the Plötzkauer succession to Albert and the Winzenburger inheritance to Henry. He did not have to make any rigorous enquiry as to who had the better claim to which inheritance, a sign of the revival of royal power.

The question of the duchy of Bavaria was considerably more difficult. Henry Jasomirgott, as a Babenberger a close relative of the Staufer, had been installed in the duchy, but Henry the Lion as heir of his mother Gertrude who had died in 1143 had never given up his claim to it. There were attempts to deal with the dispute at a general assembly, but Henry refused to acknowledge that he had been lawfully summoned. He was probably right in supposing that the new king would favour Henry the Lion in order to make his peace with the Welfs. After Henry Jasomirgott had been thrice summoned and still refused to present himself before an assembly, a judgement of the princes awarded the disputed duchy to Henry, tacitly ignoring the principle laid down by Conrad III that no one should hold more than one duchy. The question of the investiture of the Slav bishoprics of Oldenburg, Ratzburg and Mecklenburg was also decided in Henry's favour. Archbishop Hartwig of Hamburg-Bremen (1148–68) wanted to have these suffragans, whose sees had been set up by Hamburg as missionary bases, invested by the king. Henry the Lion had prevented this and claimed the right himself. In June 1154 the general assembly at Goslar conceded the right of investiture to Henry, though with the explicit qualification that he exercised the right on behalf of the king. Frederick's desire to come to terms with the Welfs had already been seen in 1152, when he invested the most active opponent of the Staufer in the family, Welf VI, with the march of Tuscany and the duchy of Spoleto. Although the Welfs were favoured, this was not at the expense of the Staufer. Frederick's concern to preserve royal rights showed itself in the appointments to bishoprics. Even with the suffragan bishoprics of Hamburg, as we have seen, there was a reference to royal rights, which were exercised by proxy by Henry the Lion. In Mainz, Minden, Hildesheim and Eichstätt royal candidates were elected. In Magdeburg there was a disputed election at the beginning of 1152, and both parties turned to Frederick, who according to the Concordat of Worms was supposed to give his consent and help to the candidate chosen by the 'better part' (*senior pars*) of the electors. But

Frederick acted otherwise; he rejected both candidates and pushed through the election of a third, Bishop Wichmann of Zeitz-Naumburg, whom he invested with the *regalia*. This was an interpretation of the Concordat which went well beyond what had been agreed with the pope; Otto of Freising explicitly justified this on the grounds 'that it lay in the king's discretion to appoint the man he wanted'. Pope Eugenius III immediately refused his consent and gave as his reason the prohibition of translations of bishops from one see to another; it was an old-established principle of canon law that Bishop Wichmann could not move from Zeitz-Naumburg to Magdeburg without a good reason and without the prospect of benefit for the church. It was left to Eugenius' successor, Anastasius IV, to consent to the election and grant Wichmann the pallium. Frederick had won, and Archbishop Wichmann of Magdeberg (†1192) became one of the most dedicated supporters of royal power.

Wichmann's case was symptomatic; the papal *Curia* had to deal with a new self-confidence on the part of the German ruler, which had already shown itself in the fact that no papal legate was present either at the election or at the consecration of Frederick. An Italian expedition for autumn 1154 was agreed on at the assembly of Würzburg in October 1152. Negotiations with the *Curia* began in the winter of 1152–3, and led to the Treaty of Constance of 23 March 1153. A German delegation, led by the Premonstratensian Bishop Anselm of Havelberg (†1158), who had been a close adviser of the German kings since the time of Lothar III, and by Ulrich IV of Lenzburg, a childhood friend of Frederick's, as the chief lay member, had negotiated the text of a treaty with papal plenipoten-tiaries in Rome; this was confirmed by Frederick in Constance. The royal obligations are balanced by corresponding papal ones. Freder-ick promised to make no peace with the Romans or Normans without the pope's consent and to subdue the Romans 'as well as they have ever been in the last hundred years'; and to defend the *honor papatus* and the patrimony of St Peter in his capacity as advocate of the Roman church. In return the pope promised to give Frederick imperial coronation, coupled with assistance in extending the *honor imperii* so far as his office allowed it; and to use ecclesiastical sanctions against all those who injured the *honor regni*. Both sides undertook to make no territorial concessions in Italy to the 'king of the Greeks'. The Treaty of Constance, whose language clearly reveals the juristic and diplomatic training of the royal as well as the papal negotiators, was a large-scale programme of restoration on both sides, which in traditional fashion took no account of any powers other than emperor and pope. The most important papal promise for Frederick was that to assist him to extend the *honor imperii*, which evidently included both the rights and the territorial extent of the Empire.

The agreement reached at Constance was accompanied by accommodating gestures on both sides. While still in Constance the curial representatives consented to the dissolution of the marriage between Frederick and his wife Adela of Vohburg-Cham-Nabburg; Frederick had alleged that they were too closely related, and in order to prove this breach of canon law had had a family tree drawn up which showed that he and Adela descended from a common ancestor, who had probably lived in the tenth century. The marriage was declared null and void. But Frederick was also willing to fulfil the spirit of the Treaty of Constance, as can be seen in his behaviour towards the Byzantine emperor. Manuel I sent an embassy to Frederick in 1153, to try to win him for a common attack on the Normans, and there was even discussion of a proposed marriage between Frederick, now free again, and a Comneni princess. But Manuel evidently insisted on his territorial claims in Italy, especially as Conrad III had once conceded them to him. Frederick treated these approaches with reserve, and avoided an open breach of the Treaty of Constance.

FREDERICK AND THE EMPIRE BEFORE THE ALEXANDRINE SCHISM

1 *The revival of imperial rule in imperial Italy and the breach with the* Curia

The extension of the *honor imperii*, mentioned in the Treaty of Constance, was evidently a preoccupation of the new king, and one which could only be realized in Italy. Barbarossa went on six Italian expeditions and spent sixteen of the thirty-eight years of his reign there. From the time of Henry IV, who had spent the period 1090–6 more or less imprisoned in Italy, German rulers had only visited Italy for short periods and none had made any serious attempt at building up a new basis for government there.

Only a comparatively small army took part in the first Italian expedition, which set out in October 1154 from Augsburg. Its make-up reflected the new political constellation: the largest contingent among the 1,800 knights was provided by Henry the Lion, duke of Bavaria and Saxony, while the Babenberger Henry Jasomir-gott was absent. With such a small force Barbarossa could not risk any substantial military undertakings, but he was at least able to pose as the emperor and judge. Several of the cities which had been oppressed by Milan – Lodi, Pavia and Cremona – made accusations against her, and Frederick invited Milan to send representatives to answer these charges before him. Milan refused and was consequently outlawed, though there was no immediate prospect of enforcing the sentence. Frederick had a meeting near Bologna which was to have important consequences for the future: he made the acquaintance of a number of teachers of Roman law, probably including Martinus and Bulgarus, both of whom were pupils of the almost legendary Irnerius, and it was now, if not before, that he became aware of the opportunities inherent in his role as successor to the legislating emperors of antiquity.

In Rome there had been a change of pontiff: the ageing Anastasius IV (1153–4) had died after a short pontificate and had been succeeded by Hadrian IV (1154–9), the only Englishman ever to have become pope, who only a few years previously had carried out an epochal legation in Scandinavia in which he paved the way for national Scandinavian churches without regard to the missionary and metropolitan aspirations of Hamburg-Bremen. Hadrian, himself not a man who much favoured compromise, was increasingly influenced by the cardinal priest Roland Bandinelli, who had become chancellor of the Roman church in the last months of Eugenius III's pontificate. Bandinelli was a lawyer who had written a commentary on Gratian's *Decretum* and established a reputation for himself in Bologna. The rise to power of these two men marked the end of the contemplative interlude in papal history under Eugenius III; increasingly the Roman church saw its own greatness measured in the number and extent of its possessions and privileges. But the pope's position in the city of Rome was still precarious, for the populist movement led by Arnold of Brescia whose aim was to restore the ancient glory and independence of Rome had reached a dangerous position of strength. Hadrian IV tried to force the Romans to break with Arnold by putting the city under interdict. It was in this uncertain situation that Frederick and Hadrian met in Sutri in June 1155, at the normal final staging-post on a journey to Rome from the North. Both sides were willing to accept the validity of the agreement reached at Constance. The pope demanded merely the observation of certain formalities in order to clarify his relations with the future emperor. Frederick was to do the service of a marshal and groom, as Lothar had done; he refused, however, pointing to the vassalitic implications of such an act. Only on being assured by the *Curia* that it was purely a gesture of respect and after having been shown ancient records, probably including the Donation of Constantine, could Frederick be brought to hold the pope's stirrup and lead his horse a distance by the bridle, in the scene which had to be specially restaged. In order to avoid future misunderstandings Hadrian agreed to remove the offending picture in the Lateran which described and depicted Lothar III as the vassal of the pope.

The agreement between the pope and the king seemed once more endangered in the days before the imperial coronation, when a delegation from the Romans came to Frederick and offered him the imperial crown (just as they had Conrad III) in a deal which entailed a secular coronation on the Capitol in return for 5,000 pounds of pure gold. Frederick was outraged and turned the offer down brusquely; according to Otto of Freising he answered that he was the rightful owner of the city of Rome and that the imperial title belonged by right of conquest to the Frankish-German kings. Frederick had kept the Treaty of Constance, but only at the cost of offending influential circles in Rome. On the day of the coronation in St Peter's, 18 June 1155, there was an uprising, repressed largely by Henry the Lion and his troops. The Romans, however, were divided. Arnold of Brescia had been allowed to fall into Frederick's hands, and Frederick handed him over to the city prefect. Arnold was hanged, a common punishment for heretics, his corpse burnt and the ashes scattered in the Tiber, in order to prevent any possibility of a cult of his relics growing up; already a religious group which later merged with the Cathars had declared in favour of Arnold and his ideal of poverty. For the papal party the fall of Arnold was proof that God destroyed the opponents of the Roman church, and in a poem that circulated at the time it was said:

> He shall perish, whoever endangers the faith
> Committed to you, blessed Peter, the rock, by Christ.

In accordance with the Treaty of Constance Frederick should have moved south against the Normans, especially since the unrest following the death of Roger II favoured an attack on the kingdom. But the German princes forced a return north of the Alps in late summer 1155. Hadrian felt himself deserted, and in Benevent made a treaty with the new Norman king William I, who was granted control over the churches of his kingdom and in return for an annual *census* was enfeoffed with the kingdom of Sicily and the duchy of

Apulia. This agreement was undoubtedly contrary to the spirit of the Treaty of Constance, just as Frederick's failure to give Hadrian help after the imperial coronation had been. Relations between emperor and pope were further strained in 1156 when the notoriously anti-imperial Archbishop Eskil of Lund (1138–81) was attacked and kidnapped in Burgundy on his way back from Rome, where he had just been recognized as primate of Sweden and papal legate for the Nordic lands, a matter which naturally affected the claims of Hamburg-Bremen. Hadrian, whose protégé Eskil was and who was well informed about Scandinavian affairs, demanded Eskil's release, but Frederick did not react.

At the general assembly in Besançon in October 1157 a papal legation formally complained about the case of Eskil. Its leaders, the cardinal priests Bernard and Roland, both knew Germany well and had taken part in the negotiation of the Treaty of Constance. They handed over a letter from the pope in which he reminded Frederick of the imperial coronation: he had given Frederick the fullness of power, 'and in spite of this we do not regret having fulfilled your wishes in everything; indeed we would have rejoiced with good reason, if your excellency had received still greater *beneficia* at our hands'. Rainald of Dassel, imperial chancellor since 1156, translated the Latin text for the assembly, and rendered the word *beneficia*, which the pope had probably deliberately chosen for its ambiguity, by the technical word 'fiefs' rather than the more general one 'good deeds'. The assembled princes were shocked, and their indignation grew still greater when one of the legates, perhaps Roland, put the provocative question, 'From whom, then, does he have the Empire if not from the lord pope?' The count palatine, Otto of Wittelsbach, drew the imperial sword from its scabbard and threatened to attack the legates: Frederick had to interpose himself to protect them, and had them placed in a kind of protective custody. Their baggage was searched, and letters were found which made it evident that they were intending to conduct a visitation of the German church in a way not favourable to the interests of the German king. Frederick ordered the legates to return home 'without going aside to the left or to the right'. In a reply couched as a manifesto Frederick rejected the papal view of the Empire: 'Whoever claims that we have received the imperial crown from the lord pope as a fief denies the divinely willed order and that of St Peter and is a liar.' Hadrian attempted to split the German church from the emperor, but what had worked in the Investiture Contest now found no echo; the German episcopate was solidly behind Frederick. Hadrian yielded. A new legation was sent, under two other cardinals, 'who were much more qualified to conduct such delicate diplomacy than the earlier legates', as Rahewin remarked. It included Hyacinth, cardinal-deacon of S. Maria in Cosmedin, a pupil of Abaelard like Rainald and many other German prelates. The word *beneficium*, Hadrian assured the German princes, had not meant 'fief' but 'favour' (*beneficium – non est feudum, sed bonum factum*).

The events in and following Besançon revealed the imperial ideology of Frederick and his advisers. The leading light among the latter was Rainald of Dassel; contemporaries praised his knowledge of 'philosophy' and certainly his study of dialectic and rhetoric will have helped him to achieve conceptual clarity. The *Curia*, normally on the offensive in the development of ideas of world rule, was forced to back down. Frederick insisted on his emperorship's being seen as directly bestowed by God, not through the mediation of the papacy; to use modern terminology, he wanted a dualism of imperial and papal power, not a hierocracy. As in the times before the Investiture Contest, the sacrality conferred by royal unction was stressed: the emperor, like a bishop, was 'anointed of the Lord'. We hear phrases which were to have a long life in later German history. In the letter of the German bishops to Hadrian written in defence of Frederick at the end of 1157 Frederick is quoted as saying: 'the free crown of our Empire we ascribe only to divine favour'; the archbishop of Mainz has the first voice in the election, the archbishop of Cologne has the right to perform the royal unction, 'the highest, which is the imperial, is for the pope; whatever is more than these is of evil', quoting Matthew 5.37. The pope here became a mere executive organ, who had to crown emperor the man whom the German princes had chosen. The German bishops continued by reminding Hadrian of the humiliating and understanding interpretation of the royal display of reverence when Lothar III had led the pope's horse and was subsequently depicted in the Lateran as a papal vassal with an appropriate inscription: 'It began with a picture; the picture was followed by an inscription; the inscription is now to become law. We will not allow it.' The pope was reminded of the pastoral obligations of his office.

The rift was unbridgeable: each of the parties was convinced that they would have to give up something essential by making any move to accept the other's standpoint. When Frederick I prepared his second Italian expedition in 1158 he could no longer be certain of papal support, especially as his coming was probably seen by the papacy as superfluous: he had already been crowned emperor, and

Hadrian had long since ceased to look to Frederick for protection. He himself had negotiated an 'eternal peace' between his arch-enemies, the Normans and the Byzantines, in 1158, so that the Roman church no longer needed the emperor's assistance. In June 1158 Frederick set out with a large army. The first step was to enforce the sentence of outlawry declared against Milan in 1155. In September the city capitulated under humiliating conditions: all Milanese between the ages of fourteen and seventy were to take an oath of loyalty to the emperor, and in future the consuls elected by the city were to be confirmed in office by Frederick. In victorious mood, Frederick held a general assembly 'in the usual place' in November 1158 on the fields of Roncaglia, near Lodi. The main purpose of the assembly was to define the extent and nature of the *regalia* in Italy. A commission consisting of four Bolognese jurists and twenty-eight representatives of the cities of imperial Italy met to produce a doom, a finding of what was valid customary law. *Regalia* were defined, following older definitions, as duchies, marches, counties, the right to nominate city consuls, the right to build roads and take tolls, the right to coin money, the right to build palaces, and so on. All lords and cities were to show that they were in lawful possession of their *regalia*.

In 1967 the text of three laws issued in Roncaglia in 1158 was rediscovered. It shows the strong influence of Roman law on Barbarossa and his thinking. This was by no means original. As early as the eleventh century the *magister* Peppo of Bologna had taken part in a court of Henry IV's and issued a judgement based on Roman law; Irnerius, later celebrated as the 'light of the law', had provided Henry V with a proof that the right of installing popes had been exercised by the Roman emperors; and in 1136 Lothar III had issued a constitution on fiefs which was heavily laced with Roman law phraseology. Barbarossa's use of Roman law was thus no novelty, but he was the first emperor who fully took up the role of the defender and source of *ius Romanum*. Constantine the Great, Valentinian and Justinian were described as 'our predecessors, the sacred emperors'.

Perhaps at this time, possibly already in 1155, Barbarossa issued a further law which stands at the beginning of the development of European universities: all 'scholars who have left their homes through love of learning, and especially those learned in law' were taken under his protection while travelling or staying at their place of study and provided with a jurisdiction of their own; at the same time Frederick ordained that this *Authentica* (supplementary law)

Habita (the title is taken from the opening word of the law, by which it was cited) should be inserted into the text of Justinian's Code. It was also at this time, according to an anecdote, that Frederick is supposed to have ridden out with the famous pupils of Irnerius, Bulgarus and Martinus, both of whom belonged to the *regalia* commission, and to have presented Martinus with his horse on being assured by him that he, Frederick, was the 'lord of the world'.

The recuperation of the *regalia* promised a huge income. Rahewin estimated the annual income from them at 30,000 talents of silver. An English source records an income for the imperial fisc in Italy of 84,000 pounds of silver in 1164, so that the annual income of the German king in Italy can be estimated at about 100,000 pounds. This held admittedly only so long as the emperor was in Italy, but it was enough to make the German emperor one of the richest rulers in the West. The French king Louis VII (1137–80) is said to have joked that 'we French only have bread, wine and joy' but in spite of that his annual income was probably around 60,000 pounds of silver; the rich great fiefs were still in the hands of the English king, whose annual income has been estimated at about 90,000 pounds. Frederick took precautions to ensure that the newly regained *regalia* were not alienated again. They were not to be granted out as fiefs but administered by royal officials. It could be foreseen that putting the Roncaglian decrees into effect would arouse the resistance of many of the north Italian cities, especially as the cities had frequently not taken the *regalia* directly from the king but from the bishop who had previously been lord of the city. Particularly resentful were Milan and her satellite city of Crema, which lay next to the pro-imperial city of Cremona. A sentence of outlawry on Crema was decreed and promptly put into effect: after a siege of several months the town was taken and razed to the ground. The execution of the sentence against Milan was deferred.

Frederick's recuperations did not stop short at the borders of the papal state, and after papal legates had complained about this Frederick accused Hadrian IV of breaking the Treaty of Constance and proposed to settle their differences by arbitration, a proposal unacceptable to the pope. On Hadrian's death on 1 September 1159 it became clear that the split ran through the college of cardinals, just as in northern Italy an imperialist group of cities (Pavia, Lodi, Piacenza, Cremona) stood in opposition to Milan and her followers. Two candidates emerged from the initial discussions: the imperial and aristocratic cardinal-priest Octavian of Monticelli and Roland Bandinelli from a bourgeois family in Siena, well known to the imperial court through the events at Besançon. The election was divided. Octavian was elected by a minority of only two cardinals and took the name of Victor IV, while Roland called himself Alexander III. The election took place in St Peter's and led to grotesque scenes: Alexander was about to don the purple mantle of the popes, one of the most important symbolic actions in the series of ceremonies associated with the consecration of a new pope, when, as he angrily reported later, Octavian behaved so shamelessly as '. . . to draw the cloak from Our Person with his own hands and to drag it off uttering loud shouts'.

Barbarossa assumed an attitude of neutrality. He summoned a council for 13 January 1160 to meet in Pavia, basing his right to do this on his succession to the emperors of antiquity, who were responsible for calling synods. It was naturally impossible for Alexander III to consider attending, for 'a pope may be judged by no one'. The confirmation of Victor IV, who took care to turn up, was no more than a farce. But the imperial action did not have much effect, especially as only some fifty prelates attended the council, and the entire clergy of the English and French churches were absent. In order to make a slightly more impressive showing, the names of absent prelates were added to the subscription list. The council of Pavia excommunicated Alexander III; Alexander in his turn excommunicated Victor IV, the emperor and his advisers. The schism which had broken out was to last for eighteen years.

In the meantime Milan continued her opposition in spite of all pressure. Not until March 1162 did she capitulate; her citizens came before the enthroned emperor to beg his mercy. 'All who heard were moved to tears, but the emperor's face did not change.' This time the punishment was harsher than in 1158. The *caroccio*, the standard-wagon which symbolized the commune, was destroyed, the walls levelled, the buildings destroyed, the legal status of the settlement annulled and the population dispersed to four villages, where they were resettled with the status of peasants. This cruel punishment was not without precedent: half a century earlier, in 1111, the Milanese themselves had done the same thing to Lodi with the same intention: that the town should cease to exist. On the fall of Milan her lesser allies gave up their resistance, and by mid 1162 the whole of Lombardy was under Frederick's control.

2 Frederick's German policy

For the first ten years of his rule Frederick divided his time equally between Germany and Italy, and it was evident that he would have to pursue a policy of reconciliation with the Welfs, not only because it was expected of him, but also so as to avoid trouble on the home front during his Italian campaigns. But the favours shown to Henry the Lion as duke of Saxony and Bavaria had been at the cost of Frederick's Babenberger relatives, who had remained faithful to the Staufer against the Welfs. Henry Jasomirgott received his compensation at the general assembly of Regensburg in September 1156. He and his wife were invested with the march of Austria, which had been raised to the status of a duchy. The Babenberger received the duchy on privileged terms, laid down in the diploma with which the investiture was confirmed, the so-called *Privilegium minus*. It is known as the *Privilegium minus* to distinguish it from the *Privilegium maius*, a forgery based on the *minus* carried out for Duke Rudolf IV of Austria in 1358/9. When the *maius* was exposed as a forgery in the nineteenth century, the *minus* also came under suspicion. This was misplaced; but the *minus* did display a number of peculiar features. The new duchy of Austria was conferred not only on Henry Jasomirgott but also on his wife Theodora, a niece of the Greek *Basileus* Manuel whom Henry had married in 1148; his first wife Gertrude died in 1143. It has been claimed that the *minus* reflects principles of Byzantine law, but similar if exceptional provisions can also be found earlier in German history. A further unusual feature was the right granted to Henry and Theodora to determine their own successor if they had no male heir (*ius affectandi*). Their feudal duties were also restricted: the new duke had to attend royal assemblies in Bavaria only and was not obliged to send troop contingents to an imperial army except in the case of campaigns in areas bordering on his duchy. The *Privilegium minus* reconciled Frederick with the Babenberger.

Frederick had succeeded in reducing tensions and ending feuds within a very short period, and the next step was obviously to bind the outlying parts of the Empire and neighbouring kingdoms more closely to the German kingdom. Frederick extended his influence in Burgundy by marrying the sixteen-year-old Beatrix in 1156, heiress to substantial possessions in upper Burgundy and in Provence. Frederick had received the homage of the Burgundian magnates at the assembly of Besançon in 1157 at which the papal legates also appeared. In the same year, 1157, Barbarossa had invaded Poland, and compelled the Polish duke Boleslav IV to acknowledge the rights of his brother Vladislav, who had sought protection with Frederick, and to recognize German suzerainty. A few years later, in 1163, Frederick summoned Boleslav to a general assembly and forced him to allow Vladislav's two sons to succeed their recently deceased father in lordships in the diocese of Breslau: Boleslav the Long received the duchy of Breslau, and Mieszko Ratibor and Teschen. Both were subject to the suzerainty of the Polish king, but they sought support from Germany. It was at this time that the German colonization of Silesia began, encouraged by the Polish dukes.

In Denmark the bloody civil war following the murder of Knut Laward in 1131 had finally been won by Waldemar the Great. His reign, a lengthy one by Nordic standards (1157 to 1182) brought a consolidation of the power of the Danish monarchy; like his predecessors, Waldemar let the German king enfeoff him with Denmark. In spite of this his relations with the German king and with his neighbour, the duke of Saxony Henry the Lion, remained cool and mistrustful. From the 1160s Waldemar had the old Danewerk, a defensive wall dating from the Carolingian period, rebuilt and extended: in the central section the technique of building in brick, new in the North, was used to create a wall some four kilometres long, several metres wide and seven metres high, an impressive if somewhat outdated piece of fortification.

Henry the Lion, duke of Saxony and Bavaria, extended his lordship with Frederick's connivance. Two of his urban foundations, both characteristic of his far-sighted planning and of his brutality in carrying it out, were to be of great significance in the future: Lübeck and Munich. Count Adolf II of Holstein had founded Lübeck at the confluence of the Wakenitz and the Trave in 1143, and it soon flourished. Henry forbade a market to be held there when it appeared that Lübeck was damaging the development of the ducal trading-centre of Bardowick north of Lüneburg. When Adolf II's settlement was badly damaged by fire Henry attempted a rival foundation, but the *Löwenstadt*, badly sited, did not prosper. Only after Henry the Lion had made a third attempt by founding a town on the peninsula between Trave and Wakenitz in 1159 was there progress: this new settlement was founded in cooperation with the merchants of old Lübeck. It is not certain that there was a formally organized consortium of merchants engaged in long-distance trade in Lübeck, such as we can observe at work as partners with the duke of Zähringen in the cooperative foundation of Freiburg im Breisgau, but it can hardly be denied that a number of mercantile families participated at an early stage, and they are soon to be found holding leading positions in the running of the market and in the town council. It is also noteworthy that Henry the Lion continued to care for the interests of his new foundation: for merchants travelling to

Gotland he negotiated parity of legal status with the native inhabitants. Munich was founded at almost exactly the same time, in 1158.
Here too the beginnings were marked by an act of violence. Henry
destroyed the bridge of the bishop of Freising over the Isar at
Föhring, which carried the salt trade from south-eastern Bavaria,
and diverted the traffic to a newly built bridge near the *villa
Munichen* (the villa of the monks) which was given market status and
soon became a merchant settlement.

Henry combined a policy of encouraging urban growth on a large
scale with one of energetic colonization on the Slav border. It was
said that his ruthless behaviour made his name more terrible 'than
the name of God' to the petty chiefs of the Abodrites. Through
colonization, founding of new markets, investiture of bishops and
endowing them with *regalia* Henry created a territory which was
virtually a separate principality under his control. Where there was
no obvious male heir Henry stepped in and took over inheritances,
ignoring the claims of daughters or collateral relatives. He also
confiscated the lands of rebellious nobles, collected advocatial and
comital rights and was able to get his own candidates elected to
bishoprics by influencing cathedral chapters; once elected, he had
them enfeoff him with church lands.

Henry's quasi-regal position corresponded to the Welfs' own
view of their status as adopted and magnified by Henry. The
Kaiserchronik, a vernacular and pro-Welf piece of historiography
written in Regensburg around 1150, depicted the history of the
Empire as if the rise in its fortunes brought about by Lothar III,
treated as an honorary Welf, had been brought to a halt by the
election of the Staufer Conrad III – 'Welf was stronger', claimed the
chronicler – and a genealogy of the Welfs set out in the manner of
contemporary tables of consanguinity stressed two names in
particular: Charles the Bald and Frederick Barbarossa, both with
Welf mothers called Judith and both claimed for the Welf family.
Like a king, Henry married in 1168 Mathilda, the daughter of the
English king Henry II; an evangeliary produced in the monastery of
Helmarshausen for the 'cathedral' of St Blasius in Brunswick,
Henry's foundation, has a picture of Henry and Mathilda with a
hand reaching down to crown each of them. In 1172 Henry made a
pilgrimage to Jerusalem with a large following, and was received
like a king by the Greek emperor. Brunswick took on the character
of a royal court, and its buildings, taken as a whole, were more
substantial and magnificent than all of the palaces newly founded by
Barbarossa. The ducal palace in Dankwarderode was unmistakably

modelled on those at Aachen and Goslar. In 1166 the famous bronze lion was set up in Brunswick, the first substantial piece of free-standing sculpture and the first dynastic symbol of the Middle Ages; the man who commissioned it had as his nickname the name of his house (*Löwe*, 'lion', from *Welf*, 'whelp'). Henry's court, his patronage of the arts and commissions from artists, put a still greater distance between him and the other imperial princes. According to the medieval idea of *nomen* the essence determined the name, so that it could be said of someone that he 'is a king and is called one'. Elevations to royalty were known to the twelfth century, and Henry's posturing could have been intended as laying claim to a supra-ducal status, at a kind of kingship, even if one still incorporated in a larger unity.

3 The Staufer idea of empire

In Frederick's diplomata and edicts a new tone can be discerned, a newly articulated self-confidence. The emperorship is depicted as the natural pillar of earthly order, created by God directly. In a diploma for Pisa issued immediately after the imperial coronation in 1155 Barbarossa talks of 'Europe, in which we have the seat and home of the Empire', and the city is said to have 'filled the peoples of Asia and Africa with fear' and to have 'extended the Empire'. Pope Gelasius I had spoken in an often-quoted definition of the 'two things by which the world is ruled', the 'sacred authority of the popes' (*sacrata pontificum auctoritas*) and the 'power of the ruler' (*potestas regalis*). Frederick's chancery transformed this into: 'There are two things by which our Empire is ruled: the divine laws of the emperors [*leges sanctae imperatorum*] and the good customs of our predecessors and ancestors [*usus bonus predecessorum et patrum nostrorum*].' If Bernard of Clairvaux had recently proposed a doctrine of the two swords in which the one was held by the pope and the other entrusted by him to the emperor, Frederick turned this into two swords which were directly conferred by God, 'especially as the Apostle Peter gave this doctrine to the world: fear God, honour the king'. Up until then it had been said only of papal writings that they were to be honoured like 'divine revelations'; now under the influence of Roman law it was claimed that the laws of the emperors from Constantine the Great to Louis the Pious were to be revered 'like divine oracles' (*tamquam divina oracula*); at the same time (1157) the expression 'Holy Empire' (*sacrum imperium*) became a standard formula. The imperial dignity was given a higher status; to offend it was to risk the death penalty, just as under the *crimen laesae maiestatis* of Roman law. When Urban III later refused to crown Henry VI emperor in Barbarossa's lifetime, Barbarossa, like an Augustus of antiquity, gave his son the title of Caesar.

Compared with the aggressive and compelling propaganda of the imperial chancery the papal counter-manifestos seem pale and bureaucratic. However much Frederick himself may have been in agreement with the new ideas, they were worked out and propagated by a group of clerics at the court and in the chancery. At the outset the leading figure was probably Abbot Wibald of Stavelot and Corvey (†1158), the chief adviser to Conrad III; one might also mention Bishop Eberhard II of Bamberg (1146–70), who, however, was always concerned to mediate between emperor and pope and who knew how to preserve his independence: he declared at the council of Pavia in 1160, which was under heavy pressure from the emperor, that his recognition of Victor IV was conditional on the latter's being acknowledged as pope by the rest of the Catholic church. The most fanatical member of the circle, who soon eclipsed Eberhard of Bamberg, was Rainald of Dassel. He was the son of a rising Saxon comital family, educated in Hildesheim and in France, and held canonries in Hildesheim, Goslar, Münster, Maestricht and for a time also in Xanten, before becoming chancellor in 1156 (he was the main actor in the scene in Besançon in 1157) and in 1159 archbishop of Cologne and archchancellor of Italy. Rainald was a *vir litteratus* but also a man of war: on his last Italian expedition he and ten of his knights took three hundred Ravennatese militiamen prisoner, and he showed his ability as a general in the battle of Tusculum in 1167. Rainald's radical attitude gave clarity to the ideas of empire being developed, but at the same time prevented compromise. He made use of the antipopes for a special project, the canonization of Charlemagne. At Christmas 1165 the Frankish emperor was translated from his crypt in Aachen and venerated as a saint, a very definite sign that Charlemagne was regarded as a German emperor and predecessor of Frederick. This was, to say the least, a hostile act towards France, which saw itself as the upholder of Charlemagne's tradition. Frederick and the Empire might have become still more isolated had not Rainald died in 1167 immediately after his triumph at Rome. Barbarossa described him as 'our most faithful prince Rainald', but contemporaries blamed him for the schism, and an anecdote related how he had said in his sleep while still in the cathedral school 'I am the ruin of the world', on which his schoolfellows gave him the nickname of *ruina mundi*.

The Staufer imperial idea and the striving for world domination found literary expression in the works of a number of authors: the court poetry of Gunther and Gottfried of Viterbo were inspired by it. The most mature productions were the poems of the Archpoet and the play *Ludus de Antichristo*. We know virtually nothing about the origins or career of the poet known from a title in one manuscript as the Archpoet: possibly a German, perhaps the son of a *ministerialis*. His poems – ten in all from the period 1160–5 – all seem to have some connection with Rainald of Dassel. They display a brilliant mixture of verbal skill, freshness and melodiousness; even a died-in-the-wool classical philologist like Wilamowitz could say of them that they managed to produce sound effects in Latin unknown to antiquity. Life in the archbishop's entourage was not without its tensions: on the one hand the Archpoet was by his own confession the 'poet and servant' of the archbishop, on the other hand he was a personality which needed freedom, a representative of the wandering clerics who toured the land looking for gifts and bene-fices and whose fate is well described in a poem written by one of them, Hugo Primas of Orleans, at the end of his life: 'I was rich and well loved, elect among equals; now I must submit to senility and be worn out by old age. My stomach is hollow ... and if I starve to death, I shall blame you.' The Archpoet's most famous poem, included in the *Carmina Burana*, is his 'vagabond's confession', written probably in Pavia in 1163. An envious rival had denounced the Archpoet to Rainald of Dassel for his sinful way of life; the poet addresses his patron, confesses his sins, and asks for a mild penance. The most famous strophe is the drinking-song

> In a tavern I shall die, so at least I've vowed it;
> wine to wet my thirsty lips, before I am enshrouded.
> May the angels in their choirs sing these joyous verses:
> 'To this wretched drunk, we pray, show, O Lord, your mercies'.

Rainald asked the Archpoet to compose an epic on Frederick's deeds in Italy, but the poet refused. Perhaps as a substitute he wrote around this time his hymn to the emperor:

> Hail to thee, lord of the world!
> Hail to thee, our Caesar!
> You whose yoke to all good men
> Gentle is and easy!

The Christological tendency of the poem is unmistakable; the same expressions and metaphors are used for Christ and for the emperor.

Otto of Freising had compared Barbarossa to the cornerstone of the building, following Ephesians 2.14ff; the Archpoet used Christ's saying: 'my yoke is easy, and my burden is light' (Matthew 11.30).

The dramatic *Ludus de Antichristo* struck a deeper, more eschatological note. It was written around 1160 in Tegernsee, perhaps on the occasion of Frederick's coronation in 1152. The history of man's salvation is depicted on stage. First come the heathen with the king of Babylon, next the synagogue with the Jews, and finally the church with the emperor and pope, both of whom follow the figure of the church as equals. The Last Emperor, the king of Germany, subdues the kings of Greece, Jerusalem and the rebellious king of France. But he in his turn is defeated, not by force of arms, but by the Antichrist and his miracles; in its turn the rule of Antichrist is interrupted by the Last Judgement. Here, as with Otto of Freising, we find a pessimisic streak; even the victorious forces of order are subject to decline and decay when their time is done.

The idea of empire implies that kings are subordinated to the emperor. The writings of the period occasionally use the words 'petty kings' (*reguli*) and 'kings of the provinces' (*reges provinciarum*) for the other rulers of Europe. And Rainald spoke at a meeting with the French king of the 'arrogance of the kings of the provinces'. There was a corresponding rise in resentment and rejection of the hegemonial claims of the German emperors, in England and especially in France. The most famous expression of this came from John of Salisbury (†1180), an Englishman by birth but one who had studied in France and who was to finish his career there as bishop of Chartres. John, a man learned in political thought and one who had for his time an unusually comprehensive knowledge of Aristotle, did not consider Frederick the heir to the emperors of antiquity; for him Frederick was an arrogant and pretentious German, a 'German emperor', a 'German tyrant'. And in biblical language he asked: 'Who has made the Germans to be judges over the peoples? Who has given this crude and violent race the right arbitrarily to choose a lord over the children of man?' It is difficult to assess the political content of the Staufer idea of world dominium, and it is not very helpful to use the classical idea of the emperor as the *princeps* who ranks above others in authority. Whatever imperial pre-eminence was supposed to imply, there was soon an answer to it in the doctrine of the king as 'emperor in his own kingdom' (*rex est imperator in regno suo*). But whatever their vagueness there was a hard core given to these ideas by the existence of an empire in a more narrow sense: Germany, Burgundy and Italy.

EMPIRE AND PAPACY IN THE STRUGGLE FOR SUPREMACY

The two decades following the Roncaglian decrees were marked by the attempt to set up a proper governmental basis for Staufer rule in Italy. It was not just a matter of rights and possessions; there was also the intention of establishing a proper imperial administration carried out by men whose powers were delegated to them by the emperor, in other words, an arrangement which should act as a replacement for the vanished church system of the Salians without suffering the drawbacks of a feudalized administration. Frederick Barbarossa was in a position similar to that of Henry II of England, who had built up a territorial lordship on the Continent which was also outside his own main kingdom. The schism was not a struggle for the right ordering of the world, as the Investiture Contest had been, and there was in consequence no revival of the *Libelli de lite*; the dispute was one over definite and concrete rights of rulership.

1 Papal schism and diplomacy to the death of Alexander III (1181)

There were two main obstacles to Frederick's attempt to put the edicts of Roncaglia into practice, the Lombard cities and Pope Alexander III. By 1162 both of these opponents appeared to have been defeated. Milan had had its fortifications razed and had ceased to exist as a commune; Alexander III had had to leave Italy in early 1162. He went to France, which together with England, Hungary, Norway, Spain and the Latin East and of course the Normans and the Lombard cities made up his obedience. Only the satellites of the German kingdom, Denmark and Bohemia, recognized the antipope Victor IV, and there were supporters of Alexander even among the German episcopate, such as the archbishops Eberhard of Salzburg and, later, Conrad of Mainz. It was therefore of considerable importance for Frederick to win over the French king Louis VII. It was agreed between the two rulers that they should meet for a settlement of the schism by arbitration on a bridge over the River Saône, the border between the two kingdoms, near St Jean de Losne, on 29 August 1162, together with the two popes: Frederick was to bring Victor IV, Louis, Alexander III. But Alexander refused to come and pointed to the canon law principle that the pope might be judged by no one; the French clergy also offered resistance. The meeting in the end did not come off, and the negotiations which went on into the following weeks did not come to anything; it was here that Rainald made his remark about the 'kings of the provinces' (meaning Louis VII), who arrogantly claimed for themselves the rights of a Roman emperor by presuming to judge the papal schism. The fact that a synod summoned by Frederick to Dôle in Burgundy declared Alexander III to be deposed simply underlined Frederick's failure. Frederick remained obdurate, in spite of an embassy sent by Alexander III to the general asembly in Nürnberg in the summer of 1163 and in spite of the divisions among the German episcopate. He may have thought that he would be able to bring Italy and Rome firmly under his control and so be able to establish his antipope there permanently, along with his own power. In the autumn of 1163 he travelled to northern Italy without an army, expecting to be able to raise one on the spot, but the wind was changing. The Patriarch of Grado, Henry Dandolo, whose see had been shifted to Venice in 1156, used the financial resources of his city to bring together a number of cities in the anti-imperial league of Verona: Vicenza and Padua as well as Verona itself.

Victor IV died on 20 April, and without informing Frederick, Rainald had had a successor chosen even before the end of the customary three days' funeral ceremonies: Paschal III, who came from an aristocratic family in Crema. Frederick gave his consent *ex post facto*, since the chances of a reconciliation were gone in any case. He returned north of the Alps in 1164 without having improved his position.

It was evident that neither Alexander nor the League of Verona could be defeated without help from outside. The most likely candidate was Louis VII's most powerful vassal, the English king Henry II, who was successfully building up a centralizing royal administration. He laid down in the Constitutions of Clarendon of 1164 that clerics had to appear before royal courts when charged with crimes within these courts' competence: felonies and forest offences. This threatened the clergy with a loss of privilege, for by the early twelfth century they had succeeded in having their right to be judged in their own courts (*privilegium fori*) recognized. It was alleged that the crime rate among clerics had risen sharply since then, because ecclesiastical courts, which operated on quite different principles from royal ones, only imposed inadequate penalties. Henry's main opponent was Thomas à Becket, archbishop of Canterbury since 1162, who before that had been Henry's chief

adviser for several years. Becket retracted his acceptance of the
Constitutions and fled to Louis VII in France: he did not return to
England until 1170; at the end of the year he was struck down by
royal knights before the altar in Canterbury cathedral, a martyr's
death which put Henry hopelessly in the wrong, thanks to the
intensive and in part libellous propaganda put out by Becket's
friends (who were also partisans of Alexander III), and forced him to
repudiate the Constitutions and do public penance.

In the year in which the Constitutions were issued, 1164,
Alexander's enemies, Frederick and Henry, quickly drew together.
The negotiations which Rainald of Dassel conducted at Rouen early
in 1165 led to a treaty. Henry the Lion was to marry Henry II's
older daughter Mathilda, and the younger daughter, the three-year-
old Eleanor, was betrothed to Frederick's recently born son Frederick. Henry promised to bring the English clergy into Paschal III's
obedience. In the euphoria which followed the successful sealing of
this alliance, a general assembly met at Wurzburg in May 1165. The
princes were forced to take an oath never to recognize Alexander,
only the pope supported by Frederick; those who refused the oath
lost their offices and fiefs. Archbishop Conrad of Mainz, the brother
of Frederick's faithful supporter Otto of Wittelsbach, was replaced
by the royal chancellor, Christian of Buch. Alexander felt his
position in France to be so precarious that in 1165 he returned to
Rome and to the protection of his Sicilian vassals. But the death of
William I in 1166 was followed by the minority of his son William
II, and Alexander had to look for additional supporters. The young
king was to marry a daughter of Manuel I and Manuel proposed to
Alexander that the churches of East and West should be reunited and
that he should crown him, Manuel, emperor. These radical projects
were dropped as soon as the danger was over.

Barbarossa looked for a decisive solution in Italy. An army of
over 10,000 knights, reinforced by *Brabanzoni* (i.e. mercenaries
from Brabant), set out in the autumn of 1166. It advanced in two
columns: the emperor marched along the coast, Rainald of Dassel
and Christian of Buch, straight for Rome. They won a brilliant
victory over the Romans at Tusculum, and Alexander was forced to
flee the city disguised as a pilgrim; the Leonine city was captured
after heavy fighting. Paschal III was enthroned and on 1 August
1167 he crowned Beatrix empress in St Peter's. Only a few days later
the German army suffered a catastrophe, a turning-point not only
for this Italian expedition, but for the whole of Barbarossa's reign.
The stifling summer heat was broken by a sudden thunderstorm,

and an epidemic of malaria broke out in the German camp. Over two thousand knights are said to have perished. Among the dead were Rainald of Dassel, Frederick of Rothenburg (duke of Suabia and Barbarossa's cousin), Bishop Daniel of Prague, who had just been appointed chief justice for Italy, and Welf VII, Welf VI's young son. The army was so decimated that it was incapable of further action; there could no longer be any thought of a campaign against the Normans. The Alexandrine party saw the catastrophe as a divine judgement; the League of Verona expanded to become a league of the Lombard cities, and as a demonstrative gesture of support for Alexander III a new fortification with the name Alessandria was built in a strategically important site on the Tanaro. Frederick had to sneak through northern Italy disguised as a servant in order to get back to Germany through Burgundy.

Rainald's death was a great personal loss for Frederick, but it freed the emperor from Rainald's uncompromising assertion of principle, which in spite of the effort and imagination devoted to it had brought no great success. The policy followed from then on, aimed at bringing about a satisfactory compromise, was much more Frederick's own work. He was favoured by disputes within the Lombard League – particularly between Cremona, which was more tolerant to him, and Milan, which had been rebuilt with English and Byzantine subsidies. In 1174 Barbarossa moved on Italy for the fifth time, with a powerful army of about 8,000 soldiers. He did not succeed in taking Alessandria, which would have been a victory of great symbolic importance, but the perpetual fighting, which seriously disturbed trade, had made the Lombard cities tired of war as well. In 1175 a truce was negotiated at Montebello, and on the assumption that this would soon be followed by a permanent peace Frederick dismissed a large part of his army. But the arbitration judgement delivered by the consuls of Cremona was not accepted by the Lombard League; it would have had to give up Alessandria and to abandon Alexander III. Frederick was in an awkward position. He was almost without troops and needed military assistance urgently. He turned to the richest German prince, Henry the Lion, duke of Bavaria and Saxony. At the beginning of February 1176 Frederick and his most prominent vassal met in Chiavenna north of Lake Como for a conference. Frederick asked Henry for help; he may even have gone on his knees to do so. Henry was not obliged to give it, as a matter either of feudal or of tribal law. He offered Frederick a deal: the latter should hand over the imperial city of Goslar and the surrounding silver mines in return for help.

Frederick refused, and Henry the Lion in turn denied him assistance. This was certainly not due to any fundamental opposition to Frederick's Italian policies, which had after all more or less allowed him a free hand to build up his lordship in Germany. From Frederick's point of view Henry was not legally obliged to help him, but he was certainly morally obliged to do so; his refusal was not a crime, but sheer ingratitude.

Frederick resumed military activities but with a greatly reduced army; in spite of this he took the offensive. But the Milanese foot-soldiers grouped around their standard-wagon defeated the attacking German knights at Legnano, north-west of Milan, in May 1176.

The commune had triumphed over the state. The Italians, with short-sighted patriotism, see in this victory one of the great moments of national history, but never has a people paid so dearly for its victory. Instead of becoming a state Italy became a bundle of petty city-states and feeble principalities; it suffered for centuries from the consequences of victory

was Albert Hauck's judgement. It is remarkable how skilfully Frederick managed to compensate for military defeat in the following months. In a preliminary treaty made in Anagni in November 1176 the pope and the Lombard League still appear as partners. The final peace treaty made at Venice in July 1177 revealed a considerable improvement in Frederick's position. The question of his relations with the Lombard League was set aside; all that was agreed was a truce of six years, together with one of fifteen years with the kingdom of Sicily. Frederick was also to remain in possession of the Mathildine lands for fifteen years. The German bishops recognized Alexander and in return kept their bishoprics; Bishop Ulrich of Halberstadt, who had been replaced by a candidate of Henry the Lion's, was reinstated, a definite sign that the tide was turning against Henry the Lion. The peace settlement was completed with great ceremony in Venice on 24 July 1177. The emperor kissed the pope's feet and did the service of a groom and marshal. Emperor and pope remained together in Venice for several weeks. In early 1178 an army under Archbishop Christian of Mainz led Alexander in triumph back to Rome. Frederick stayed a whole year in northern Italy after the conclusion of peace, probably to make sure that it really was a peace; on his way back he had himself crowned in Arles as king of the *regnum Arelatense*, symbolically laying claim to lordship over the whole of Burgundy.

It was standard practice to hold a great council after a schism or dispute in the church. Alexander III summoned a synod to the Lateran in March 1179, later counted as Lateran III and as the eleventh ecumenical council. The canons were of particular importance for the later history of the church, as would be expected from a pope who was by training a lawyer and whose pontificate, in spite of all its difficulties, showed an unbroken flood of privileges and decisions. About a fifth of all the papal privileges and letters issued before 1200 were issued during the twenty-two years of his pontificate, amounting to almost 4,000, and the number of decretals he issued – legal decisions with the status of precedents for ecclesiastical law – was several times larger than the number of those issued by all his predecessors put together. The circumstances of his disputed election had left a deep impression on Alexander. It had not previously been laid down how many votes from the college of cardinals a candidate had to have to be elected; the council determined that a two-thirds majority was necessary. There was a very noticeable attempt to deal with abuses of other kinds as well. Pluralism was forbidden, and the council began the transformation of the right of the proprietary church owner to name the priest of a church he or his ancestors had founded into a mere right of patronage, which 'in gratitude' allowed the founder only the right to propose a candidate.

2 Staufer government in Germany

Frederick tried to build up the basis of his rule in other directions as well. He frequently interpreted privileges more widely than they had originally been intended: the Concordat of Worms, for example, had by no means provided for a German king's choosing a third candidate for a bishopric after a divided election, as happened in the case of Wichmann of Magdeburg in 1152. Following the example of the French and Anglo-Norman kingdoms he demanded that prelates invested with the *regalia* should provide corresponding services and managed to force even Burgundian bishops to do homage. During a vacancy, i.e. following the death of a bishop or of the abbot of an imperial monastery, he exploited the *regalia* himself and demanded the right of *spolia*, of confiscating the movable property of a prelate on his death. He also clearly attempted to build up closed territories in rivalry to the princes, just as the French kings were doing in the crown domain in the Île-de-France. Crown and family lands were administered together, even though the distinction between the two was acknowledged. Like other princes, Barbarossa systematically rounded off his territories by exchanges of property. A good example of such an operation is found in the exchange between Frederick and Henry the Lion in 1158: Frederick got the dowry of Henry's first wife Clementia of Zähringen in southern Suabia, and Henry in return received possessions in the southern Harz. The lands in southern Suabia were particularly valuable to Frederick as a bridge to the newly acquired lands of his wife Beatrix in Burgundy, while Henry was able to round off his Saxon allods with what he got. A further means of acquiring land was to exploit the right of escheat. A number of Suabian noble families became extinct in the direct male line during Frederick's lifetime, such as the counts of Pfullendorf; Frederick claimed to inherit their lands, and took over not only their lands but also their advocacies. A number of his faithful supporters made him their heir, such as the last count of Lenzburg, Ulrich IV (†1173), who had carried out an unusually intensive and brutal policy of clearance and land colonization south of the upper Rhine. Barbarossa even managed to derive advantage from the disaster at Rome in 1167. Frederick of Rothenburg, the son of Conrad III and duke of Suabia, had died there; Barbarossa immediately conferred the duchy on his own eldest son Frederick, who because of his feeble health had been passed over for the succession to the throne. When he died at the age of about seven Frederick gave the duchy to his fourth son Conrad, whose name was changed on the occasion to Frederick, the Staufer leading-name and the name borne by all the dukes of Suabia since 1079. The epidemic at Rome had also carried off Welf VI's only son, the young Welf VII, who died childless at the age of twenty-seven. Welf VI lost all interest after this in extending his family lands: 'he sought above all to live in state, devoting himself to hunting, banqueting and other pleasures and to displaying his generosity in the giving of feasts and presents', as the continuator of the *Historia Welforum* reported. He became short of cash, and by degrees handed back his Italian fiefs, Tuscany, Spoleto and other scattered lands, to Frederick: from 1173 he no longer used these titles in his charters. After lengthy negotiations Henry the Lion agreed in 1175 or 1176 to pay a large sum of money in return for being made Welf's heir; but the money did not materialize, and Welf VI turned to Frederick. Agreement was reached before 1180; Henry the Lion had been outmanoeuvred. Some of the Welf allods passed into Frederick's hands, but the use of the main Welf lands around Ravensburg remained with Welf VI until his death in December 1191 at the age of seventy-six. This was too late for the Staufer, for Frederick

Barbarossa and his son Duke Frederick V of Suabia were no longer alive, and the new Staufer king, Henry VI, husband of Constance of Sicily, attended Welf's funeral but did not incorporate the newly acquired Welf lands into a comprehensive ducal territory; his interests lay in Italy.

This rigorous policy of acquisitions, which was carried out with particular thoroughness in the years following the catastrophe at Rome, revealed the outlines of a new kind of state. A number of territorial complexes were expanded to form 'royal regions': the family lands in Alsace and Suabia, greatly extended and consolidated, and in Franconia. There were Staufer possessions in the region around Nürnberg – it was here that Conrad III had been able to defend himself so successfully in the days of his antikingship. To these were added crown lands in Thuringia around Altenburg and along the Pleiße. On the death of Frederick of Rothenburg Barbarossa took over the Egerland. The whole complex was run from the imperial castles at Altenburg and Eger. We can see in outline the idea of a broad strip of Staufer family lands and imperial possessions running from the upper Rhine in the South-West through Franconia to Thuringia, a barrier which would cut Henry the Lion off from Bavaria and confine him to the North-East. Bavaria was in any case after the transformation of Austria into a duchy no longer a frontier duchy; it could become a more powerful state only through internal consolidation.

The most important element in the newly extended lordships were the *ministeriales*, who were in the process of shaking off the last traces of their former unfreedom and of turning themselves from a nobility of service into a nobility of birth. In the course of time they frequently managed to get their service tenements converted into genuine fiefs, which they ran as landlords, with serfs bound to tenements doing labour services. *Ministeriales* who had risen in status sought to protect their lands in the traditional way; they built castles. One of the most prestigious royal *ministeriales* of Barbarossa's time, Werner of Bolanden, owned seventeen castles and had 1,100 knights in his service; the chronicler Gislebert of Mons, who reports this, calls him a 'very wise man'. Frederick made still greater use of *ministeriales* than his predecessors had done: the high nobility were preoccupied with their own territories and after the Concordat of Worms the bishops were no longer available as agents of government. In Italy, where absolute reliability was essential, the use of *ministeriales* was even more obvious. They were largely responsible for the administration of the crown lands. Together with the chancellor and notaries they formed the executive organ of royal rule and policy. They took over the court offices; only the so-called 'arch-offices' were left to the high nobility. Werner of Bolanden, a typical newly rich and powerful *ministerialis*, became steward of the Empire (*dapifer imperii*); the office of marshal was taken over by another *ministerialis* family, the Pappenheimer. It was especially in times of crisis that the *ministeriales* proved their value as supporters of the throne. After Barbarossa's death the group around Henry of Kalden-Pappenheim, imperial marshal (his family held the office until 1815) and Markward of Annweiler, imperial steward, were the chief supporters of the Staufer crown. In Germany as well *ministeriales* were the backbone of Staufer government. In the 'royal regions' there were numerous castles belonging to royal *ministeriales*, and in keeping the king's peace, a concern of Frederick's which found expression in a series of laws and edicts from 1152 onwards, *ministeriales* were employed, as in the Pleißenland in 1172, where we find a *ministerialis* as *iudex terrae*, 'judge of the region'.

New heights were reached in the development of both the rural and the urban economy, as well as in legislation and administration. The income from the *regalia*, the connections with Italy and its highly developed money economy, the continuing increase in the output of craft workers, which could not be traded in without money, and the foundation of towns and markets all led to a rapid increase in the demand for money. In the first half of the twelfth century there were around two dozen mints in the kingdom of Germany, of which only Goslar and Nürnberg were royal. Barbarossa's reign saw a rapid increase in the number of mints. For the period between *c.* 1140 and 1197 about 215 mints on German soil are known: 106 were ecclesiastical, 81 secular, and 28 royal. The output as well as the number of mints seems to have increased sharply. The annual output of the most productive German mint, that of the archbishop of Cologne, was around two million pennies, which meant about 3,000 kg. in silver. The fee the archbishop took for coining, about 7%, meant an annual income for him of some 200 kg. of silver. Once again *ministeriales* played a leading role in the expansion of the money economy, men who 'carried out administrative tasks for their lords either in the towns or in castles. During the Staufer period they were the real administrators in town or countryside; and in particular they controlled the trade in precious metals, the running of the mints, the exchange of currency, the policing of currency and markets, the control of weights and measures and the steps taken against forgers' (E. Nau).

Economic advance, growth in population, increased security of rights and possessions all meant, almost inevitably, a period of urban growth between the reigns of Conrad III and Henry VI. The town privileges which Barbarossa conferred were very diverse; for obvious reasons they were most numerous in the years between 1178 and 1184, a period when Frederick was trying to consolidate his rule in Germany after the Peace of Venice. His experiences with the communes of northern Italy had taught him what leagues of towns and burghers were capable of, and he was evidently not prepared to grant burghers freedoms which could endanger the crown. He was an opponent of sworn communes and of town leagues, but he was cautious even in the question of urban legal autonomy. The most normal form of privilege was a reduction in dues, or improvement in the legal position of the individual burghers, or permission to build walls. He reacted allergically to any displays of independence. When the burghers of Mainz refused to pay their army tax in 1158 Barbarossa had the city walls torn down, and when in 1160 they went so far as to murder their over-strict lord, Archbishop Arnold, Barbarossa held a court in 1163, cancelled all the city's privileges, and razed the city to the ground. One of the most characteristic features of Barbarossa's urban policy was the transformation of palaces into cities. No palace was visited more frequently by Barbarossa than Ulm, where he stayed no fewer than thirteen times and held six general assemblies; Ulm became a town in his time. The palaces of Gelnhausen, Kaiserslautern, Eger and Wimpfen were raised to the status of towns, as were Chemnitz, Altenburg and Zwickau in Thuringia. Barbarossa encouraged towns not so much for their own sake or because he felt particularly drawn to urban culture, but because they provided bases for his government.

It was not only kings who encouraged towns.

All who had the right and the opportunity, from king and princes to *ministeriales*, from bishops to monasteries, took part in the development. Schauenburger in the North, Askanier and Wettiner in the East, Babenberger in the South-East, Zähringer in the South-West, Welfs in the South and in the North were the dynasties who beside the king played the most important role in the founding of new towns. (E. Maschke)

Not only did the Welfs found new towns and give settlements within their territories town status, as with Ravensburg in the Welf heartland and Landsberg, there were also foundations associated with the violent displacement of other lords' rights, as at Lübeck or Munich or at Stade. Henry the Lion even tried to found towns in regions of colonization. The settlement at Schwerin among the Abodrites, where Germans had already begun to live, was raised to the status of a town. Henry evidently gave preference to places which were important in long-distance trade and exerted a pull of their own.

The peasant as well as the burgher became an instrument of territorialization. In the 'royal regions' Frederick neutralized the nobility, and controlled the lower classes without any intermediaries, assisted in this by his peace legislation. He installed free peasants organized in communities under an imperial advocate (*Freivogt*) on newly cleared settlements in his imperial and family lands. Alongside his own large-scale territory stretching from Suabia in the South-West to Thuringia in the North-East Frederick established a number of medium-sized territories, some formed by breaking off sections of the territories of the old tribal units. In 1156 the march of Austria was split off from the duchy of Bavaria and turned into a duchy, and the privilege of 1168, the 'Golden Freedom', gave the bishop of Würzburg ducal powers within his own diocese, although there was no tribal basis for them. In 1180 Styria was separated from Bavaria and became a duchy, and at about the same time the count of Andechs, margrave of Istria, was given the title of duke of Croatia, Dalmatia and Meran. Such lordships and others like the Zähringer duchy show the way in which the tribal duchy was ceasing to be of significance compared with the new territorial state.

NEW FORMS OF GOVERNMENT

Helmuth Plassner called the Germans a 'delayed nation'. The French and English had managed to achieve political unity by the time of the high Middle Ages, whereas the Germans only became a nation in the nineteenth century, and even that did not include all Germans. What caused the delay?

Frederick I had quickly succeeded in making good the losses caused to the Empire by the Investiture Contest. But his income from the *regalia* was uncertain, and there were no large-scale closed crown domains. The lack of a fixed residence was also detrimental to establishing a proper administration. Staufer kingship retained a number of archaic elements in its make-up. The *ministeriales* could have acted as a bureaucracy, but this would have required kings who devoted themselves over a longer period of time to the internal consolidation of the Empire.

The history of France and England shows a sharp contrast to the 'German path'. The Capetian king rounded off the crown domain just as a lesser noble might have done his family lands, and took care to see that the crown vassals did not cut him off from the lower classes. An administration with a fixed central point and a royal residence were built up, and the royal income was put on a reliable footing. England, in any case a very progressive country in administration and legislation, found its way to Magna Carta in spite of, or rather because of, being gradually cut off from its continental possessions. France and England became states; Germany became an agglomeration of petty states scarcely ruled by the king.

1 The fall of Henry the Lion and the so-called 'new estate of imperial princes'

Henry the Lion, a 'super-vassal' whose lordship was based on two tribal duchies, who had built up a compact and intensively organized territorial lordship, who conducted colonization in the East on a grand scale, and whose ostentatious court outshadowed Barbarossa's itinerant kingship, was in many ways exceptional. Frederick could not punish a quasi-regal duke like Henry by legal means for his refusal of help at Chiavenna in 1176 and his attempt at blackmail. The refusal cannot have entirely surprised Frederick, for Henry the Lion had not taken part in the Italian expeditions since 1161, had broken with Barbarossa's foreign policy, and had allied himself with a different group of European ruling houses. He had kept his promise to marry the English princess Mathilda, but the marriage between Frederick's weakly son of the same name and Mathilda's sister Eleonore had not come about. Barbarossa sought a *rapprochement* with the French king, while Henry II, Henry the Lion's father-in-law, spun a wide network of alliances to encircle Staufer and Capetians. Eleonore was betrothed to Alfonso VIII of Castile, another daughter married William II of Sicily, and English subsidies helped to rebuild Milan, Barbarossa's chief enemy in Italy.

Barbarossa let the princes who were antagonists and rivals of the double duke do his work for him. In 1168/9 he had ignored complaints from the princes about Henry's breaches of the law, but by 1177, when the Treaty of Venice provided for the reinstatement of Ulrich of Halberstadt, who had been driven out by Henry, the two were set on collision-course. The cause of Ulrich, a stubborn and unpleasant man, was taken up by the archbishop of Cologne, Philip of Heinsberg (1167–91). At the general assembly of Speyer in

November 1178, the first held by Barbarossa since his return from Italy, Philip brought charges against Henry, and Barbarossa allowed them to go forward. The course of Henry's trial, a typical political trial, can be reconstructed from the Gelnhausen diploma of April 1180, which survived in the original until its destruction in 1945; it set out the division of Henry's lordships and possessions. The charges brought by the princes in Speyer led Frederick to summon Henry to Worms in January 1179, following tribal law; Henry was accused of having infringed another man's rights and so of breach of the peace. As expected, Henry did not appear in Worms; the princes passed a provisional judgement that if Henry refused further summonses he should be outlawed. After Henry had ignored a number of citations outlawry was pronounced in June 1179. It may be that Henry underestimated the seriousness of his position, for he did not give way at a meeting between himself and Frederick, when the latter demanded payment of a fine of 5,000 marks of silver. The king now accused Henry on the basis of feudal law of not having attended his courts, which as Frederick's vassal he was obliged to do. Henry ignored this second trial as well; after a triple summons he was condemned for *contumacia*, contempt of court, and his peers the princes pronounced the loss of his imperial fiefs. One year after outlawry Henry fell automatically under the more severe form of outlawry, *Oberacht*, which meant not just the passive penalties of loss of honour and of legal rights but the active one of dispossession in the name of the Empire. Execution of the *Oberacht* began promptly in the summer of 1180. Frederick led an expedition to Saxony, and Henry was rapidly deserted by his allies. In August 1181 the ducal city of Lübeck capitulated and became an imperial city; impressed by the royal campaign – it was several decades since a German ruler had appeared in the North – Waldemar I of Denmark, the Abodrite prince Niklot of Werle and Bogislav of Pomerania came to Lübeck to receive their lands from Frederick as fiefs. Henry submitted at the general assembly of Erfurt in November 1181. He did not get the duchies and other imperial fiefs back, as they had already been disposed of, but did recover the allodial lands around Brunswick and Lüneburg. He was also compelled to leave the country for three years, and went to his father-in-law Henry II; he returned temporarily for the general asembly at Mainz in 1184 before coming back permanently in the following year.

The fall of Henry the Lion from the status of a 'super-vassal' to that of an outlawed man whom anyone might strike down with no penalty has produced an enormous literature. A nationalist school of historiography saw in Henry's fall a 'fatal blow' (J. Haller), for it interrupted the German eastern colonization and created the conditions for a Danish empire in the Baltic. And indeed Waldemar I's son Knut VI (1182–1202) refused to recognize German suzerainty in spite of a number of requests to do so. On the contrary the Danish king laid claim to Wagrien, Holstein, Stormarn and Polabia, and in a campaign of 1200–3 advanced as far as Hamburg, Lüneburg and Ratzeburg. In 1214 the German king conceded Transalbingia to him, but the battle of Bornhöved in 1227 restored the situation and the counts of Schauenburg to their lands. The territorial and constitutional consequences were more significant. Even before Henry fell under the *Oberacht* his imperial fiefs had been disposed of at the assembly of Gelnhausen in April 1180 and their distribution set out in the diploma recording the trial already mentioned. The duchy of Saxony was divided. The western part, covering the dioceses of Cologne and Paderborn, became a new duchy of Westfalia and came to the archbishop of Cologne, Philip of Heinsberg, an early representative of the new type of ecclesiastical prince with a strong interest in building up his own territorial state. Eastern Saxony went to Count Bernard of Anhalt, the younger son of Albert the Bear. Bavaria, finally, was given half a year later to the count palatine Otto of Wittelsbach, whose descendants continued to rule there until 1918.

The dividing of Bavaria and Saxony meant the disappearance of the last of the tribal duchies and the replacement of tribal by territorial organization in all parts of the kingdom. Feudal law became definitively the basis of royal government, and the kingdom was parcelled out into territories. Henry's deposition shows how significant feudal law had become, for the judgement was pronounced by Henry's peers for contempt of the royal court. It was not the cumbersome procedure under tribal law with *Acht* (oulawry) and *Oberacht* which brought about Henry's downfall, but the exclusion of Henry from the circle of his peers and the redistribution of his fiefs; the imperial princes denied him their support. In these events we can already see the 'new estate of imperial princes' in action as a defined and closed group; the term was coined by the constitutional historian Julius von Ficker (1826–1902) to distinguish this group based on feudal law from the older estate of imperial princes based on office-holding. Admittedly the fiefs returned to the king as the suzerain, but he did not retain them, but redistributed them, even if in a divided form. It was long thought that there was a legal obligation on the king to regrant fiefs (*Leihezwang*); though this belief probably rests on a misreading of Eike von Repgow's *Sachsenspiegel*, there was certainly a custom of regranting fiefs, and this was often backed up by private arrangements. The imperial principalities were regarded as '*membra imperii*, that is, as the limbs which made up the body of the Empire and were an essential part of it' (H.-G. Krause). The imperial principalities took over a number of the functions previously associated with the office of king, and this became their distinguishing feature. These crown vassals received their fiefs from the king, symbolized either by a banner (for secular princes) or by a sceptre (for ecclesiastical princes). It was this which determined their status, not ducal rank or the size of their possessions. The vassals of these imperial princes, counts and free lords, could not hope to become direct vassals of the king on the death of a crown vassal; a new crown vassal had to be found, and they were permanently mediatized. This hierarchical ordering of estates was expressed in the so-called *Heerschild*, developed by the end of the twelfth century and defined fully in the law-codes of the thirteenth. The *Heerschild* ranking defines whose vassal one may be, without 'lowering' one's 'shield' (*Schild*). At the top of the pyramid, bearer of the first *Heerschild*, stands the king, who is no one's vassal and can only give fiefs, not receive them. Below him come the imperial princes; they are the king's vassals but their shield is divided, with the ecclesiastical princes taking the second and the secular ones the third, thus enabling secular princes to hold fiefs from ecclesiastical ones. The fourth *Heerschild* was made up of counts and free lords; the bottommost, consisting of men who could only receive fiefs, not grant them, included the *ministeriales*, who were thus finally emancipated from their servile status and incorporated into the feudal hierarchy.

2 Kingship and feudalism in France and England

France and England also experienced far-reaching constitutional changes in the second half of the twelfth century, which increased the differences between them and Germany. The French kings had been able to win back the crown domain in the Île-de-France and consolidate it, but Louis VII was faced with the danger of being swallowed up by his most powerful vassal, the English king. It was the achievement of Philip Augustus (1180–1223) to have extracted the French monarchy from 'Angevin encirclement'. After binding the French nobility to him by insisting on their duty to him as their liege lord, he went over to the attack from 1187. In 1202 he had

John's fiefs pronounced forfeit by a judgement of his court, and drove him out of most of his continental possessions. Philip kept the confiscated fiefs and thus greatly extended his lordship.

The Anglo-Norman kingdom possessed at the beginning of the reign of Henry II a huge advantage, both in its size and in the degree of its organization. Henry proceeded step by step to turn England into a country under a unified system of law. The most important development was the introduction of itinerant justices. These toured the country and made use of the jury of presentation, i.e. a sworn jury which accused all those suspected of crimes. Those accused had to prove their innocence, if necessary by an ordeal; if they could not do this, even if there was no positive proof against them, they normally had to leave the country. Henry II thus was able to eliminate undesirable elements from his kingdom. In the second half of his reign, however, Henry II suffered a number of setbacks. The murder of Thomas à Becket weakened his moral position. Becket's friends spread propaganda hostile to the king throughout Europe, and Alexander III canonized Thomas with unusual speed, at the same time reserving the right of canonization of saints to the pope. The wave of feeling against Henry was exploited by his sons and his independent-minded wife Eleanor for a dangerous rebellion, which he suppressed only with difficulty. And at the end of his reign Henry II experienced the beginnings of Philip's campaign to drive him out of his continental possessions.

Henry II's successor was his son Richard I the Lionheart, the king of Ivanhoe and Robin Hood, an itinerant knight and the 'personification of his age', in Stubbs's phrase. He spent precisely seven months in England during the ten years of his reign. He was the ideal knight of chivalry, a terror to the Muslims in the Holy Land, who gave him the name of 'the pale death of the Saracens', but he was also an ineffectual politician, who could see no further than the chivalric code. His death, characteristically, occurred while he was besieging a small though not unimportant castle near Limoges in 1199. His successor was his younger brother John, who had been nicknamed 'Lackland' by his father. In contrast to Richard, John was a talented administrator; it is in his reign that the long series of rolls, the administrative archives of the crown, begin. John moved ruthlessly against the barons. He increased scutage, the sum to be paid by those who did not fulfil their military obligations in person, and other feudal incidents. Whereas in Germany it was the vassal who chose between service or payment, in England it lay in the king's discretion whether he took scutage or military service.

Through high scutage-payments John forced many barons to renounce their fiefs; this group of dissident nobles was swelled by the failure of John's continental campaigns. Their growing resistance forced John to issue the most famous document of English constitutional history, Magna Carta, in 1215; the history of England, in Stubbs's judgement, was from now on a 'commentary of Magna Carta'. It should be seen not so much as the origins of modern parliamentarism as a document of feudal law. This is clear from the prehistory of the document. In the autumn of 1214 the barons had sworn to renounce their fealty to John, and after a deadline ignored by the king they proceeded with *diffidatio*, a formal renunciation of the feudal tie; the barons had exercised their right of resistance. The negotiations which followed led to the issuing of Magna Carta on 19 June 1215. It contained general provisions about law and order, but also specific ones regulating such feudal incidents as heriots and wardships. A particularly important provision for the future was the clause which made the granting of aids dependent on the *commune consilium regni*, the king's feudal court, the functions of which were later to be absorbed by parliament. The English barons displayed a solidarity which did not and could not exist in Germany. In England there were far more secular than ecclesiastical barons – the ratio was about four to one – whereas in Germany the ratio was about six to one the other way: the new estate of imperial princes comprised about ninety ecclesiastics and only sixteen lay princes, a figure which later rose to thirty. Consequently the German princes could not be affected by a king's arbitrary use of feudal powers in the same way as the English magnates were.

3 International alliances and the Third Crusade

Following the Peace of Venice and the fall of Henry the Lion Barbarossa stood at the height of his power. This found its expression in the assembly held in Mainz at Whitsun 1184, at which his two eldest sons, Henry VI and Frederick, duke of Suabia, were made knights. Contemporaries were greatly impressed by the pomp and size of the assembly; the sources mention 40,000, even as many as 70,000 participants. Poets like Henry of Veldeke and Guiot de Provins sang of the feast; no assembly, says Henry in his *Eneid* of the marriage between Aeneas and Lavinia, was so magnificent, save for the one at which Frederick knighted his two sons. The feast was accompanied by tournaments, dances and music, the expression of a new courtly and chivalrous culture in which the lay element found a more self-confident expression than it had previously done.

Frederick was indeed in a favourable position at Whitsun 1184. The six-year armistice with the Lombards made in 1177 had been turned into the Peace of Constance of 25 June 1183. Frederick formally renounced the execution of the Roncaglian decrees and allowed the cities to keep the *regalia*, but he had managed to preserve most of his governmental powers. For this renunciation the cities had to pay him 15,000 marks of silver initially, and an annual commutation-payment of 2,000 marks. All members of the Lombard league had to swear an oath of loyalty to Frederick and to agree to provide *fodrum*, hospitality for the king and his entourage, so that the provisioning of Italian expeditions was assured. There was even agreement on the league's fortress of Alessandria; it submitted, and, unharmed, was renamed Caesarea. The ownership of the Mathildine lands remained disputed. Frederick had been granted usufruct for fifteen years in Venice in 1177; he now made the proposal that his possession should be made permanent and that in return the pope should receive a tenth of the imperial incomes in Italy. The pope refused, for acceptance would have meant that Rome would have become dependent on the Empire. In spite of this setback, Frederick was able steadily to improve the extent and intensity of imperial rule in Italy. The imperial lands, for example, were reorganized under the control of an imperial legate – the first was Christian of Buch, while later the post was entrusted to imperial *ministeriales*. In 1184 Barbarossa set off for his sixth and last Italian expedition. In Verona he met Pope Lucius III, the aged Bernadine successor of Alexander III. It must remain uncertain whether Frederick still wanted an agreement with the *Curia* on the Mathildine lands; what he did was to make a radical change of policy to seek a marriage alliance with the Normans. The German king Henry VI was betrothed in 1184 to Constance, daughter of Roger II and sister of William I (†1166), who was the aunt of the reigning king of Sicily, William II, himself married to Joanna, a daughter of Henry II of England. It could not have been foreseen in 1186 when the marriage took place that it would have such far-reaching consequences; quite unexpectedly William's marriage remained childless and William was outlived by his older aunt, who was thirty-two at the time of her marriage.

The papacy was bound to see the alliance between Normans and Staufer as a great danger, and it was all the more a sensitive issue as the new pope, Urban III (1185–7) was a Milanese by birth and had

experienced the destruction of his native city in 1162. He took up a
public stand against Frederick, and denied his right to the *spolia* and
regalia of vacant abbeys and bishoprics. The Staufer exerted counter-
pressure; Henry VI occupied the papal state. But Urban was able to
ally himself with one of the most powerful imperial princes, the
archbishop of Cologne, Philip of Heinsberg, who had been one of
the principal beneficiaries of the fall of Henry the Lion but since then
had come more and more into opposition to Barbarossa. Barbarossa
regarded this alliance as so dangerous that he returned to Germany
and made a counter-alliance with the French king Philip Augustus.
Philip had his own interest in a pact with Barbarossa, for he wanted
allies against the English king, who in his turn supported the
archbishop of Cologne. Faced by superior forces Philip of Cologne
had to submit; a treaty was negotiated with Urban's successor
Clement (1187–91) in April 1189, which put off a decision about the
Mathildine lands, but conceded the rights of *spolia* and *regalia* to
Frederick.

The speed with which the compromise was reached may seem
surprising, but the whole of the western world had been shaken by a
catastrophe. Saladin (1169–93) had inflicted an annihilating defeat on
the combined crusading armies at the battle of Hattin in July 1187,
and had taken Jerusalem in December. By 1188 the Frankish
possessions in the Holy Land consisted only of a few fortresses, like
Krak des Chevaliers, the great castle of the Templars, and the cities
of Tyre, Tripoli, Tortosa and Antioch with their surrounding
territories. Heathen victories were, according to the Christian view
of things, a proof that men had been living sinfully, and at the next
assembly, held at Mainz in March 1188, there was much discussion
of the obligations of the emperor and of the Christian knight. At the
assembly of Jesus Christ, as it became known, Frederick I and many
knights took the cross, a decision celebrated in poetry by Friedrich
of Hausen, who was to die on the crusade, and by Hartmann of Aue.
Barbarossa had set an effective example. Although at odds with each
other, the kings of England and France took the cross and concluded
an armistice, though Richard Lionheart, who had succeeded his
father in 1189, and Philip Augustus did not set out until the middle
of 1190. By this time the fate of the German crusading army had
already been decided. The affairs of the Empire were dealt with at an
assembly at Goslar in 1188 before Frederick set out. The main
danger was Henry the Lion, for Frederick's son Frederick, duke of
Suabia had taken the cross along with his father, and only the young
king Henry VI, aged twenty-four, remained in Germany. Henry the

Lion was given the choice of taking part in the crusade or going into exile for three years. He chose exile. In May 1189 the army set out from Regensburg. Chroniclers report an army of 100,000, which is certainly an exaggeration, but it was probably as large as 12,000–15,000, including 3,000 mounted knights. They were put to the test on the way, for the new Byzantine emperor, Isaac Angelos (1185–95) had broken with the pro-western policies of his Comnenan predecessors and sought a reconciliation with Saladin. Isaac treated the crusaders with hostility, and Frederick ordered the storming and plundering of Adrianople. The Turks were impressed by the strength of the army, which followed the legendary route taken by Godfrey of Bouillon straight across Asia Minor. Saladin evacuated the frontier fortifications. But Frederick drowned in the Saleph, a small river in Cicilia, on 10 June 1190, probably while trying to take a short cut. An Arab historian wrote: 'Had not Allah in his mercy showed the Muslims his goodness by bringing the king of the Germans to his end just as he was on the point of conquering Syria, one would have to write today: Syria and Egypt once belonged to Islam.' The author of the Royal Chronicle of Cologne was also overwhelmed by the news: 'at this point and on this news our pen fails us and our speech is turned to silence'.

The superiority of the German army depended on its strict organization and on a well-planned commissariat. Both now collapsed. The crusaders were disheartened and whole contingents allowed themselves to be taken captive by the Muslims without a struggle. Some princes and their contingent turned back for home. The young duke Frederick, whose authority was not great enough to hold the army together, went on and joined up with the English and French crusaders. Philip and Richard had come by ship from Sicily, where they had paused for half a year. *En route* Richard took Cyprus from the Byzantines; later he set up the failed king of Jerusalem, Guy of Lusignan, as king there. Philip and Richard joined forces to lay siege to Acre; Frederick of Suabia joined them here, but died of a fever before the city fell. Philip returned to France in 1191; Richard made three attempts to advance on Jerusalem, all of which failed. Nothing was achieved in spite of great bravery and much bloodshed. In the end a three-year armistice was negotiated with Saladin in 1192. The status quo was to be respected; during the three years the Christians were to be allowed to visit the holy places as pilgrims. In the same year Richard Lionheart left the Holy Land; the Third Crusade had definitely ended in failure.

4 *The chivalric ethos of the Staufer period*

Medieval thinkers saw society as divided into estates (*ordines*), which were regarded as being of divine creation. Christian society was divided into two groups, clergy and laity, or into three classes: 'those who pray, those who fight and those who plough' (*oratores, pugnatores, agricultores*). This phrase was the fruit of much theological discussion, and it continued to be used in spite of the contradictions between it and reality. The estate a man assigns himself to does not necessarily say anything about his social and legal status, especially as an estate can come to define a whole epoch, not in the sense used by historical materialism, but in the self-understanding of the epoch. Knight, noble or plebeian could say *civis Romanus sum* in ancient Rome, and the bourgeois of the nineteenth century could include the king. The knight was the ideal of the high Middle Ages, so much so that many literary historians have claimed that chivalry and knighthood did not reflect social reality but literary tradition.

The knight (*Ritter*) was originally defined by his function: he was a rider, a warrior on horseback. The expense necessary for his armament separated him from the mass of fighting men. His fighting value was high, and the high Middle Ages cited the proverb 'A hundred horses are worth a thousand foot-soldiers.' To fight on horseback was always expensive: in the eighth century a full set of equipment for a cavalryman was equivalent in value to forty-five cows or fifteen mares. In the eleventh century a horse was worth five to ten oxen, and a mail-shirt anything from twenty to a hundred. When in 1100 Count Robert of Flanders undertook to provide 500 knights, it was assumed that each would have three horses, and this seems to have been normal for the Staufer period: one to travel on, one to fight on and one to carry baggage. It has been calculated that an estate would have to be a minimum of 400 acres in order to support a knight who was ready to fight at all times. From the second half of the eleventh century onwards the knight was a clearly defined figure. In combat he sat on a heavy box-like saddle, with his feet in stirrups (the advance of which in the eleventh century has even been suggested as one of the causes of the 'second age of feudalism'); he was protected by a shirt of linked iron rings, a helmet and a shield which tapered to a point at the bottom. Only strong and well-rested horses could move under such a weight, which was why the fighting horse was spared during the march and led by the hand (hence *dextrarius*, destrier). Individuals were not recognizable in the all-enveloping armour, so that coats-of-arms, plumes and pennants had to be worn. The first noble who is known for certain to have borne arms was Geoffrey V of Anjou on being dubbed knight by Henry I of England in 1127, a ceremony which corresponded to the conferring of the knight's sword or belt in Germany. The Angevin bore a sprig of broom (*Planta genistae*, hence 'Plantagenet'). The weapons of the knight were sword and spear at first, later the heavy lance; distance weapons like the bow were regarded as dishonourable. War generally followed fixed rules; just putting on armour took a considerable time, so that the time and place of battle were generally agreed in advance. It was neither usual nor honourable to set ambushes. Combat was a combat between groups, occasionally between individuals as in a tournament. The first known tournament in Germany was in 1127 outside Würzburg, held by the Staufer brothers Duke Frederick II the One-Eyed of Suabia and his brother the antiking Conrad. Tournaments were not without danger; sixteen knights died in tournaments in Saxony alone in the single year 1175. The knight in his defensive feudal castle needed large-scale logistic support; it has been calculated from the number of castles built between the mid eleventh century and 1300 that the class which lived a knightly life-style cannot have made up more than 1% of the population as a whole.

The era of the knight, or the *miles*, began in France with its flourishing feudalism. The *ordo militiae*, the warrior caste, became a general notion that covered groups very different in their legal and social standing. The *ministeriales* who functioned as knights were at first distinguished from the *Edelfreie*, but this distinction soon became blurred. They all belonged to the *ordo militaris*, even if they were still distinguished, for example in a constitution of Lothar III's, as *ordo equester maior et minor*. *Ministeriales, Edelfreie*, counts and dukes were all referred to as knights, as *milites*. The proportion of *ministeriales* was naturally very high. 'Since *ministeriales* were unfree, they were, even in the twelfth century, still frequently made over as gifts. A lord could give away as many as twenty, fifty or even a hundred *ministeriales* at a time to another lord or to a church. It is therefore probably not an underestimate when we put the ratio between older noble families and *ministerialis* families at 1:50 or even 1:100' (J. Fleckenstein). Frederick I reserved judicial duels to knights of knightly origins, and it was decreed in 1186 that the sons of priests, deacons and peasants could not become knights. A few decades later knightly birth was the normal prerequisite for membership of the knightly class.

An essential feature of the western knight was his religion: Bernard of Clairvaux praised the role of the *miles Christianus* as one through which a man could achieve salvation. The purest form of such engagement for the Christian faith was found in the knightly orders, the Hospitallers, the Templars, and the Teutonic Knights. The Hospitallers were in their origins primarily devoted to charitable works; they had been active in the care of the sick in Jerusalem from the time of Gregory I (†604), and only in the mid twelfth century did they take up service with the sword, in contrast to their rivals, the Templars, with whom they were frequently at odds, mostly over the possession of fiefs. The latter order was from the time of its foundation intended to protect pilgrims in the Holy Land. It took its name from the place of residence of the Grand Master of the order, on the site of the temple of Solomon in Jerusalem. Hospitallers and Templars were recruited almost exclusively from the French nobility; in 1190 a German community of Hospitallers was founded in the camp before Acre, and in 1198 this became the knightly order of S. Mariae Theutonicorum in Jerusalem, following the Rule of the Templars.

Along with the practice of arms and charity went the courtly honouring of women, found first at the beginning of the twelfth century in the songs of the troubadours. The earliest troubadour we know of in some detail was Duke William IX of Aquitaine, the grandfather of the loose-living and politically talented Eleanor of Aquitaine, and the court of Aquitaine was one of the first centres at which a knightly ceremonial was developed. From here it was transmitted via the court of the dukes of Burgundy to that of the counts of Champagne. Frederick's Burgundian wife Beatrix certainly played a large part in turning the itinerant Staufer court into a centre of chivalric culture. Beatrix had literary tastes, and in the course of her thirty years of married life (she died in her early forties) evidently took an active part in the cultural life of the court, which she generally accompanied even on the exhausting Italian expeditions. Barbarossa allowed her free reign, so that he came to acquire the reputation of being a man under his wife's thumb, a *vir uxoratus*. A chivalric court culture also flourished in the Welf residence at Brunswick, where Henry the Lion was married to a Plantagenet princess, and at the courts of the dukes of Austria and landgraves of Thuringia. The troubadour, in Germany the *Minnesänger*, sings the praises of the beautiful women, the lady who belongs to another and does not return his love. The distant lady became the object of a kind of cult, so that the secular courtly poetry praising her uses much the same language as that found in the religious poetry honouring the Virgin Mary.

Knightly culture was full of ritual, and scholars have tried to establish the existence of a code of honour. Some, like G. Ehrismann, have thought they could trace a 'system of knightly virtues' derived ultimately from a literary tradition going back to Cicero, while others, like Ernst Curtius, have denied that there was ever a formally defined code of conduct. Certainly there was a great increase in the number of treatises written on sins and virtues in the high Middle Ages, which made use of a number of general notions and terms connected with one another, even if the question of whether this consisted a system is left undecided. The knight was expected to show *mâze* (*moderatio* or *temperantia* in Latin), moderation, and *staete* (*fides* in Latin), constancy of purpose; the two are often summed up in the word *zucht*, translated in Latin by the complex word *virtus*, virtue.

HENRY VI AND THE SHIFT IN THE EMPIRE'S CENTRE OF GRAVITY

The young king Henry VI who had stayed behind in Germany was of a quite different stamp from Barbarossa, although it is reported that he was Frederick's favourite son. They differed even in their appearance: his contemporary Burchard of Ursperg says of him that 'his face was pleasant but very thin, and he was only moderately tall and with a slight and frail physique'. A Byzantine author describes him as a Cassius: 'He was always active, so that he thought it enough when he satisfied his bodily needs late in the evening, a man who despised all self-indulgence, pale and mediative.' Highly educated, eloquent, he spoke Latin fluently and was at home in Roman and in canon law. Three vernacular love-songs are attributed to him, and a number of important manuscripts of Middle High German lyric poetry have miniatures of him at their head. He was a failure as a warrior, but a politician and planner of high quality, with a bad reputation for being merciless when it suited his purposes. In Karl Hampe's judgement, no German ruler 'possessed to such a high degree the ability to seize political opportunities and calculate the means necessary as Henry VI'.

1 *The German kingdom and the Sicilian inheritance*

The crusading army had set out in May 1189; in October 1189 Henry the Lion broke his word, returned to Germany and destroyed

Bardowick, the market settlement he had established as duke. Before Henry VI could move against him a new situation arose: William II of Sicily died childless on 18 November 1189, aged just over thirty. His heir was his aunt Constance, Henry's wife, and Henry immediately claimed the inheritance. But there was a national and anti-Staufer party in Sicily which raised a bastard half-brother of William II, Tancred of Lecce, to the throne, in agreement with the *Curia*. In order to free his rear for an Italian expedition Henry VI made a peace settlement with Henry the Lion: Henry received part of the royal revenues but had to hand over his sons Henry of Brunswick and Lothar as hostages. The news of Barbarossa's death further delayed Henry's departure, and in the mean time Tancred's position grew stronger. Richard Lionheart, the brother-in-law of William II, made an alliance with him, and he could also expect support from his suzerain, the pope. It was a misfortune for Henry that Clement III, with whom he had negotiated an imperial coronation, died while he was on his way to Rome. Clement's successor Celestine III (1191–8), flexible and imaginative in spite of his eighty-five years and a tough negotiator, delayed the coronation, so that Henry was forced into inactivity. In order to win the pope over Henry handed over the town of Tusculum, which was at odds with the pope and occupied by an imperial garrison, to the pope and the Romans. Celestine was consecrated pope on Easter Sunday (14 April 1191) and on the following day Henry VI was crowned emperor; shortly afterwards Tusculum was evacuated and destroyed. On the next stage of the march southwards the German army was attacked by a typhus epidemic, and Henry himself fell dangerously ill. He had to turn back, and his wife Constance fell into the hands of the rebellious town of Salerno. The disaster was complete when Celestine III came off the fence, recognized Tancred, and invested him with the kingdom of Sicily. Henry of Brunswick, the oldest son of Henry the Lion, had left the army at Naples and fought his way back to Germany, where the rumour spread that the young emperor had died; Henry came under suspicion of having organized a murder. After a disputed election to the bishopric of Liège he had pushed through his protégé, while the papal candidate was murdered by episcopal *ministeriales*: a second Becket. By the end of 1192 there was a rapidly growing alliance against Henry. The princes of the lower Rhine and the archbishops of Mainz, Trier and Cologne joined Tancred of Lecce, Celestine, Richard Lionheart and his brother-in-law Henry the Lion. Henry must have been thankful for the support he received from the French king Philip II, and a happy accident, which was not entirely unplanned, altered the situation dramatically. Henry VI and Philip II had arranged to capture Richard, who had insulted Philip at the siege of Acre, even though returning crusaders were supposed to enjoy safe conduct. Richard was recognized near Vienna in December 1192 and held prisoner by Duke Leopold V of Austria, whose banner he had had hauled down after the storming of Acre in the castle of Dürnstein in the Wachau valley. A show trial was staged to justify the action against Richard and the claim for ransom to the world; Henry VI and Leopold V agreed to divide the ransom of 100,000 marks of silver between them. Henry now proceeded to blackmail Richard mercilessly with the threat of handing him over to his suzerain, the French king. Richard was forced to agree to support Henry against Tancred of Lecce, his own ally, and when the ransom payment was further delayed Henry raised the price to 150,000 marks. Richard's position was desperate, for neither Philip II nor John had any interest in having him released. Henry increased his demands still further: Richard had to promise to hold the kingdom of England from Henry as a fief and pay an annual rent for it of 5,000 pounds of silver. Richard was only released after the ransom, some 35,000 kg. of silver, had been paid in full in February 1194.

Faced with this situation, the opposition of Saxon, Welf and lower Rhenish princes began to break up. An unexpected love-match brought a reconciliation between Welfs and Staufer in 1194. Henry the Lion's eldest son married Agnes, the daughter of Conrad, count palatine of the Rhine and a half-brother of Barbarossa, against the opposition of Henry VI. Agnes had already been promised as a bride to Philip Augustus, and not only that but her marriage meant that the Pfalz passed into Welf hands. Peace was agreed with Henry the Lion in March 1194; a year later he died at the age of sixty-six. Immediately after reaching an agreement with the Welfs Henry VI set out for Italy and Sicily, for the situation had altered in his favour there as well: Tancred of Lecce had died in February 1194. Henry reached the straits of Messina, where he was met by a combined Pisan and Genoese fleet under the command of the imperial steward Markward of Annweiler, which ferried the troops across. Palermo was soon taken, and on Christmas Day 1194 Henry had himself crowned king of Sicily in the cathedral of Palermo. He had left his wife Constance in Jesi in the March of Ancona, where she gave birth to a son on 26 December 1194: he was originally called Constantine, but was later renamed Frederick Roger after his two grandfathers, kings of Germany and of Norman Sicily. A great assembly at Bari in March 1195 settled the future administration: Constance was made regent, and the Suabian *Edelfreier* Conrad of Urslingen was appointed governor. Henry's youngest brother Philip, who had originally been destined for an ecclesiastical career (he had been provost of Aachen and bishop-elect of Würzburg before becoming a layman again in 1193), was made duke of Tuscany and administrator of the Mathildine lands. In a general reorganization, imperial *ministeriales* were appointed to important positions in a new official hierarchy, based on and incorporating the arrangements already existing in Norman Sicily. Henry of Kalden-Pappenheim appeared as imperial marshal, Henry of Lautern as butler; Markward of Annweiler received the March of Ancona and the duchy of Romagna as hereditary fiefs. A large number of imperial *ministeriales* took over the confiscated fiefs of rebellious or exiled Norman nobles. The general position had improved so much for the better that Henry could turn to the role of 'defender of the church' which his father had taken up with such tragic results. The moment also seemed right for the reconquest of Jerusalem: the truce arranged in 1192 expired in 1195, and after Saladin's death in 1193 the Muslims were plagued with succession struggles.

2 Plans and beginnings

Henry VI was a reserved man; he did not reveal his aims or discuss them with anybody, and contemporary historiography does not have much to say about his intentions. What he began was impressive, but because of his early death it remained only a beginning.

The first thing that stands out is his consistent policy of developing 'royal regions'. The union of the family lands of the Staufer with the rich Welf inheritance had made the duchy of Suabia immensely powerful. When Henry's younger brother Conrad of Suabia died in 1196 (he succeeded Frederick V in 1191), the youngest brother Philip, duke of Tuscany, immediately took over the office. In central Germany Henry was also able to build up his lordship by retaining escheated fiefs. The escheated march of Meißen was joined with the *Land* of Pleißen to form a royal territory, and Henry even attempted to retain the county of Thuringia in his own hands. A continuation of this process would have helped greatly to stabilize the basis of royal power, as it did in France.

Internally, Henry built up the administration of the Empire and consolidated royal power; externally, he tried to give the imperial title a new meaning. It is an open question whether the first Italian expedition was not already the expression of a new imperial policy and not just the claiming of an inheritance (which is D. Clementi's view). To talk of plans for world domination would be to give Henry's intentions too much ideological content: he was interested in concrete, feudally expressed dependence, even though he may also have been influenced by the eschatological ideas of the Cistercian abbot Joachim of Fiore (†1202), who saw the approach of the 'age of John' (i.e. the author of the Apocalypse), the era of the Holy Spirit, in which there was a place for the Last Emperor. In 1194 Richard Lionheart had recognized German suzerainty and agreed to pay an annual rent of 5,000 pounds of silver. Henry encouraged the warlike Richard to attack Philip II, obviously with the idea that a threatened king of France would also have to look to him for protection. Henry laid claim to Tunis and Tripoli, once conquered by Roger II, and the Almohad Caliph Al-Mansur, himself under pressure from the fanatical Almoravids, agreed to pay tribute. But it was the eastern Mediterranean that his power was most greatly extended. In capturing Palermo he had captured Tancred's widowed daughter-in-law Irene, the daughter of the Byzantine emperor Isaac II Angelos. When shortly afterwards Isaac was deposed by his younger brother Alexis III and Irene had been married to Henry's youngest brother Philip, duke of Suabia and subsequently king of Germany, Henry was able to proceed against the usurper as the representative of the rights of Philip and Irene, and Alexios, who was also faced with bitter internal opposition, agreed to a huge tribute-payment of sixteen hundredweight of gold, which he collected by imposing a new tax, the *Alamanikon*. Such successful brutality made an impression on others. The Byzantine vassal King Leo II of Cilicia-Armenia and King Amalric of Cyprus both offered Henry their kingdoms as fiefs; a crusade was all that was needed to set the seal on Henry's success. But before that it was necessary to settle the affairs of the Empire.

Henry's plan was to unite the kingdoms of Germany and Sicily in a hereditary kingdom, that is, to make the kingdom of Germany as hereditary as the Sicilian kingdom already was. At the assembly at Mainz in February 1196 Henry VI made an offer to the German princes: if they would recognize the heritability of the crown, he in turn would concede that imperial fiefs might be inherited in the female as well as the male line and, where there were no direct heirs, even by collaterals. The ecclesiastical princes were offered a renunciation of the right of *spolia*, which Barbarossa in particular had exercised rigorously. These concessions were individually and in themselves not new, as a comparison with the *Privilegium minus* of 1156 shows; what was new was their being coupled together and made available not as individual privilege but for the whole of the estate of imperial princes. The plan had good chances of success: a majority of the princes spoke in favour of accepting the proposals at the assembly of Würzburg in April 1196. Henry's main opponent was Adolf of Altena, archbishop of Cologne, a member of the anti-Staufer opposition group from the lower Rhine, who would have had to renounce for himself and his successors his chance of influencing subsequent royal elections. Henry VI treated the acceptance of the plan by the princes as a certainty, and began negotiations with the *Curia*; the pope would have to agree not only in his capacity as suzerain of the Norman kingdom of Sicily but also because he would have to crown the hereditary kings of Germany emperors. In the summer of 1196 Henry negotiated with Celestine III, then ninety years old but not easy to bargain with. It was in the course of these negotiations that Henry made what has been called his 'final offer to the *Curia*'. It is recorded only in an anecdote told by the Welsh cleric Giraldus Cambrensis (†1223), but this is generally held to be plausible. Henry offered the pope and the *Curia* the best prebend in each bishopric in the Empire, and held out the prospect of an extension of this arrangement to the whole of the western church. In return he required the pope to renounce all territorial claims outside the papal states, most of which he was still occupying. Celestine III turned the offer down; he would obviously have placed himself in Henry's hands had he accepted. Resistance also grew in Germany; a meeting of the princes rejected the plan for a hereditary kingdom in October 1196. However, they did agree to elect Henry VI's two-year-old son Frederick II as German king, something they had previously refused to do.

The plan for a hereditary kingdom had not been realized, but at least Henry had cleared the decks. He gave orders to the crusaders to collect in the cities of southern Italy. The transport arrangements were thoroughly planned, and all the maritime cities of Italy were made to supply shipping. An advance troop set out under Archbishop Conrad of Mainz; the main army was under the leadership of the chancellor and bishop of Hildesheim, Conrad of Querfurt, and of the imperial marshal Henry of Kalden. Just before the expedition was due to set off there was a rebellion of disgruntled Norman nobles. Henry had left the Sicilian administration, the most effective in Europe, undisturbed, but the fiefs of rebellious Normans had been confiscated and given to imperial *ministeriales*. The Normans were thus under constant control and scrutiny, and besides this they had to put up with high taxes and a review of their privileges. The conspiracy was said to have involved the pope and even Constance herself. Henry VI reacted firmly, though it is only an atrocity tale that he had all the members of Tancred of Lecce's family, who had previously been deported to Germany, murdered. Part of the army was already *en route* when Henry died of a typhus-like fever in Messina on 28 September 1197. On his death-bed he had made a testament which appointed Markward of Annweiler as regent; Constance and Frederick were to do homage to the pope for Sicily and be prepared to make concessions; they were also to give up the occupation of the Mathildine lands and the papal state. But subsequent developments were to show that the whole conception depended on Henry's own personality, on his imaginativeness and decisiveness. Even contemporaries felt that his death was a turning-point: 'his death should be mourned by the Germans and all the peoples of Germania for all time', wrote Otto of St Blasien. Shortly before his death a rumour went round Germany that Henry had had princes who planned to murder him executed, that he was constantly being thwarted in his intentions, that he was in danger of his life, 'and the empress was behind it all'. In the Moselle region it was reported that several people had seen a ghostly rider on a black horse: 'they shrank back, but he rode boldly up to them and said that they should not fear for themselves. He said he was the old king Dietrich of Bern, and had come to announce that the whole Roman Empire would soon suffer misery and catastrophes of many kinds.'

Henry VI's death was a catastrophe for Germany. The young king had initiated new policies, had given the imperial administration new structures, had found a new power-base for the emperorship in the Norman kingdom of Sicily, whose institutions served as models for the imperial government in Germany, and given it new perspectives through his hegemonial policy; he was in the process of stabilizing the monarchy by making it hereditary, and of turning the pope into a pensioner of the imperial church. His death revealed the weakness of the Staufer dynasty: Beatrix had borne Frederick Barbarossa at least ten children, including eight sons, but only Henry VI continued the family in the male line with a single son, who was marooned in distant Apulia. A disputed succession was not to be avoided, for the Welfs and a hierocratic papacy stood ready to intervene.

BIBLIOGRAPHY

The present work in the first edition of 1978 had a bibliography of some twenty-five pages, which was expanded in the second edition of 1983 by a further thirteen pages. It has not seemed useful to reproduce this here, for two reasons. First, the works listed on German history are almost all in German: most of those who will make use of the present translation are unlikely either to find such works in the libraries available to them or to be able to read them if they do. Second, much of the bibliography consists of titles on the history of countries other than Germany, notably England and France; and in these areas English-speaking readers are already well served by other publications. What is offered here instead is a bibliography of works in English on German and imperial history during the period. It is in consequence much shorter; on many of the issues dealt with in the book either there is nothing in English, or what there is is so out of date that it can no longer be recommended.

Timothy Reuter

ABBREVIATIONS

EHR	*English historical review*
Land and work	M. Block, *Land and work in medieval Europe* (London 1967)
Leyser, *Medieval Germany*	K. J. Leyser, *Medieval Germany and its neighbours, 900–1250* (London 1982)
Medieval Germany	G. Barraclough, *Medieval Germany 911–1250*, vol. 2 (Oxford 1938)

Medieval nobility	T. Reuter (ed.), *The medieval nobility: Studies on the ruling classes of France and Germany from the sixth to the twelfth centuries* (Amsterdam 1978)
Pullan	B. Pullan, *Sources for the history of mediaeval Europe: from the mid-eighth to the mid-thirteenth century* (2nd edition, Oxford 1980)
Renaissance and renewal	*Renaissance and renewal in the twelfth century*, ed. R. L. Benson and G. Constable (Oxford 1982)
Tierney	B. Tierney, *The crisis of church and state, 1050–1300* (Englewood Cliffs, NJ, 1964)

GENERAL SURVEYS

K. Hampe, *Germany under the Salian and Hohenstaufen emperors*, translated by R. F. Bennett (Oxford 1973), is a traditional history giving essentially a narrative of high politics; both the approach and the content are now somewhat outdated. It does, however, replace the relevant chapters in volumes 5 and 6 of the *Cambridge Medieval History*. From the same period, and not to be recommended, is J. W. Thompson, *Feudal Germany* (Chicago 1928), which was criticized as soon as it appeared for not being abreast of current scholarship, and has not worn well since. G. Barraclough, *The origins of modern Germany* (2nd edition Oxford 1947) is an impressive survey written from the standpoint of a constitutional historian. It can still be recommended, though the author is perhaps excessively preoccupied with the power of the central state. Also to be recommended by the same author is his two-volume work *Medieval Germany 911–1250* (Oxford 1938): the first volume is an original and learned survey of political and constitutional developments in Germany during the high Middle Ages, and the second contains slightly abridged translations of nine pieces by German scholars, several of which can now be regarded as classics. An excellent short introduction to the period is given by J. B. Gillingham, *The kingdom of Germany in the high middle ages* (Historical Association pamphlet, London 1971). The volumes preceding and following the present work in the original German series have both been translated into English: J. Fleckenstein, *Early medieval Germany* (Amsterdam 1978), and J. Leuschner, *Germany in the later middle ages* (Amsterdam 1980).

The subtitle of H. Mitteis, *The state in the middle ages: a comparative constitutional history of feudal Europe* (Amsterdam 1975), gives a good idea of the approach and content of the work: Mitteis was the leading legal historian in Germany between the wars, and his survey, though covering the whole of Europe, pays particular attention to German developments. S. Reynolds, *Kingdoms and communities in western Europe, 900–1300* (Oxford 1984), also deals with Europe as a whole, but is especially worth reading for her refusal to assume that German history in this period was necessarily radically different from that of other parts of western Europe. On many aspects of the period covered here, not just on ecclesiastical history, the best modern survey in English is often to be found in the *Handbook of church history*, ed. H. Jedin and J. Dolan, vols. 3, *The church in the age of feudalism*, by F. Kempf and others (London 1968), and 4, *From the high middle ages to the eve of the Reformation*, by H.-G. Beck and others (London 1970); the dividing-point between the two volumes for the western church is the Concordat of Worms and the first Lateran Council.

POLITICAL AND CONSTITUTIONAL HISTORY

There is little in English on the reigns of the individual rulers dealt with in this book. Henry IV's conflict with Gregory VII has naturally received the attention of historians (see below under ecclesiastical history); his problems with the Saxons and with his nobility have not been given a great deal of coverage in English, though see now K. J. Leyser, 'The crisis of medieval Germany' (Raleigh Lecture 1983, *Proceedings of the British Academy* 69 (1983)), which deals with the Saxon uprising of 1073. The anonymous Life of Henry IV, together with his surviving letters and the biography of Conrad II by Wipo, are translated in *Imperial lives and letters of the eleventh century*, translated by T. E. Mommsen and K. F. Morrison, ed. R. L. Benson (Columbia records of civilization 67, New York 1962). On Henry V, Lothar III and Conrad III there is even less, except for a number of articles on the negotiations between Henry V and the papacy (see below under ecclesiastical history). *The two cities: a chronicle of universal history to the year 1146 A.D. by Otto, bishop of Freising*, translated by C. C. Mierow (Columbia records of civilization 9, New York 1928), gives an account of the late Salian and early Staufer period from the point of view of a Cistercian bishop who was also related to the Staufer. On Frederick Barbarossa there is rather more. The major source for the early years of his reign is available in translations as *The deeds of Frederick Barbarossa by Otto of Freising and his continuator Rahewin*, translated by C. C. Mierow (Columbia records of civilization 49, New York 1953). Among modern works there is a dull and rather thin biography by M. Pacaut, *Frederick Barbarossa* (London 1969), and a fuller but highly idiosyncratic one by P. Munz, *Frederick Barbarossa: a study in medieval politics* (London 1969). Munz's view of Frederick as a 'rational' politician who operated in accordance with long-term plans is difficult to sustain, and the book is marred by frequent errors of detail. J. B. Gillingham, 'Why did Rahewin stop writing the *Gesta Friderici*?', *EHR* 83 (1968), 294–303; P. Munz, 'Why did Rahewin stop writing the *Gesta Friderici*? A further consideration', *EHR* 84 (1969), 771–9; and J. B. Gillingham, 'Frederick Barbarossa: a secret revolutionary?', *EHR* 86 (1971), 73–8, discuss the question of Otto of Freising's intentions in his biography of Frederick and the validity of Munz's approach. On Barbarossa see also the brief essay by G. Barraclough, 'Frederick Barbarossa and the twelfth century', in *History in a changing world* (London 1955), 73–96, which perhaps

overstresses the backwardness of the twelfth-century Empire by comparison with the kingdoms of England, France and Sicily; other comparative
views can be found in A. Brackmann, 'The birth of the national state in
medieval Germany and the Norman monarchies', in *Medieval Germany*,
281–300, and K. J. Leyser, 'Some reflections on twelfth-century kings and
kingship', in Leyser, *Medieval Germany*, 241–69. On Barbarossa's early
years see also K. J. Leyser, 'Frederick Barbarossa, Henry II and the hand of
St. James', in Leyser, *Medieval Germany*, 215–40. W. Ullmann, 'Cardinal
Roland and Besançon', *Miscellanea Historiae Pontificiae* 18 (1954), 107–25, is
the only full discussion in English of the incident at Besançon in 1157,
though the author's view that Hadrian IV had no intention from the
beginning of setting a 'feudal' interpretation on the imperial title is
questionable. See also the same author's 'The pontificate of Adrian IV',
Cambridge Historical Journal 11 (1955), 233–52, and R. L. Benson, 'Political
renewal: Two models from Roman antiquity', in *Renaissance and renewal*,
339–86. On the schism of 1159 see *Boso's Life of Alexander III*, translated by
G. M. Ellis (Oxford 1973), a contemporary biography of Frederick's great
opponent.

The idea of empire is well surveyed by R. Folz, *The concept of empire in
western Europe from the fifth to the fourteenth centuries* (London 1969), which
has an appendix of documents in translation; many of the central documents
are also translated in the collections by Pullan and Tierney. See further the
articles by M. Bloch, 'The empire and the idea of empire under the
Hohenstaufen', in *Land and work*, 1–43; G. Barraclough, 'The mediaeval
empire: idea and reality', in *History in a changing world*, 105–30, and
W. Ullmann, 'Reflections upon the medieval empire', *Transactions of the
Royal Historical Society*, fifth series, 14 (1964), 89–108.

On the German nobility see K. J. Leyser, 'The German aristocracy from
the ninth to the early twelfth century: a historical and cultural sketch', in
Leyser, *Medieval Germany*, 161–90 and K. Schmid, 'The structure of the
nobility in the earlier middle ages', in *Medieval nobility*, 37–60. Both articles
deal with the change in the sense of family in the course of the eleventh and
twelfth centuries towards a more strictly agnatic family consciousness with
greater stress on descent in the male line. J. Freed, *The counts of Falkenstein:
noble self-consciousness in twelfth-century Germany*, Transactions of the
American Philosophical Society, 74.6 (Philadelphia 1984), investigates
these problems in the twelfth century, taking as an example a well-
documented noble family whose status lay between that of the very highest
aristocracy and that of the *ministeriales*. Family consciousness is also
explored in an article by K. Hauck, 'The literature of house and kindred
associated with medieval noble families, illustrated from eleventh- and
twelfth-century writers on the nobility', in *Medieval nobility*, 61–86, a
difficult but rewarding piece showing how a largely non-literate lay
aristocratic culture can be recovered, at least in part, through careful
attention to the literature and historiography of the period. Two key works
referred to by Hauck are available in English translation. There are two

translations of the *Ruodlieb*: *Ruodlieb, the earliest courtly novel*, edited and translated by E. H. Zeydel (North Carolina studies in the Germanic languages and literatures 23, Chapel Hill 1959), and *The Ruodlieb, the first medieval epic of chivalry from eleventh century Germany*, translated by Gordon B. Ford, Jr (Leiden 1965). The other work is *Ecbasis cuiusdam captivi per tropologiam: Escape of a certain captive told in a figurative manner, an eleventh-century Latin beast epic*, edited and translated by E. H. Zeydel (North Carolina studies in the Germanic languages and literatures 46, Chapel Hill 1964). Both works, besides being interesting literature in their own right, offer many insights into the aristocratic mentality and life-style of the eleventh century.

There are a number of articles on the *ministeriales*: M. Bloch, 'A problem in comparative history: the administrative classes in France and Germany', in *Land and Work*, 82–123; J. Freed, 'The origins of the European nobility: the problem of the ministerials', *Viator* 7 (1976), 211–42 and 'The formation of the Salzburg ministerialage in the tenth and eleventh centuries: an example of upward social mobility in the early middle ages', *Viator* 9 (1978), 67–101; K. Bosl, '"Noble unfreedom": the rise of the ministeriales in Germany', in *Medieval nobility*, 291–312.

On the constitutional developments of the twelfth century see the classic studies by G. Tellenbach, 'From the Carolingian imperial nobility to the German estate of imperial princes', in *Medieval nobility*, 203–42, which shows how a new kind of ducal power emerged in the course of the eleventh and twelfth centuries; T. Mayer, 'The state of the dukes of Zähringen', in *Medieval Germany*, 175–202, which surveys one of the earliest examples of the territorial principality which was to become the normal form of state organisation in late medieval Germany; O. Freiherr von Dungern, 'Constitutional reorganization and reform under the Hohenstaufen', in *ibid.*, 203–34; and H. Mitteis, 'Feudalism and the German constitution', in *ibid.*, 235–80. See also the study by Hirsch noted below under 'Ecclesiastical history'.

On regional history, one of the most important developments in German medieval historiography in the last two generations, there is almost nothing in English. The only regions which have received some attention are those lying on the border between the kingdom of Germany and the surrounding Slav principalities and kingdoms. On the missionary, colonizing and crusader activities here see W. Urban, *The Baltic crusade* (DeKalb 1975); E. Christiansen, *The northern crusades: the Baltic and the catholic frontier 1100–1525* (London 1980); and A. P. Vlasto, *The entry of the Slavs into Christendom* (Cambridge 1970). Economic developments are also covered in the essay by H. Aubin (see below, 'Social and economic history'). G. Barraclough (ed.), *Eastern and western Europe in the middle ages* (London 1970), contains five essays by F. Graus, K. Bosl, F. Seibt, M. M. Postan and A. Gieysztor on various aspects of the Germans' relations with their Slavonic neighbours; it covers the whole of the middle ages and not just the century and a half of the present book. A number of primary sources for the

Drang nach Osten and the conversion of the Slavs have been translated into English. Adam of Bremen (see below under ecclesiastical history) is valuable on missionary work up to the late eleventh century. *The life of Otto, apostle of Pomerania, 1060–1139, by Ebbo and Herbordus*, translated by C. H. Robinson (London 1920), is an important source for the revival of missionary work by the German church in the post-Gregorian era. *The chronicle of the Slavs by Helmold, priest of Bosau*, translated by F. J. Tschan (Columbia records of civilization 21, New York 1935) is a very valuable source for the career of Vicelin, for the Wendish crusade of 1147 and especially for the career of Henry the Lion. Saxo Grammaticus, *Danorum regum herorumque historia*, translated by E. Christiansen (3 vols., Oxford 1980–1) is informative on the relations between Germans and Danes and on their rivalry in the Baltic and in Slav colonization.

ECCLESIASTICAL HISTORY

On the 'church system' of the Ottonian and Salian rulers see T. Reuter, 'The "imperial church system" of the Ottonian and Salian rulers: a reconsideration', *Journal of ecclesiastical history* 33 (1982), 347–74, who argues that the elements of plan and system in the German rulers' control of their church in the tenth and eleventh century have been exaggerated. Two articles by E. N. Johnson deal with the career of eleventh-century bishops: 'Adalbert of Hamburg-Bremen', *Speculum* 9 (1934), 147–79 and 'Bishop Benno II of Osnabrück', *Speculum* 16 (1941), 389–403; for Italy see H. E. J. Cowdrey, 'Archbishop Aribert II of Milan', *History* 51 (1966), 1–15. Adam of Bremen, *History of the Archbishops of Hamburg-Bremen*, translated by F. J. Tschan (Columbia records of civilization 53, New York 1959) gives among other things a colourful picture of the activities of Adalbert of Bremen.

   G. Tellenbach, *Church, state and Christian society at the time of the Investiture Contest* (Oxford 1940) is still a stimulating introduction to the spiritual upheavals of the period of the Gregorian reform. See also the articles by G. B. Ladner, 'Gregory the Great and Gregory VII: a comparison of their concepts of renewal', *Viator* 4 (1973), 1–27; 'Terms and ideas of renewal', in *Renaissance and renewal*, 1–33. H. E. J. Cowdrey, *The Cluniacs and Gregorian reform* (Oxford 1970), deals among other things with the German version of Cluniac monasticism which spread from the monastery of Hirsau in Suabia; see also H. Hirsch, 'The constitutional history of the reformed monasteries during the Investiture Contest', in *Medieval Germany*, 131–73. H. E. J. Cowdrey, 'The papacy, the patarenes and the church of Milan', *Transactions of the Royal Historical Society*, fifth series 18 (1968), 25–48, covers a movement both important and interesting in itself and of great significance for the conflict between Gregory VII and Henry IV. Remarkably, there is no modern biography of Gregory VII in English, but many of his letters are available in translation: *The correspondence of Pope Gregory VII; selected letters from the Registrum*, translated by E. Emerton (Columbia records of civilization 14, New York 1932); H. E. J. Cowdrey, *The 'Epistolae vagantes' of*

Bibliography

193

Pope Gregory VII (Oxford medieval texts, Oxford 1972). On the polemics see I. S. Robinson, *Authority and resistance in the Investiture Contest: the polemical literature of the late eleventh century* (Manchester 1978) and K. J. Leyser, 'The polemics of the papal revolution', in Leyser, *Medieval Germany*, 138–60. Robinson has also published a number of articles on Gregory VII: 'The friendship network of Gregory VII', *History* 63 (1978), 1–22; '*Periculosus homo*: Pope Gregory VII and episcopal authority', *Viator* 9 (1978), 103–32; 'Pope Gregory VII, the princes and the Pactum 1077–1080', *EHR* 94 (1979), 721–56. On Canossa see K. F. Morrison, 'Canossa: a revision', *Traditio* 18 (1962), 121–48, who argues that Gregory VII's actions during and following the excommunication and reconciliation of Henry IV were consistent, a sentiment open to doubt. Still worth reading is P. Joachimsen, 'The Investiture Contest and the German Constitution', in *Medieval Germany*, 95–129. Also to be recommended, though somewhat idiosyncratic in their approach, are the later chapters of W. Ullmann's *The growth of papal government in the middle ages* (3rd edition, London 1970). See also his *A short history of the papacy in the middle ages* (London 1972), and, for the history of the papal patrimony, P. Partner, *The lands of St. Peter: the papal state in the middle ages and the early renaissance* (London 1972). The final stages of the Investiture Contest have been dealt with in a number of articles: M. J. Wilks, '*Ecclesiastica* and *regalia*: papal investiture policy from the council of Guastalla to the first Lateran council (1106–23)', *Studies in Church History* 7 (1971), 69–86 (with a rather unconvincing argument that Paschal II did not really intend to give very much away in 1111); U.-R. Blumenthal, '*Patrimonia* and *regalia* in 1111', in *Law, church and society: essays in honour of Stephen Kuttner*, ed. K. Pennington and R. Somerville (Philadelphia 1977), 9–20; S. Chodorow, 'Ecclesiastical politics and the ending of the Investiture Contest', *Speculum* 46 (1971), 613–40. Rather older, but still to be recommended, is Z. N. Brooke, 'Lay investiture and its relation to the conflicts of empire and papacy', *Proceedings of the British Academy* 25 (1939), 217–47.

There is little specifically on the German church in the period following the Concordat of Worms, though the recent study by J. H. van Engen, *Rupert of Deutz* (Berkeley 1983), gives a good idea of the reactionary flavour of much of German monastic life in the early twelfth century. The effects of the Concordat of Worms are dealt with *en passant* by R. L. Benson, *The bishop-elect: a study in medieval ecclesiastical office* (Princeton 1968); for an episode of some significance in the reign of Henry VI see R. H. Schmandt, 'The election and assassination of Albert of Louvain, bishop of Liège', *Speculum* 42 (1967), 639–60.

SOCIAL AND ECONOMIC HISTORY

There is virtually no work in English which deals primarily with Germany, and recourse has to be had to general surveys of European social and economic history. A. Verhulst and F. L. Ganshof, 'France, the Low Countries and western Germany' and H. Aubin, 'The lands east of the Elbe and German colonization eastwards', in chapter 7 of the *Cambridge economic history of Europe* vol. 2 (2nd edition Cambridge 1966; the additions on pp. 790ff should also be noted), reflect essentially the state of scholarship at the end of the 1930s. G. Duby, *Rural economy and country life in the medieval west* (London 1970) gives slightly less full coverage to Germany than to France and England, but is nevertheless still probably the best account in English of the medieval German agricultural economy; the author also includes a number of documents in translation. B. H. Slicher van Bath, *The agrarian history of western Europe, 500–1850* (London 1963), should also be mentioned. On population see J. C. Russell, 'Population in Europe 500–1500', in *The Fontana economic history of Europe*, ed. C. Cipolla, vol. 1, *The middle ages* (London 1973). C. T. Smith, *An historical geography of Western Europe before 1800* (Harlow 1978) is especially good on town development. M. W. Barley (ed.), *European towns: their archaeology and early history* (London 1975) contains a number of articles on German towns. P. Dollinger, *The Hansa*, translated and edited by S. S. Ault and H. Steinberg (London, 1970), deals mainly with the later Middle Ages. P. Strait, *Cologne in the twelfth century* (Gainesville 1974) is a very solid study of a single important German town. Galbert of Bruges, *The murder of Charles the Good, count of Flanders*, translated by J. B. Ross (Columbia records of civilization 61, New York 1967), is an invaluable source for town development in the twelfth century, though Bruges lay in royal, not imperial Flanders, and hence the source is only indirectly applicable to Germany. For the material culture of the period see the exhibition catalogues noted in the following section.

INTELLECTUAL AND CULTURAL HISTORY

On the intellectual history of Germany see also many of the titles listed above under 'Ecclesiastical history', especially the works by Robinson and van Engen. On Honorius Augustodunensis, a significant figure in the intellectual life of Germany in the first third of the twelfth century, see E. M. Sandford, 'Honorius, presbyter and scholasticus', *Speculum* 23 (1948), 397–425 and V. I. J. Flint, 'The place and purpose of the works of Honorius Augustodunensis', *Revue Bénédictine* 87 (1977), 97–127. On Otto of Freising see the articles and translations noted above under political and constitutional history, and also K. F. Morrison, 'Otto of Freising's quest for the hermeneutic circle', *Speculum* 55 (1980), 207–36. P. Classen, 'Res gestae, universal history, apocalypse: visions of past and future', in *Renaissance and renewal*, 387–417, deals with a number of historical writers of twelfth-century Germany, including Otto of Freising and Gerhoch of Reichersberg.

One of the earliest medieval treatises on the techniques of the fine arts, *Theophilus, De diversibus artibus*, edited and translated by C. R. Dodwell (London 1961), was probably written by a German monk and goldsmith, Roger of Helmarshausen; see also J. H. van Engen, 'Theophilus Presbyter and Rupert of Deutz: the manual arts and Benedictine theology in the early twelfth century', *Viator* 11 (1980), 147–63.

Finally, mention should be made of a number of exhibition catalogues which have appeared in recent years; they are so lavishly illustrated that it seems appropriate to include them, even though the texts are in German, for the information they provide on the artistic and intellectual life of the period and on its material culture: *Rhein und Maas: Kunst und Kultur 800–1400* (2 vols., Cologne 1972); *Monumenta Annonis* (Cologne 1975); *Die Zeit der Staufer* (5 vols., Stuttgart 1977–9: vol. 2 contains the illustrations to the catalogue, and vol. 4 is genealogical tables and maps); *Ornamenta Ecclesiae* (3 vols., Cologne 1985).

INDEX